CRICFITSPORT

#UNLOCKPOTENTIAL

MULTINATIONAL CRICKET EDUCATION FIRM

CRICFITSPORT (CFS) IS A CRICKET BASED EDUCATION FIRM FOCUSING ON GRASSROOTS AND BEYOND PLAYER DEVELOPMENT

LOCATIONS

- CFS Academy, London/ Essex
- CFS Academy, Bucks/ Northants
- LSG Academy, Gr Noida/Delhi,(Operated by CFS)

KEY PARTNERS

FOCUS AREAS

- Academy operations with unique coaching courses.
- Domestic & International tours & tournaments.
- Boutique high end cricket equipment.
- Player, Officials and Coach Education Courses.

 Scan the QR code to visit our website
//www.cricfitsport.com/

 Follow us on social media to know more about us
https://www.instagram.com/cfs_cricket

 Email ID: info@cricfitsport.com

'This book is unique and has really struck on something special: unlocking the difficult ability to get the key fundamentals of bowling across in a simple yet detailed way. There is something here for all abilities – it is relevant to players at the beginning of their bowling journey all the way through to providing nuggets of advice for experienced players. It is a super and interesting read'

MARK PATTERSON, SURREY & IRELAND

'The authors have a vast knowledge and delightful passion for the game and this recent instalment of their series of books is excellent. From grassroots to elite level cricketers, anybody could pick this book up and learn a snippet or two. I highly recommend'

JACK BROOKS, SOMERSET, YORKSHIRE, NORTHANTS CCC & ENGLAND LIONS

'Another comprehensive guide which blends in-depth knowledge of all bowling disciplines and insight from elite players and coaches'

RICHARD HUDSON, CEO OF BUCKS CRICKET

'This third book in the series is a great addition offering both technical and tactical coaching all described in a clear and understandable manner. The book is a valuable addition to the coach's toolkit but is equally useful for parents and players alike. The drills section offers a welcome number of options and the photos ensure it is easy to follow. Whether you are new to coaching or have years of experience, this book will further your self-development and the way it is written means you can dip in and out whenever you have the opportunity'

CHRIS MALTON, NORTHANTS PERFORMANCE COACH

'Another masterpiece. A comprehensive guide to the art of bowling – invaluable for both coaches and players alike. Bowling has evolved so much in recent years and this guide covers every aspect to enable all bowlers to take their game to the next level. Practical, insightful and hugely relevant. As a coach, I love the ongoing guidance notes which enables me to understand the context in order to be player-centric'

NICK BROOME, NORTHANTS PERFORMANCE COACH AND COACH DEVELOPMENT

BOWLING

A COMPREHENSIVE MODERN GUIDE FOR PLAYERS AND COACHES

JAMES KNOTT & ANDREW O'CONNOR

FOREWORDS BY
DARREN GOUGH
SAQLAIN MUSHTAQ

*With contributions from
David Willey, Martin Bicknell, Gareth Batty,
Ian Salisbury, Brenden Fourie, Chris Liddle & Phil Rowe*

This edition first published in 2024 by

POLARIS PUBLISHING LTD
c/o Aberdein Considine
2nd Floor, Elder House
Multrees Walk
Edinburgh
EH1 3DX

www.polarispublishing.com

Text copyright © James Knott & Andrew O'Connor, 2024
Photography copyright © Stowe Studio 100, 2024
Follow on Instagram #stowestudio100

ISBN: 9781915359223
eBook ISBN: 9781915359230

The right of James Knott & Andrew O'Connor to be identified as the authors of this work has been asserted by them in accordance with the Copyright, Designs and Patents Act 1988.

All rights reserved. No part of this publication may be reproduced, stored or transmitted in any form, or by any means electronic, mechanical, photocopying, recording or otherwise, without the express written permission of the publisher.

The views expressed in this book do not necessarily reflect the views, opinions or policies of Polaris Publishing Ltd (Company No. SC401508) (Polaris), nor those of any persons, organisations or commercial partners connected with the same (Connected Persons). Any opinions, advice, statements, services, offers, or other information or content expressed by third parties are not those of Polaris or any Connected Persons but those of the third parties. For the avoidance of doubt, neither Polaris nor any Connected Persons assume any responsibility or duty of care whether contractual, delictual or on any other basis towards any person in respect of any such matter and accept no liability for any loss or damage caused by any such matter in this book.

Every effort has been made to trace copyright holders and obtain their permission for the use of copyright material. The publisher apologises for any errors or omissions and would be grateful if notified of any corrections that should be incorporated in future reprints or editions of this book.

All names and trademarks are the property of their respective owners, which are in no way associated with Polaris Publishing Ltd. Use of these names does not imply any cooperation or endorsement.

British Library Cataloguing-in-Publication Data
A catalogue record for this book is available on request from the British Library.

Designed and typeset by Polaris Publishing, Edinburgh
Printed in Great Britain by MBM Print, East Kilbride

CONTENTS

FOREWORD BY DARREN GOUGH	viii
FOREWORD BY SAQLAIN MUSHTAQ	x
INTRODUCTION	xii
ONE: THE BASICS	1
What is a Bowler?	2
The Grip	8
The Gather	9
Completing the Action	10
When to Release the Ball – the Timing of Release	11
The Bound	12
The Run-Up	15
The Follow-Through	18
Front-Arm Variations	20
Midway and Front-On Bowling Actions	22
TWO: SEAM AND SWING BOWLING	25
Outswing	26
Inswing	29
Varying the Amount of Swing	32
Wrist Flick	33
Shining the Ball	34
Reverse Swing	35
Changing the Ball	35
Seaming and Cutting the Ball	36
Wobble Seam	37
Cross Seam	38
Use of Crease and Bowling to Left-Handed Batters	39
Slower Balls	41
Off Cutter Slower Ball	42
Leg Cutter Slower Ball	42
Split Finger	43
Knuckle Ball	44
Back of the Hand Slower Ball	44
Bowling the Bouncer	45
Bowling with Purpose and Adding Pace	48
Picking the Right Ball	51
THREE: OFF SPIN BOWLING	52
The Grip	52
The Action	54
The Front Arm	57
The Run-Up or Approach to the Wicket	58
Completion	59
Where to Look and How to Respond	60
Bowling with Purpose and Spinning the Ball Hard	60
Variations	62
Bowling to Left-Handers and Left-Arm Orthodox Spin Bowlers	67
Shining the Ball	70
Bowling with the New Ball	70

FOUR: LEG SPIN BOWLING	71
The Grip	71
The Action	73
Stock Ball	74
Run-Up or Approach	76
Bowling with Purpose and Spinning the Ball Hard	76
Variations	77
Bowling with the New Ball	85
FIVE: BOWLING PRINCIPLES	87
Finding Top of Off	87
Wind and Slope	88
Bowling with a Wet Ball	89
The Three-Second Rule and the Power of Visualisation	90
Should I Bowl with the Wicketkeeper Up or Back?	90
Run-Ups and Dealing with No-Ball Problems	91
Bowling Principles	92
The All-Rounder	94
Verbals	94
SIX: BOWLING TACTICS	96
Before Play (Deciding Whether to Bat or Bowl First)	99
During play (General Bowling Tactics for All Formats)	102
How Will a Batter Try to Counteract the Bowling Plan?	133
How Will the Bowler Try to Counteract the Batter's Plan?	133
Additional Bowling Tactics Relevant to Each Format of Cricket Played	134
T20 Match (White ball)	135
T20 Bowling Tactics	135
The Hundred (White Ball)	139
The Hundred Bowling Tactics	139
50-Over Match (White Ball)	141
50-Over Bowling Tactics	141
Multi 2, 3, 4, or 5 Day Test Match (Red Ball).	141
Multi-Day Bowling Tactics	144
Field Placings Can Be Used as a Guide for Both Adult and Junior Cricket	149
SEVEN: MENTAL ASPECTS OF BOWLING	151
Mental Toughness	153
Motivations	155
Confidence	160
Visualisation or Mental Imagery	164
Concentration	167
Anxiety Control	173
Act Like a Professional	176
The Role of the Coach in the Bowler's Mental Development	182
Getting to Know your Bowler	183
The Use of Open-Ended Questions	184
Listening intently to the Answers	185
Reacting to the Answers with Appropriate Thoughtful Responses	185

Use of Funnelling Questions to Self-Empower the Bowler	185
Ensuring a Positive Learning Environment	186
Dealing with Bowlers' Non-Selection	187
Summary	188

EIGHT: LOOKING AFTER YOURSELF — 193

Pre-Match Preparation	193
Pre-Match Bowling Warm-Up Routines	194
Post-Match Bowling Cool-Down Routines	197
Weekly Workload Record Sheets (Summer Matches and tTaining)	198
Rehabilitation Work Routines	199
Strength and Conditioning (S&C) work	200
Weekly Workload Record Sheets (Winter Training and Body Conditioning)	206
Fitness	207
Nutrition	211
Bowling in Hot Temperatures	215
Bowling in Cold Temperatures	215
Sleep	216
Bowling Equipment	217

NINE: BOWLING DRILLS — 223

Coaching Styles	223
Bowlers Coaching Development Methods	224
Games-Based Learning	225
General Technical/Tactical Net Drills	227
Technical Remedial Work Drills	252
Fitness and Stability Drills	277
Useful Coaching Quotes to Remember	285

TEN: INTRODUCTION TO VIDEO ANALYSIS — 287

Filming Location	288
Key Elements to Study in the Bowling Action	289
Snaking Run-Up	291
'Cutting In' or 'Jumping In' During the Bound	293
Excessive Bound Height with Backward Body Lean	294
Excessive Back-Leg collapse	296
Falling to Off Side	298
Front Leg Not Braced	199
Front Foot Cutting Off	301
Redundant Front Arm or Non-Bowling Arm	302
Seam Bowler's Arm, Wrist and Fingers Not Vertical	304
Seam Bowlers Not Flicking Wrist	305
Off-Spinners Undercutting the Ball	307
Spin Bowler not rotating 180deg	308
Weak Follow-Through (Shoulders, Arms and Feet)	310
Weak Back-Leg Knee-Drive	312

ABOUT THE AUTHORS	**314**
ABOUT THE PLAYERS AND COACHES	**316**
ACKNOWLEDGEMENTS	**319**

FOREWORD BY DARREN GOUGH

I have been lucky enough to witness some great bowling spells as a player and broadcaster for many years and I have been involved in many great duels with some of the world's best batsmen like Brian Lara, Sachin Tendulkar, Ricky Ponting and Jacques Kallis to name just a few of them.

There is nothing more exciting in the game than to witness a great fast bowler steaming in – from Michael Holding bowling to Brian Close, to Allan Donald to Michael Atherton, Freddie Flintoff to Jacques Kallis or indeed a great spinner weaving a web like Shane Warne or Muttiah Muralitharan.

My memories of Donald versus Atherton were – 'I hope I don't have to face him!' Donald was disappointed that he didn't get a decision, so he turned up the volume on Atherton with rhythm and anger, but always maintaining control with pure athleticism and technique. Fair play to Atherton – he was always up for the challenge of facing fast bowling, as he proved a few years earlier in Johannesburg when South Africa threw everything at him.

It is important as a bowler to believe in your ability, to enjoy the challenges and always remember it only takes one ball, no matter how much the batter may be on top up to then. You've got to want to bowl at the best at any stage of the game. I've had many battles over the years – the ones against the great Australia team of the 90s arguably the greatest ever.

With the new ball there were challenges bowling to the likes of Michael Slater who played aggressively from the outset, wanting to dominate. You win some, you lose some. Then there was Ricky Ponting and Steve Waugh in the middle overs, when the new ball had gone, knowing they were huge scalps – you had to get them early or they usually went big. Then there was Adam Gilchrist coming in at seven, when you're tiring, runs are already on the board, and he wants to take the game forward quickly.

You have to be strong, positive and have a plan A and a plan B. I was lucky enough to dismiss Ricky Ponting and Brian Lara on quite a few occasions, of which I'm immensely proud as they are two genuine greats of the game.

No two bowlers are alike, and these differences can make a devilish duo when bowling together. Wasim Akram + Waqar Younis, Alan Donald/Dale Steyn + Shaun Pollock, Glen McGrath + Jason Gillespie, Courtney Walsh + Curtly Ambrose, Jimmy Anderson + Stuart Broad, and even Darren Gough + Andy Caddick.

The most destructive for me was Akram and Younis. In their pomp both bowling 90mph+, swung the new ball, and when the pitch got flat, in any country, they could bowl deadly reverse swing, a real skill to devastating effect – often teams went from 100-1 to 150 all out!

Dale Steyn and Shaun Pollock from South Africa are a close comparison. Steyn with his pace and skill in all conditions. Pollock with his height and accuracy gives you no freebies along the same lines of McGrath, Walsh and Ambrose.

Both of my sons, Liam and Brennan, were coached by the two authors, Andy and James, whilst they were at Stowe School. They are both highly committed coaches with decades of experience between them. They have created a book that will provide you with all of the fundamentals of bowling and also highlight the various different options in how to go about your craft. No stone has been left unturned as the book delves into the technical, tactical, mental, physical attributes required as well as a large drills section to help you improve your game.

My inspiration for bowling fast came from watching the fast bowlers of the 80s on TV – Botham, Willis, Marshall, Lillee and Hadlee. By working hard with my coaches, especially Steve Oldham (who was the one that discovered me and turned me into the finished article) and some inspiration along the way from Waqar and Wasim bowling to England in the early 90s, as well as chatting to Malcolm Marshall about fast bowling and Richie Richardson, our overseas captain, who pushed me to bowl faster.

Darren Gough
Surrey & England

FOREWORD BY SAQLAIN MUSHTAQ

In the vibrant tapestry of cricket, where legends are born and battles are fought, a new chapter unfolds with *Bowling: A Comprehensive Modern Guide for Players and Coaches*. This book, crafted by my dear friend and teammate, James Knott, and his co-author, Andrew O'Connor, delves deep into the intricate art of bowling, be it the relentless seam attack or the mesmerising spin wizardry.

Cricket, they say, is a game of uncertainties, where no two bowlers are exactly alike. James and Andrew embody this truth in their work, emphasising the beauty of individuality and the ever-evolving journey of self-discovery on the cricketing path. As we journey through the pages of this guide, we are reminded that cricket is not just a sport; it's a way of life.

The book's approach is as diverse as the field of play itself. From the technical nuances that define a great bowler to the tactical acumen required to thrive in the ever-changing forms of the game. It touches on the physical attributes that can make or break a cricketer's career and delves deep into the mental fortitude that sets champions apart.

For me, cricket has always been more than a game – it's an art form. James's book captures this essence as it unravels the intricate web of spin bowling. The challenges I faced and conquered during my career are stories that find their place in these pages. Spin bowling is a dance of deception, and the book's exploration of variations is a treasure chest for aspiring spin maestros.

As I look back on my journey, I can't help but reminisce about the drills and methods that shaped my craft. The enigmatic doosra, a delivery that left batsmen perplexed, was born from thinking beyond the ordinary. Mental drills and spot bowling became my allies on the relentless quest for control and precision. These insights, shared within these pages, serve as a guiding light for those who seek to master the art of spin.

Beyond the technical aspects, what shines through the book is the enduring camaraderie that cricket nurtures. Memories of sharing a room with James, of conversations that transcended language barriers, remain etched in my heart. Cricket has a unique ability to bridge divides and forge friendships that last a lifetime.

James and I share a history not only on the field but also off it. His father, Alan Knott, was a beacon of knowledge, illuminating the path for everyone. James himself is a consummate professional and a sophisticated mind who extended his wisdom beyond the cricket pitch. I learned from him not just about the game but also about life's nuances. He was the guiding star, always there through the moments of frustration and triumph.

As for James, the man who donned multiple hats – a seam bowler, an off-spinner, a leg-spinner, and a wicketkeeper for Surrey – he is a testament to cricket's enduring legacy. His commitment to the sport and the values it embodies is commendable. His co-author – Andrew – is a Northants Academy coach and has been coaching at the county for 20 years. His rich experience and knowledge shines through in these pages.

In the grand tapestry of cricket, every cricketer, be it the seasoned pro or the eager novice, finds their unique journey. This book, with its insights and stories, paves the way for each one to carve their path in the world of cricket. It is a tribute to the sport we hold dear and the memories we cherish.

With that, I extend my heartiest thanks to James and Andrew for this remarkable contribution to the cricketing world. To all those who embark on this journey through the pages of *Bowling*, I offer my best wishes. May this book be your guiding star as you step onto the field, armed with knowledge, passion and the indomitable spirit of cricket.

Saqlain Mushtaq
Former International Cricketer
& Specialist Spin Bowling Coach

INTRODUCTION

The bowler is the most important player of any cricket match. Without the bowler delivering the ball the game would not start, runs could not be scored and wickets not taken. Coaches will often talk about setting the right tone from the first ball of the match and it is always the opening bowler (whether seam or spin) who is charged with this. It is hard for a team to stay 'energised' and 'vocal' or 'create an environment' if a bowler is not performing.

Bowling, whether seam or spin, is very exciting. The most enticing viewing in a cricket match is watching a great spell of bowling. Witnessing the likes of James Anderson swing and seam the ball – setting the batsman up, or Mark Wood bowling 90mph+ and having the batsman ducking and swaying before getting the yorker in and sending the stumps flying, or Ravindra Ashwin extracting bounce and turn and working through all his variations. When a bowler is on top it is always very captivating viewing.

This book is aimed at all bowlers and coaches, wherever you are on your cricketing journey, be that a beginner or a senior player. The book provides detailed analysis of technique, tactics, game plans and variations for all types of bowling, as well as how to adapt to the various formats of the game. If you are just starting to learn to bowl this will give you a great insight into seam and spin bowling – give them all a go – there is no need to specialise yet.

Further, there are chapters on the physical and mental aspects of bowling, as well as training. For more experienced bowlers there is an advanced section and for coaches a comprehensive drills section which will help keep training fun and varied. Throughout the book there are contributions from players and coaches, past and present.

As with any aspect of cricket there are several ways of achieving the same thing, and there are so many different bowling styles out there. Watch any current international match – no two bowlers are the same. We will give you various options on bowling actions for seam, swing and spin and the many variations available to bowlers of all types. Hopefully, from the various methods suggested you will find as a player what works for you. Ultimately, you need to understand your own game and play to your strengths. As coaches we need to understand the various styles and adapt our approach to different players – finding out what works best for them.

> **Note for players and coaches**
> Remember, whatever level you are currently playing or coaching, you can always learn something new. Learn from watching video of the best players, learn from the players and coaches you play with and against, and always strive to be better tomorrow than you are today.

Throughout this book, all technical descriptions and drill references are for bowling right-handed to a right-hand batter unless stated otherwise.

ONE
THE BASICS

'Practise, practise, practise! Having a repeatable action is key to consistency. You won't get any better by not bowling so go hit some target areas and learn that skill.'

MARTIN BICKNELL

Surrey & England

Director of Cricket at Charterhouse School

What is a Bowler?

In every official game of cricket played all over the world, from the first ball of the match to the last, the bowler bowls the ball which subsequently initiates all the proceeding action. The batter can only react to what is bowled at them.

Their role is to take ten batters' wickets and stop them from scoring runs. To help achieve this, the bowler has ten fielders who can be strategically positioned anywhere within the perimeter of the pitch. The bowler can bowl the ball at any speed and induce any ball movement available.

All of this takes place under variable weather and pitch conditions.

There are 11 methods of taking a batter's wicket, the bowler being **directly** involved in eight of them. These are: **Bowled, Caught, LBW, Stumped, Run Out, Hit Wicket, Handled the Ball, Hit the Ball Twice.** (The remaining forms of dismissal are; Obstructing the Field, Timed Out, Retired Out).

The bowling action and number of deliveries bowled, methods of dismissal, pitch and ground dimensions, ball type, match format and duration, and finally the time of play, are all governed by the Laws of Cricket.

To bowl the ball consistently in the same spot or where you want it to go you need a strong, repeatable action where everything is the same every ball in terms of your grip (unless deliberately bowling a variation), your run-up, your bowling action and then your follow-through. As with any skill these take a lot of practice. To get better at bowling you need to bowl.

*'Practice is a balance between exploring (adding skills)
and having a strong repeatable action that you can rely on.'*
GARETH BATTY
Surrey & England, Surrey CCC Head Coach

The Grip

To be able to bowl the ball the first thing you need to know how to do is how to hold the ball – commonly called the bowler's 'grip' of the ball.

In this book we will detail various different grips for the various types of bowling – seam, swing and spin, and all of the variations therein. For the purposes of this chapter we will only be dealing with the grip for a 'seam-up' delivery.

If you are reading this as an absolute beginner, the seam of the ball is the middle part where the leather is stitched together and creates a pronounced part of the ball known as the 'seam' of the ball. The photo below highlights the seam of the ball.

To grip the ball correctly for a seam-up delivery you should only use three fingers. Your index finger, your middle finger and your thumb as in these photos:

Try gripping the ball in both hands to see which feels the most comfortable. In terms of bowling, nearly all players bowl with their dominant hand (usually the one they write/throw with, but not always). Note that the ball is placed towards the ends of the fingers, with the second knuckle touching the ball, and there should be a gap between the ball and the hand. To start with have your two fingers slightly apart but so they are still touching the outer parts of the seam. Angle your thumb it a little so the side of the thumb is on the middle part of the seam. The grip needs to be tight enough so the ball does not fall out of the fingers but not so tight that it is hard to let go. Your third finger is bent and nestled lightly against the side of the ball. Ultimately, experiment to see how far into the fingers the ball goes until it feels comfortable.

'The grip is quite individual – more so than many non-bowlers might suspect. In general, I would encourage a starting point of the inside of the fingers sitting on the outside of the seam, so slightly apart. You will find plenty of bowlers who have a narrower grip with their fingers more on top of the seam. There is no right and wrong here and I definitely encourage experimentation with the grip, in particular when looking to achieve different outcomes.'
PHIL ROWE
Former Northants Bowling Coach

Note for players and coaches
For a young player to be able to grip the ball correctly it is important that they use the correct size ball that enables this. This table below shows the correct weight and size for varying age groups.

Cricket ball specifications

	Weight	**Circumference**
Men, and boys 13 and over	5.5 to 5.75oz (156 to 163g)	8.81 to 9in (224 to 229mm)
Women, and girls 13 and over	4.94 to 5.31oz (140 to 151g)	8.25 to 8.88in (210 to 226mm)
Children under 13	4.69 to 5.06oz (133 to 143g)	8.06 to 8.69in (205 to 221mm)

The Bowling Action

There are three main actions that bowlers adopt when bowling the ball. They are front-on, side-on and midway. The three photos below show each one:

For the purposes of this chapter we are going to detail a side-on action. To begin with place your feet wider than shoulder width apart with your left shoulder pointing at where you want the ball to be delivered. If you are in a net this would be towards the stumps at the other end. If in your garden or bedroom use something to act as the stumps and angle your shoulder towards that. Your head should be turned into the shoulder looking at where you want to bowl the ball. Although there are variations to this – start by looking at the spot where you want to land the ball:

> *'Where you look is important, some bowlers rely on feel, others on focusing on where you want the ball to land.'*
> MARTIN BICKNELL

From this point raise your left arm (referred to as your 'front arm' and can be either completely straight or slightly bent) so it is pointing at the sky. It needs to be slightly angled so you can look over your arm at the target as in these photos:

In this photo the player has an open fist, but it can be a clenched one as well. Now place the hand with the ball on under your chin as in these photos:

This position of the ball is often referred to as 'biting the apple'.

At this your bowling arm is bent, but to be within the laws of the game it must be straight throughout the action. So, from here the bowling arm unfurls until, with a straight arm, it is pointing in the opposite direction to your front arm as in these photos:

Now, imagine both of your arms are working together. Your front arm should move towards the target and your bowling arm should move in time with it until eventually it is your front arm that is pointing down to the ground and your bowling arm above your head:

Note that the bowling arm is very close to the right ear, so you can maximise height on ball release and making it much easier to bowl straight and keep the seam upright. Some bowlers do have a lower arm but initially think of your shoulders working vertically not horizontally as in this photo:

Think of your arms as arms of a clock – working together around the clock face.

Note for players and coaches

When teaching a player to bowl for the first time, doing so in front of a mirror is a powerful tool for the player to see for themselves the technical aspects of their action. At first practise the action without involving the legs or a run-up, just to get used to how the arms work in the action.

Note at this stage we have not engaged the legs or hips – we just want you to get used to the action of the arms and how they work together and the importance of having a straight bowling arm. Practise this without letting go of the ball (or you can practise without bowling the ball). Just one thing to remember is when your bowling arm is above your head the ball and the palm of the hand must be facing the target and not rotated in any way. Lock the wrist tight. This is because we want the ball to go down the wicket straight and with the seam upright. An upright seam gives the ball a chance to move in the air (called swing) or move off the wicket (called seam movement). The reason we want the ball to have a chance to move in the air or off the pitch is that a moving ball is much harder to play.

Throughout the bowling action keep your front arm tight to the body – it should brush the outside your left thigh as it comes down – do not allow it to arc away. It should go towards where you want to bowl. Imagine if your left hand fell off whilst you were bowling it would hit off stump. Think of staying as compact as possible with both arms staying close to your body.

'Line and length comes down to the repeatability of your action. If everything is the same each time, you've got more chance. Factors that influence this are your alignment, momentum and balance, which all incorporates a physical element. When that's all nailed down, then it's just repetition.
Practise, practise, practise!'
DAVID WILLEY
Northants & England

The Gather

Once you have mastered the arm movement now it is time engage the lower parts of your body – your legs and hips. Now when you raise your front arm and place your bowling hand under your chin also raise your left leg up to waist height:

From here step forward towards the target (off stump at the batter's end) and at the same time start unfurling your arms. Your front foot should land flat with your toes pointing at the target. Try and keep your knee straight, not bent – known as a 'braced' front leg. If you can't manage that it is fine to have a slight knee bend on landing. A braced front leg is good for bowling fast and maintaining height in your bowling action.

Your front arm should be waist height pointing at the target as your foot lands. Your bowling arm should be straight – pointing in the opposite direction:

As you can see in the photo the head remains upright (although most bowlers' heads lean away slightly to allow the bowling arm to come over) but moving towards the target. From here complete the arm movement but do not move the legs any more:

Completing the Action

We are not quite ready to add a run-up, but we do need to engage our other leg and hips to enable more momentum in our bowling action and generate more pace. This time, as we move our bowling arm from hip height up above our head, bring your right leg forward in line with your other leg:

Note that the right leg is not splayed out, it is close to the left leg. Practise that a few times to get the feel of it and then add a drive through with the right knee and hips towards the target and allow your arms to go full circle so that your front arm is now behind you pointing directly behind your bowling arm to finish in line with your left hip. Your right foot should now be pointing at the target:

Note that, although your upper body has moved forward toward the target, ideally the head should be angled upright looking at the target. At all stages of the action aim to keep your eyes focused on where you want to bowl the ball, even after you have let go of it. For all pace bowlers it is important to emphasise that it is a drive through with the back leg.

When to Release the Ball – the Timing of Release

The mechanics of your action can help determine the line that you bowl, but the timing of when you let go of the ball determines its length. This will vary depending on your height and strength initially. The main factor to consider is we want the ball to bounce, but only once. We want it to be straight and in a perfect world be hitting the 'top of off stump' as this is the length, if the batter is stood in their crease, that is the hardest to play. This will be the ball that you bowl most often – referred to as your 'stock' ball. If you can repeatably hit this length and move the ball in the air or off the pitch you will cause problems for the batter. As a guide to the different types of length please refer to this diagram.

GOOD LENGTH IN CRICKET

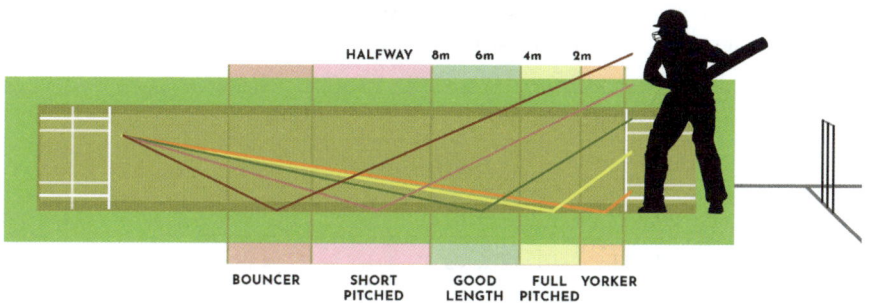

So, if you are a young player starting out then you're likely to need to release the ball just before your bowling arm is completely vertical above your head so that the ball's flight goes up slightly first before coming down. If you are older, taller and stronger then you would need to release the ball slightly after the vertical point so the ball has a downward trajectory to achieve the length we are after. It is very much about 'feel'.

Varying your length depends on the timing of release. To bowl a fuller length (closer to the stumps and the batter) then your release needs to be earlier, and to bowl a shorter length a later release is required. However, these are only small changes – all release points are close to the vertical.

As noted earlier, to start with, have your eyes fixed on the spot where you want to land the ball throughout all parts of the bowling action. If you were throwing a ball to a friend then you would be looking at them and more precisely at their hands that are going to catch the ball. So initially that's where you should focus your eyes when bowling – on the spot where you want to land the ball. You can adjust from there. If the ball is going fuller than where you are looking, then look at a shorter length. If it is going shorter, then look fuller. Some bowlers like to have a broader area in mind to target but the principle remains the same.

Before we add a full run-up move back from the stumps a few steps and walk a few steps towards the crease before performing and competing the action. Get used to having an approach to the crease before bowling.

Note for players and coaches

It is important the players practics on the correct length wickets for their age groups. The chart below shows these:

Age Group	Boys	Girls
Under 9	15 Yards / 17 Yards*	15 yards
Under 10	17 Yards*	17 yards
Under 11	17 Yards*	17 yards
Under 12	18 Yards*	18 yards
Under 13	19 Yards*	18 yards
Under 14	21 Yards*	20 yards
Under 15	22 Yards*	20 yards
Under 17	22 Yards*	22 yards

Please note that U9 hardball cricket will take place on 17-yard pitches, with all softball on 15 yards.

The Bound

Before running in, though, we need to discuss the 'bound'. To achieve a side-on position for your bowling action you will have had to leave the ground a little to achieve this whilst running at pace. As a right-arm over, side-on bowler you will take off from your left foot and rotate your body side-on in mid-air to land on your right foot, which should be parallel to the crease. This photo sequence shows from take-off to landing:

So having tried a few walk-throughs previously, now move back a bit further adding a few more steps and add some more pace to these steps (still walking, not running) and practise your left-foot take-off and right-foot landing. You should approach the crease square-on and then turn in mid-air to gain the side on position. If you turn too early it will be harder to align towards the batter's off stump.

It is important not to lean back too much as you bound or bend your right leg too much as you land, although some bending is required. You will see in these photos the position of the front arm and bowling have begun moving into position. One important aspect of the bound is not to jump too high so that you lose momentum going towards where you want to bowl. Also, the higher you jump the more the right knee needs to bend to absorb the landing, which can lead to you falling away and not aligning to the target.

> **Note for players and coaches**
> A good method for learning the bound and getting into a side-on position is to introduce a small hurdle that bowlers need to jump over and towards the target. Approach the hurdle square-on and then take off from your left foot over the hurdle and complete your bowling action having landed on your right foot the other side.

The Run-Up

'The run-up plays a huge part in how we bowl, we have to gain enough momentum to allow the bowler to maintain that through back-foot and front-foot contact. Each bowler will have an optimum pace that allows them to feel control of their base at the crease. Athletic running strides that the bowler can maintain form at when they are at their optimum pace is very important.'

CHRIS LIDDLE

Northants Bowling Coach

Now that the basics of the action are in place we can start thinking about adding a run-up. For all types of bowlers a run-up is important so we can gain the required momentum to add pace on the delivery. Some spinners may walk up to the crease, but for seam bowlers it is a run.

The run-up is not a sprint, it is a controlled running approach that should accelerate as you get closer to the crease and be quick enough to add pace to your bowling, but not too quick that you cannot perform the bowling action correctly and you are out of control of your body's movements.

To begin with, start at the point where your front foot would ideally land upon release (this is usually cutting the popping crease in half). Do not have a ball in hand. Begin running away from the crease in a straight line, gradually accelerating until you reach around 75% of your maximum pace and then complete your bowling action. Don't stop immediately – allow yourself to keep going until you naturally come to a stop.

Note for players and coaches

One of the important parts of a run-up is it is the same every ball. Therefore, it is important to always begin your run-up with the same foot each time and that step is always the same length. This can be marked if necessary. Also encourage your bowlers to lean forward slightly with chest and head before stepping so they lead the way in the approach to the wicket.

No two bowlers have the same length run-up (and yours will most likely change as you get older, grow and become more experienced) but to begin with start your bowling action when you reach 75% of maximum pace and very importantly when it feels natural to do so. It has to feel right for you. Do this a few times – still with no ball in hand. The reason to do this without a ball in hand is so that you run naturally as you would in a race with arms and legs pumping in a straight line.

> *'A bowler's run-up is very individual but the most important thing is your alignment and momentum. Everything should be working towards where you want to deliver the ball – the direction you run and the direction you follow through. Very often you put a ball in somebody's hand and they run completely different. Try and keep it relaxed and natural – it should feel good.'*
> DAVID WILLEY

> *'Rhythm is the key, followed by good balance through the crease, maintaining a straight line through to the target. When you hit the crease, make sure you drive through with your landing leg, and get your bowling shoulder all the way through, following through towards the target. To improve accuracy, balance through the crease is crucial. Keep your head as upright as possible, driving it, your front and bowling arms again in a straight line towards the target.'*
> BRENDEN FOURIE
> *Border and Leicestershire CC*

One major aspect to avoid is your legs crossing over as you run up:

You will now need a coach, parent or friend with you, then ask them to mark with a flat marker where your front foot lands as you run away from the crease. Do this for six balls, asking them to mark each one. There will most likely be some variation to begin with but identify which one 'felt' the best and most natural. Leave that marker there and do six more – thinking of the timing to land your front foot on that same marker. With more repetitions the run-up will start to gain more consistency.

Now try a few from the mark to the crease. You should land on or behind the line. If you land over the line it will be called a 'no-ball'. Each time remember to allow the momentum to carry you forward down the wicket – do not stop still. In terms of how close to land your front foot in relation to the stumps then start 'mid-crease', which is a point equal distance from the stumps to return crease as marked on this diagram:

THE CRICKET PITCH

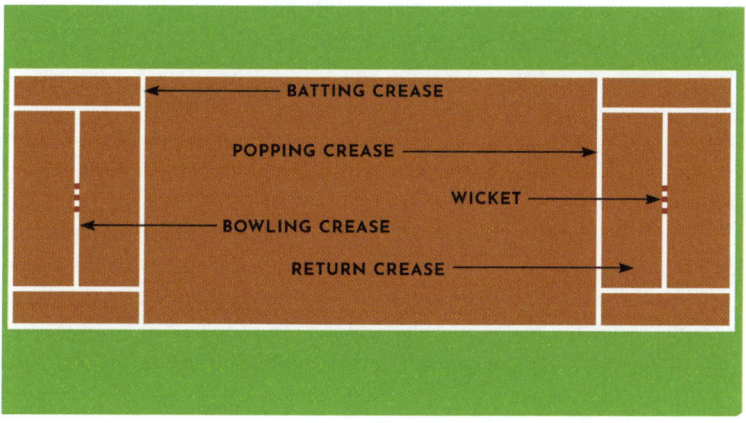

There are variations to this, which are discussed later in the book.

At this point you also need to take note of the length of your run-up. Taking even strides (as in every stride the same length), count how many back to the crease and make a note of this number. Now next time you are playing you can pace out your run-up.

We identified earlier that the ideal line and length is one where the ball is hitting the top of off stump after bouncing once. The point where you start your run-up is the point where you can draw a straight line from that point through the middle of the popping crease to the off stump. If you have a long piece of string you can mark this out. You will notice there is a slight angle towards the wicket.

From starting the bound to gather and then completing your action you want as much of your momentum going in a straight line towards the batter's off stump. Run in a straight line to that target. Ideally, if you want to bowl the ball straight then your run-up needs to be straight. We don't want it to curve or move in to out or out to in. As well as enabling a more consistent line to your bowling, a straight approach makes it easier to gain optimum momentum and therefore more pace to your bowling, as well as good alignment of your feet from back-foot contact to front-foot contact.

It should also be noted that if your back foot, upon landing, whether grounded or raised, cuts the return crease, this is also a no-ball. As mentioned earlier, if your front foot oversteps the popping crease this is also a no-ball – you must have some part of your foot, whether grounded or raised, behind the popping crease. A batter cannot be dismissed off a no-ball. It will cost you one run and you will have to bowl the ball again.

Another type of no-ball is if you deliver the ball and it bounces twice before reaching the batter and also if you bowl a delivery above waist height to the batter without bouncing. Lastly, if you deliver the ball with a throwing action (arm bent to straight on release) this also can be signalled a no-ball by the umpire. Your bowling arm must not straighten throughout the bowling action.

A wide is different to a no-ball. It is called by the umpire if it is perceived by the umpire to be wide enough that the batter cannot play the ball with a legitimate stroke. In some limited overs matches the wide is brought closer into the batter and maybe signalled any time you bowl a ball down the leg side. A wide costs you one run and the ball must be bowled again.

The Follow-Through

Despite happening after you have let go of the ball the follow-through is still an important part of the bowling action. For a lot of bowlers, concentrating on the follow-through keeps them upright at the crease and driving towards the target. That is the key point – the follow-through is a drive through to where you are bowling and then you naturally slow down.

The principle is – 'follow the ball down the pitch'. The caveat to this is when playing on turf wickets then there is an area of the pitch that you are not allowed on, so your follow-through does have to move from this area. The following photos show the path of a good follow-through:

Even in the follow-through you should have your eyes still drilled on where you want to land the ball.

The following diagram highlights the area of the pitch that you are not allowed to follow through into:

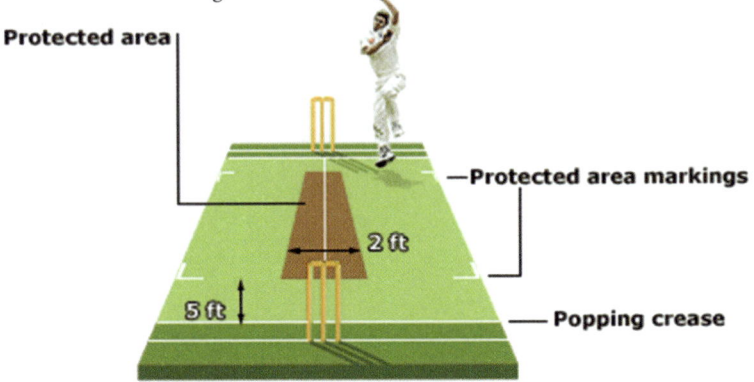

Front-Arm Variations

If you have watched any cricket live or on TV, you will have noted that bowling styles are very different and vary greatly from player to player. One of these differences is the use of the front arm. When discussing the front arm earlier in the chapter it was very much about keeping this arm (as well as the bowling arm) straight. However, most pace bowlers do not do this – they pull their elbow into the side of their body. For some this happens when the arm is vertical above the head while others keep the arm straight until waist height and then the elbow is pulled in. The following show the differences between all three.

One of the reasons bowlers use these methods is to gain more pace. So do try both and see what you prefer – you might use a combination like a hard pull-down for your bouncer. The important aspect is for it not to allow the head to drop as you pull in. Pull in hard but keep your head up and momentum going forward.

The other reason bowlers use a pull-in rather than straight front arm is it can help keep them 'compact' and keep the front arm tight to the body so they do not fall away in the action. A straighter arm for longer can lead to the front arm arcing away from the body and not going in a straight line to the target.

In terms of the front arm starting position, it can start bent, but the important part is having the elbow high – ideally at least to eye level as in this photo:

The important part here with a bent front arm is that the bend does not result in the hand starting to point to the leg side because when pulling in from here the natural arc of the arm is to go to the off side with the shoulders working horizontally not vertically, which will affect your wrist position on release and decrease accuracy.

Midway and Front-On Bowling Actions

Again, if you've watched some cricket you will have definitely noticed that all bowlers are side-on – some are partially side-on (called midway) or completely front-on. Perhaps your favourite bowler is the England fast bowler Gus Atkinson and you would rather bowl like him. That is fine – the principles for all three are very similar and in terms of the bound is actually easier when front on. The key is not to be mixed with your bottom half landing side on and your top half front-on, or the other way round. This stresses the back, which can cause problems later in life.

The following photos show the full sequence of both midway and front-on bowling actions. Note the differences in feet position on back-foot landing and where the front arm is in relation to the head. With any action it is important to avoid a cross over of arms as you run in and then gather.

> **Note for players and coaches**
> If you find a player with a mixed action and feel they are putting a lot of stress on their back, then it is usually (although not always) easier to then align the top half with the feet rather than the other way around. These are mixed actions and can put a lot of stress on the back.

The bowling action, particularly the path of the arms, shoulders and hands, is quite a complicated series of movements for both bowling and non-bowling (front) arms.

A simple and effective way of visualising this for very young bowlers is by using a plastic hoop (size suitable for age and size of bowler) to provide a track for the hands and arms to run around. The importance of trying to move each arm in relatively vertical alignments, moving towards the target, can be both seen and felt by the bowler.

Firstly this should be demonstrated by the coach, holding the hoop in the following manner:

- Bowling arm. The hoop is held in the non-bowling hand (front arm) across to the appropriate ball-starting position for the bowling arm. The hoop is held slightly away from the body, creating a big vertical circle for the ball and bowling arm to track around. The coach demonstrates the tracking movement from the bent-arm gather position, through to the high, straight-arm release. This can be done with or without a ball.

- Non-bowling (front arm). The hoop is now held in the bowling hand across to the appropriate starting position for the front arm and hand. The hoop is held slightly away from the body, creating a big vertical circle for the non-bowling (front arm) to track around. The coach demonstrates the tracking movement from the raised vertical front forearm and elbow position, through to the high, follow-through finishing position.

The bowler can then try this themselves or with the assistance of the coach holding the hoop in its approximate position. This visual method of coaching should help the young bowler to feel the arm and body movements necessary to deliver the ball from a vertical arm position, and with practice develop an efficient action co-ordinating both arm movements simultaneously.

Another successful method of coaching a young bowler the importance of balance and the vertical movement of the bowling and non-bowling arm is to ask them to imagine bowling through a single doorway. Ask them what would happen if they fall to the side or lean or lower the angle of their arms. They always answer, 'I'll smash my hands into the door frame!'

With this in mind suggest to them that a good principle to remember would be to 'stay tall and narrow and go straight'. Even discussing bowling through airport customs X-ray machines can help them understand these bowling principles. Ask them, 'What is the first part of your body to go through the beam?' The answers are invariably 'foot, hand or head'. Any answer is fine, as long as all three are going straight!

Finally, another method of helping to attain a 'tall, narrow and straight' bowling alignment is to use an intervention pole corridor. This method is shown in the Bowling Drills and Video Analysis chapters.

TWO
SEAM AND SWING BOWLING

'As a fast bowler you must be willing and able to push your body to gain the most out of what you have, and, when under pressure, be able to know what your best options are and how to deploy them.'
CHRIS LIDDLE
Northants & England Women's Bowling Coach

In this chapter we will discuss the various technical components of pace bowling, which incorporates the art of swinging the ball, seaming the ball, bowling variations (use of the crease, slower balls, bouncers and yorkers) and how to add pace. Tactical advice is in chapter six. All of the skills below can only be mastered with lots of practice and this should often be done when a batter is not present to allow you to hone skill without the consequence of what the batter is doing.

'Wrist position is the absolute key. Seam presentation either angling towards fine leg or slip depending on which way you want to swing the ball. The seam must not wobble so ensure the ball is released off the end of your fingers. Practise with a red and white ball for an idea of what your seam does.'
MARTIN BICKNELL
Surrey & England

'To maximize any swing that is available, a good wrist position is critical, ensuring that you keep your fingers behind the ball.'
BRENDEN FOURIE
Border & Leicestershire CC

Outswing

In the last chapter we looked at a side-on action predominantly with a grip for a seam-up delivery. A side-on action, to generalise, assists outswing bowling with the way the shoulders work and how that can affect the wrist and release of the ball. However, it is possible to bowl an outswinger with a midway or front-on action. It is all to do with the grip you have on the ball and wrist position on release of the ball.

> *'The conventional view here is that a bowler needs to be 'side-on' to swing the ball out and more 'front/chest-on' to swing the ball in. My opinion is that it's possible (not always easy) to swing the ball either way with almost any bowling action. The less the bowler changes their action to achieve a different outcome, the more difficult things become for the batsman. The arm path and in particular the wrist position/ball presentation are crucial factors.'*
> PHIL ROWE
> *former Northants bowling coach*

An outswinger is a ball that swings away from the batter as it comes down to them. The England great Jimmy Anderson is a great exponent of the outswinger (as well as inswing and other variations) so do watch some video of him. The diagram opposite shows what the path of the ball should be like for an outswinger.

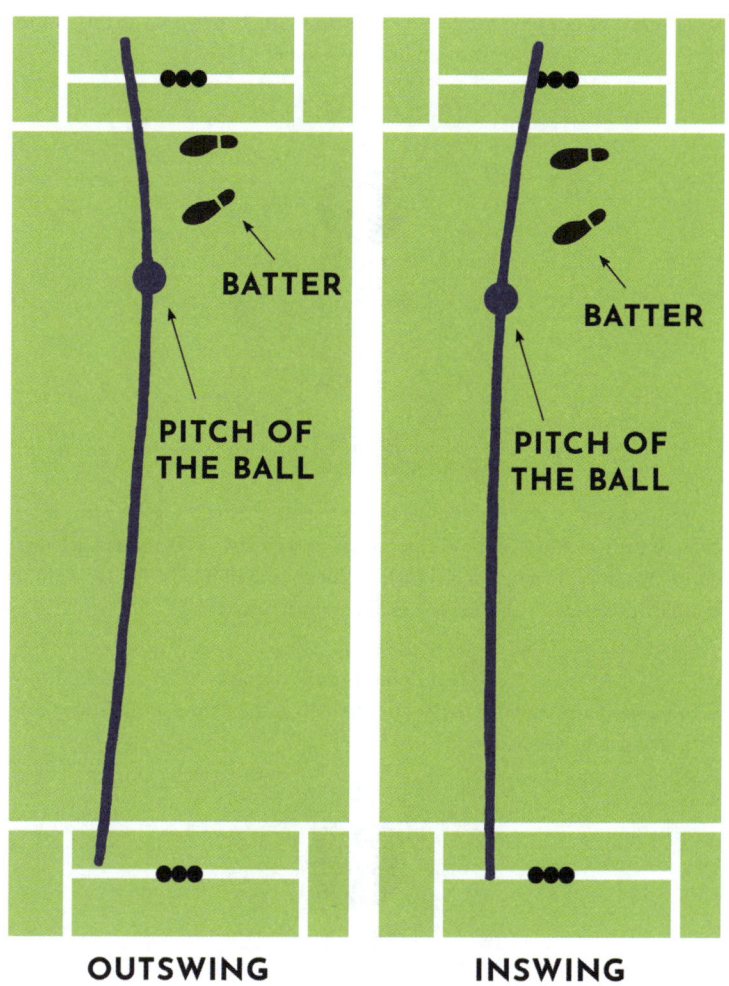

This delivery is generally used to try to have the batter caught behind by the wicketkeeper or slips. The higher the level you play the more important this delivery will become.

In terms of gripping the ball it can help to angle the seam slightly to the left – pointing to where 1st or 2nd slip would be:

In terms of your index and middle finger they can remain slightly apart or can come together on the seam – experiment to see which is better for achieving outswing – it is different for all bowlers. The thumb should be on its side in the middle of the seam – this helps lock the wrist in place.

> **Note for players and coaches**
> In terms of locking the wrist it can help to have the thumb knuckle bent on the seam as in this photo:

Note also that the shiny side of the ball (darker side in this photo) is facing towards the leg side. This is because the shiny side passes through the air quicker and therefore aids swing.

In terms of wrist position you want to keep the fingers behind the ball on release and then exaggerate the completion of the action with your bowling hand coming through past your left hip.

> *'For the ball to swing away look at the back of the ball*
> *and keep the outer part of your hand facing forward.'*
> PHIL ROWE

Depending how much the ball is swinging you can adjust how much angle you have on the seam to help you gain more swing. Sometimes with a new ball you do not need to add an angle and can rely on a strong wrist position to still get some outswing.

Some bowlers do lower their bowling arm to aid achieving outswing; however, here the ball tends to move earlier in the air – making it easier to predict where it will be by the time it reaches the batter. For both outswing and inswing the later you can achieve the movement in the air (as close to the ball pitching as possible) the harder it is for the batter to play. The other factor of outswing that makes it harder for the batter is if you can still gain away swing from a line of attack where the ball is starting on the stumps. A lot of bowlers can only swing the ball from wide of the stumps to wider, but that is easier for the batter to leave those deliveries. Practise hard at swinging the ball from straight. Angling your run-up slightly can help this so your alignment at the crease is more towards leg stump – the line where you want to swing the ball from leg to off stump.

Inswing

> *'Many experienced seamers think about gripping the ball with slightly more*
> *pressure on one finger or the other, to achieve more swing. Interestingly the*
> *best of the bunch (Jimmy Anderson) talks about having slightly more pressure*
> *on his index finger to bowl his outswinger – he likes the idea that doing so*
> *encourages the ball to head more towards the stumps (angling in) before the*
> *swing takes effect and the ball swings away from the stumps towards the slips.*

He does the opposite for his inswinger with more pressure with his middle finger. Obviously, he turns the ball over so the shiny side in on the off side. Increasing the pressure with his middle fingers encourages the ball to start outside off stump, before the swing effect kicks in and the ball swings back in towards the stumps often to devastating effect.'
PHIL ROWE

For the inswinger we now want the ball to swing in towards the batter and their stumps as in this diagram:

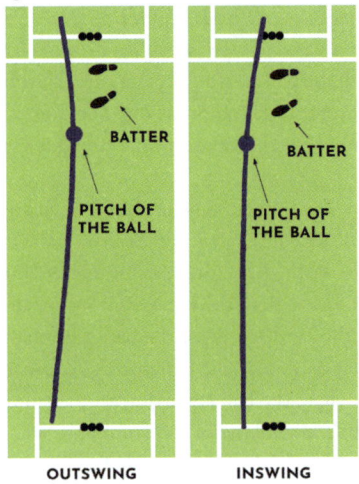

The grip for inswing is the reverse of the outswinger – this time angle the seam so that it is pointing more towards fine leg as in this photo:

Note here that the shiny side is now on the opposite side – facing the off side of the ground. Fingers can be apart or together – which works best for you.

In terms of wrist position on release it still needs to be behind the ball to achieve forward velocity but this time angled slightly to the leg side so that your fingers impart force on the left side of the ball.

When first trying the inswinger it can also help, when completing your action, that your bowling arm follows through towards your right hip rather than your left to attain the wrist action you are looking for.

It can also help to have a higher arm to achieve inswing, but again, as with outswing, it will swing earlier, and we want the ball to swing as late as possible.

If you also bowl the outswinger, ultimately you want both deliveries to look as identical to the batter as possible so work hard on your wrist position on release to attain the swing rather than changes to bowling-arm heights and follow-throughs. The less notable the changes between both deliveries the better as it is harder to bat against.

> *'It is all about your wrist position to make sure you're presenting the ball in the correct way to give it the best chance to swing. A good way to practise this is with a ball that has some tape down the seam so you can see the seam easily. Then, initially, just throwing the ball to somebody and playing around with grips and wrist position until you find something that works for you. This way you can get volume without having to bowl vast amounts of overs. You can then take that back to bowling off a short run with the same ball and eventually off your full run.'*
> DAVID WILLEY

Varying the Amount of Swing

'You can manipulate the seam for swing and scramble it for no swing. Both are very important now and need a lot of practice and experimentation.'
MARTIN BICKNELL

All balls do vary in the amount they swing and to achieve swing you may have to experiment in the game with slightly different seam positions in terms of how much you angle it (or don't) to achieve swing. However, when you do have a ball that swings it is possible to vary the amount it swings by adjusting the seam position and also your wrist position.

Small adjustments to the seam position will affect the amount of swing. Experiment by adding slightly more or less angle on the seam to see if you can vary the amount of movement you are getting.

Go further – if the ball is swinging nicely for your outswinger turn the seam more to where gully would be. To the batter it will still look like an outswinger but with this angle it is unlikely to swing – and you may even achieve some off cut.

'I would encourage the bowler to play around with the seam position. The ball is released differently out of each bowler's fingertips so by working out what angle of the seam in the grip helps present the ball better when released is the key. The other part is encouraging the bowler to bowl fuller and keep the same effort and snap – what we want is as many revolutions on the ball as possible to help the ball cut through the air and also zip off the surface.'
CHRIS LIDDLE

Wrist Flick

A lot, perhaps the majority, of professional bowlers will have a wrist flick as part of their release of the ball. A wrist flick can add pace and it imparts backspin on the ball, which helps with seam presentation and getting movement off the wicket and in the air. Whatever level you are at it is worth experimenting with and will certainly aid your bowling as long as you can keep your hand behind the ball on release and that the flick does not rotate your wrist like an off cutter.

The two photos below show how the wrist is bent back just prior to release above the bowler's head (note that it has not rotated).

Note for coaches – in terms of maintaining a good wrist position a good drill is to flick the ball up with the wrist trying to achieve a perfect straight seam whilst doing the same as in this photo:

> *'Backspin – rotating the ball backwards as you release – stabilises the ball in the air and as it rotates backwards whilst travelling through the air, the effect of the forces that make the ball swing (the air being disturbed at different speeds either side of the seam) are increased, i.e. the faster the ball is rotating backwards = the greater 'swing forces' on the ball (assuming the ball is presented well and is in a condition to swing).'*
> PHIL ROWE

Shining the Ball

An important part of swinging the ball is to have one side of the ball very shiny as this will make it travel through the air quicker. At the start of the innings the ball still has its lacquer on and you will be able to achieve swing whichever way round you hold the ball. However, after a few overs wear to the ball will develop, then you need to pick a side of the ball to shine. As a bowler you need to take responsibility for this and make sure that it is communicated to any players responsible for shining the ball. You may go through a period of trying the ball different ways around to see which swings the best, but usually the side you will opt to shine is the one with the least wear. This can change mid-match if there is some damage to the ball.

Having one side of the ball very shiny makes a huge difference as the better the shine the quicker this part of the ball will travel through the air. The whole of one side of the ball needs to be shined, and saliva and sweat can be used to help attain this. The most important part of the ball that needs to be shined is the part nearest the seam, as this cuts the air first. This is often a rougher part of the ball than the outer part so needs more work to develop a shine. The whole circumference round the seam needs to be shined. Focus on this part of the ball before shining the rest of it.

Most fielders and bowlers shine the ball on their trousers but some shirts can now be purchased which have an elongated sleeve that allows shining. You may have seen England's Joe Root do this. This is perfectly legal, but other than sweat and saliva, nothing else can be applied to the ball such as dirt or suncream.

Reverse Swing

Reverse swing is where the ball is swinging towards the side that has been shined rather than away from it. Reverse swing is usually caused by one side of the ball getting particularly roughed up and dry. This changes the airflow dynamics and this side of the ball now goes through the air faster than the 'shiny' side.

Due to how reverse swing is obtained the ball is usually very worn before it starts to 'reverse'. So the pitch and outfield conditions will play a part in whether enough wear is generated on the ball for it to reverse swing. A hard, dry pitch with little or no live grass will scuff the ball more than a pitch with plenty of live green grass. Similarly, an outfield that is dry and hard will also wear the ball down more. If there is moisture around then it is impossible to get the ball to reverse swing as how dry the ball is plays an important part as to whether it will reverse swing.

If conditions are a green wicket with a green lush outfield you are better off sticking with 'orthodox' swing throughout the innings and keeping one side of the ball very shiny.

However, if the wicket is dry and hard and/or the outfield very dry and hard then there are some things you can do as a bowler and a fielding unit to accelerate towards trying to obtain reverse swing.

When deciding on whether to try and get the ball reversing look at how much movement you are currently getting. If the ball has stopped swinging orthodoxly and there is little seam movement off the pitch then give it a go.

Changing the Ball

Depending what level you are playing at this might not be an option, but if the ball isn't moving at all in the air then have it checked by the umpire. If it doesn't fit through his rings (i.e. it is out of shape) then the umpire will be obliged to offer a replacement of similar wear that hopefully you can get swinging. An out of shape ball rarely swings.

Seaming and Cutting the Ball

On wickets where there is seam movement (to generalise, the wickets that have more live green grass on them aid seam movement) it's maybe preferable to seam the ball rather than swing it as the movement is later and harder to play.

The grip is as described in the last chapter but the seam can be angled minutely left or right so that upon landing it hits either the left side of the seam to gain seam movement away from the right-hander or right side of the seam to move the ball back in. This can also be done with a subtle change of wrist position. This is a high-end skill and will take lots of practice.

Whether you opt for seam-up delivery will also depend on the ball. If you are using one with a high proud seam – you are more likely to gain movement from hitting it.

Throughout the game dirt can collect in the seam. It is important to get this out. You are allowed to use your fingernails to do so, but it is illegal to 'pick the seam' with the intent to raise it up further, so always clean the seam in front of the umpire so they know you are not cheating.

Sometimes the ball will not seam or swing, but we still need to try and achieve some lateral movement. Here you can try an off or leg cutter where, instead of keeping your wrist behind the ball, you come down one side of it, producing 'cut' and the ball rotates slightly left (leg cutter) or right (off cutter). The aim is have the ball move off the pitch upon landing.

This form of delivery is not used as often by bowlers as it does come with a drop of pace due to less force behind the ball on release; however, even the retired England great – Stuart Broad – bowled a leg cutter regularly as he got movement away from the bat with it and he could bowl it without dropping his pace significantly.

We want to cut the fingers down one side of the ball but still apply force behind so it is a cutter – rather than a slower ball. Some bowlers will employ both fingers on the seam and some only one finger on the seam with the other finger on the flat surface.

Wobble Seam

The skills of Jimmy Anderson have been widely acclaimed and in certain conditions he will bowl a 'wobble' seam delivery more often than his inswinger or outswinger. Here the aim is not to have the seam perfectly upright all of the way down, so that the ball wobbles in the air and the batter does not know if it is going to move in or out as any movement is usually very late whether in the air or off the pitch.

Grips can vary for this to be bowled successfully but the following has been proven to assist more often than not and is recommended by former Northants bowling coach – Phil Rowe:
- Fingers wider on the ball (off the seam – see photo below), but the seam still upright.
- Bowled with some slight off cut in the wrist action on release can help.
- A wrist flick is not usually applied.

'Similar to working out how to get more away swing, each bowler will grip the ball differently. If we think of a right-arm bowler looking to bowl away swing, the seam will be angled to somewhere around first slip. For the wobble seam it's the opposite with the seam angled towards fine leg and the fingers crossing over both sides of the seam (angle of the seam different to each individual). The key thing is that you are still pulling down the back of the ball on release and not trying to push more on one side of the ball than the other.'
CHRIS LIDDLE

'There are two main grips for the wobble seam ball, one is using a wider grip on the seam, and the other is having a looser grip. Nothing else should change.'
BRENDEN FOURIE

Cross Seam

We have talked about swinging the ball and seaming the ball, cutting the ball and 'wobbling' the ball with the point of gaining lateral movement in the air or off the pitch as this is harder for the batter to hit or hit as effectively.

It therefore seems counter-intuitive to suggest a 'cross' seam delivery where the ball has no chance of swinging and a much smaller chance of hitting the seam. However, the movement we are hoping to get here is not laterally but vertically – as in the height of the bounce. If the ball manages to hit the seam it can kick up and if it hits the flat leather can keep low. This can be very effective on wickets with uneven bounce and also commonly used when bowling bouncers as the height it reaches the batter will vary between each delivery.

The grip uses the same fingers, and we still want the index and middle finger end to be on the seam so that we can still grip the ball well. The ball is likely to slip if gripped on the leather. The side-on and front photos below show how to grip the ball cross seam:

Cross seam is also a good way of getting the ball roughed up to aid reverse swing later in the innings and many bowlers use it if they simply cannot control the amount of swing they are getting and want to get their line back.

> *'Seam bowlers have several variations they can turn to. These are variations in lateral movement (in and out), they can change their length (i.e. bouncer/yorker) and they can also change their pace (slower balls).'*
> PHIL ROWE

Use of Crease and Bowling to Left-Handed Batters

A very effective way to change the angle to a batter and disrupt their rhythm is to vary your position on the crease. For example, if you are an outswing bowler bowling near to the stumps and the batter is leaving you well, try a delivery from wide on the crease – often the change of angle makes the batter play at a ball they could otherwise have left alone.

As a rule of thumb – come wider if the ball is swinging a lot and come tighter to the stumps (to bowl more wicket to wicket) if not swinging as much. Remember you cannot cross the return crease with your back foot if coming wide or hit the stumps with hand or body if coming tighter to the stumps.

Even if the ball is not moving much in the air, changing your position on the crease and therefore changing the angle to the batter makes them have to adjust and perhaps be more watchful.

Technically most bowlers will simply start their run slightly closer or wider or change the angle of their run-up to hit a different part of the crease. There are exceptions to this such as England fast bowler Mark Wood who suddenly angles wider on the crease later in his run-up to go wider on the crease. This is a hard skill as a lot of his momentum is now heading away from the target, yet he wants to bowl straight.

Keep the batter guessing – occasionally change your position on the crease but bowl an inswinger rather than an away swinger or vice versa so it is does not become predictable which delivery you will bowl when you come wide.

As always practise use of the crease until you have perfected it and can still bowl the ball where you want it, even though you will only use it occasionally in matches. Accuracy is key.

A major use of the crease variation is coming round the wicket rather than over. This is often applied by a fast bowler bowling a lot of bouncers – targeting the rib cage and head and limiting the scoring options to mainly the leg side of the ground. It is not often used when looking to bowl length as it is harder to get LBWs and hit the stumps – however, if the ball is not swinging it is an option to get the ball going across the batter towards the slips, or if you are a big inswinger of the ball you could use to change the angle to get more LBWs and bowled. The main technical aspect is getting the angle right into which stump you are attacking and that you now need to follow through in the opposite direction to get off the 'protected area'.

For left-handers – off stump is now in a different position so we need to adjust the angle of our approach to achieve the correct alignment at the crease. It's nearly always helpful to go wider with where you start your run-up to get the correct alignment at the crease. There is of course now the option of going to round the wicket to a left-hander and again the starting point of your run-up should be aligned with a straight line to the stump you are targeting.

> *'A big change is right-arm bowlers coming around the wicket early on to left-handed batters, challenging how well they can leave or play around the off stump; this has also resulted in a lot more away swing or wobble seam deliveries being bowled.'*
> CHRIS LIDDLE

Slower Balls

Slower balls can be very effective when a batter is looking to dominate you and looking for boundaries from most deliveries – that is why they are much more common in the short forms of the game – as they keep the batter guessing as to when the ball will arrive into their hitting arc. Certain ones can be very effective depending on the wicket, where the ball might grip on the surface (soft or very dry/worn wickets that are also conducive to spin).

> *'Variations should be such a fun part of your practice! This is all about deception or getting the most out of the wicket. If there's a bit of grip in the pitch you can use your offleg-cutter or back of the hand. If there's not, you can use knuckle balls, split fingers, ball deep in the hand or something you've made up yourself! Ultimately, this is whatever works for the individual. Play around with grips, techniques and different deliveries and feedback from the batter is always useful – could they see it early, what did it look like, what did it do in the air or off the pitch. You can gain a better understanding of what works for you on what pitches against what type of batter. Where do you want to bowl your various slower balls – what line and length and where will it get hit? Practice is the time to explore. Set aside time for exploring these, it's not about outcome initially, it's about finding what works for the individual and allowing the exploration and conversations to upskill.'*
> DAVID WILLEY

Why and when to bowl a slower ball is discussed in chapter six – here we are going to look at the different options of slower balls. You will not be able to master them all – aim to have three very good ones in your armoury. The key with any slower ball is that it needs to be a surprise to the batter so having the arm speed and run-up speed the same is crucial. If you have to slow either of these down then it is a lot more obvious to the batter what you are going to bowl.

Off Cutter Slower Ball

Very similar to the off cutter described earlier but this time we are going to apply even more force down the right side of the ball and rotate our wrist to do so, which will slow the ball down but also apply the cut (like an off spinner) that will hopefully also move from off to leg upon landing. Again, the index finger on the seam and the middle finger down the ball can help bowl this delivery but do also try and bowl it with your 'stock' ball grip. If you can it will be harder to pick. Due to the similar shape of the wrist an off cutter is often more suited to a side-on outswing bowler.

Leg Cutter Slower Ball

Just the opposite of the off cutter described above. This time the cut is applied down the left side of the ball and is often more suited to an inswing bowler.

Split Finger

Due to the fingers gripping the ball being so wide apart on the leather, it causes the ball to come out slower even though arm speed is the same (you can also still apply a wrist flick). What can also make this ball very effective, if you can master it, is keeping the seam upright on release – this can create wobble seam effect, or swing the ball in either direction as well as moving off the seam when it lands. This slower ball is a more obvious one for the batter to pick.

> 'I believe in white ball cricket bowlers need the following in their armoury . . . a slower ball that has a big drop in pace, a slower ball that is able to leave the batter and create a big angle away from them, able to bowl a yorker from over and around the wicket. These are add-ons to what skill we should already have in place for red ball cricket and are fundamentals to what we are able to deliver as a fast bowler.'
> CHRIS LIDDLE

In the last chapter we talked about having a gap between your hand and the ball with the grip mainly in the ends of your fingers. For this delivery we want the ball all the way into the hand with all parts of your fingers touching the ball:

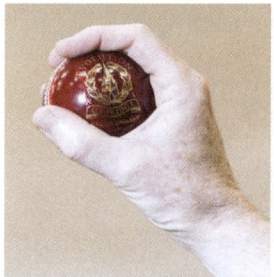 

You can see from the front-on photo that with this grip there is not much different than your stock ball and you can still hold for an inswinger or outswinger or seaming delivery. Therefore, the ball has a good chance of gaining lateral movement as well as the slower pace. England fast bowler Chris Woakes is a very good exponent of this type of slower ball.

Knuckle Ball

There are a few variations to the knuckle ball and a couple of different grips are suggested below. As with the split finger and full hand grip it is possible to keep the seam upright and gain movement. The delivery is easier to pick but does come out a lot slower than most other slower balls.

Back of the Hand Slower Ball

Probably the hardest of all slower balls to master is the back of the hand slower ball. However, if mastered, it can be one of the most effective as it does not require a change of grip (although some bowlers do prefer both fingers on the seam).

The art is to be able to turn your wrist midway through its arc so by the time of release the back of your hand is facing the batter and your fingers pointing to the sky:

If you can also bowl leg spin reasonably well then this may help you master this type of slower ball. The aim is to try and keep the seam upright on its path in the air to gain some lateral movement. With the wrist action it can also get dip in the air, which can deceive the batter, as well as the change of pace itself.

Remember that it is not just being able to bowl a slower ball, you need to master it enough so you can pitch it where you want it to go and therefore cause the batter the most problems. It will take a lot of practice and some will come more naturally than others.

> **Note for coaches**
> When setting up practice try to have a non-net situation where there is no batter and the bowler is less concerned with the outcome – the first few could hit the roof of the net or the side netting. Once competent enough a batter can be added. Here though, whilst still crafting, get them to bowl at least an over on the trot rather than just randomly bowling a slower ball occasionally. You can let the batter know this is the plan and they can work on trying to pick the slower ball and also formulating a plan as to how they would play it. The last step is to introduce the non-bowling hand hiding the ball from the batter from the moment they start their run-up, so they can't see any grip changes until the last minute. This will feel very different to the bowler and is a tough skill and will require plenty of practise and it is crucial they can still bowl their 'full speed' deliveries with a covered hand approach. Lastly, do get your players practising their slower balls with a wicketkeeper so they get used to 'picking' the deliveries.

Bowling the Bouncer

If you have pace then bowling the ball short enough to get the ball shoulder or head height will be an option for you. It adds a fear element for the batter and can alter their mindset. If used well it can also affect their footwork in terms of getting far enough forward to your good-length deliveries. It is an intimidatory delivery but can also be used as part of plan to have the batter caught out from hooking, pulling or cutting. The tactical considerations (as well as field settings) are discussed in more depth in chapter six.

It is important to remember that a bouncer is simply a change of length, this time shorter (see diagram in the last chapter). It should not have to require massive changes to your action or run-up. Just like a slower ball you want it to be a surprise so you should run in with the same pace as you would your stock ball and time the release later to achieve a shorter length. Where you look will also change – zone in on that spot from the top of your mark.

Extra pace can help to 'rush' the batter when bowling a bouncer. If you don't usually have a wrist flick you could think about adding one for this delivery as well as pulling harder into your ribs with your left elbow (especially if you don't normally do so) as long as it does not affect the basics of your action. However, even these small changes will provide visual cues for the batter.

It is important that you are able to return to hitting a good length after bowling a bouncer. If you have pushed a batter back in the crease with a short-pitched delivery (or a few of them), then the aim is they don't get forward to a length they should do, making them more vulnerable to dismissal. The myth is it is a yorker that is a good follow-up ball but, unless the batter is backing away from the stumps, if they are hanging back because of the short balls you've bowled then they are actually in a good place to play a yorker from. Get back to hitting a good length instead.

Note for players and coaches

The art is getting into the business area as much as possible – shoulder and head, or higher if the batter is a compulsive hooker/puller. Just like the slower ball, practice is good. If leg-side wides are not an issue in the format then an angle in towards the batter is a good ploy – especially if a compulsive hooker/puller, as they can only hit these deliveries square, or behind square on the leg-side, making it easier to set a field for the top-edge catching opportunity or popping the ball up for a catch on the leg-side. Coming round the wicket for regular short-pitch bowling is also a reasonable option in determining mainly where the ball can be hit to and can help take out the uppercut option for the batter. A good practice is to take the batter out of the equation and tie a target to the back of the net that correlates to where the ideal bouncer would end up. Six balls at a time with a break in between for two to three overs is good practice to finding the right length and line consistently. Remember that ideal length will change on each different surface you play on.

> *'For yorkers I load up with my bowling hand a bit higher in my gather, keep my eyes fixed on a yorker length and try to drive my chest and eyes directly to that. I also try and bowl it harder/faster than my stock delivery. Very often we can try and 'put the ball there', which is counterproductive.'*
> DAVID WILLEY

Similar to the bouncer, see the yorker as simply another change of length. If you can adjust your length enough to bowl a bouncer you can certainly do it to go fuller for a yorker. The ideal length is one where it has a chance of getting underneath the batter's bat (as in the diagram in chapter one). The ideal line will depend on match situation, boundary size and the batter's strengths, but in terms of getting a dismissal from a yorker, you need to be targeting the stumps – middle stump to be precise, so you have some leeway if you are slightly wider. When executed well it not only brings the stumps into play but it is also very hard to bat against. This is why it is often used at the death of limited-overs matches, and line can vary depending on ground dimensions and a batter's strengths. This is discussed more in chapter six.

Just as with the bounce, do not aim for radical changes to your action, but some extra pace can help the ball get under the bat, so a wrist flick and hard elbow pull-in can add pace, and the timing of the release needs to be slightly earlier than your stock ball. In terms of where you are looking, again go for the spot where you want to land the ball, but some do find it easier to get the ball full enough to be a yorker to look at the base of stumps or even higher up the stumps. Find what works for you on a consistent basis.

> *'Not one size fits all. I have encouraged our bowlers to use different angles to allow them to access the yorker easier. Right-arm round the wicket to a right-hand batter has been effective for some in getting that feeling separating the stock ball release point and the yorker release point. Focus points are also different for everyone and it's key the bowler explores and find out what works for them. Some people look at the feet and others the top of the stumps.'*
> CHRIS LIDDLE

> **Note for players and coaches**
>
> As with any delivery, a good practice for the yorker is to bowl at a target on the ground; however, what can help create the sense of getting under the bat is to also have a chair over the target that the bowler has to get underneath to hit the target.

Bowling with Purpose and Adding Pace

'If you want to bowl fast, you have to practise bowling fast. Firstly, make sure your action is safe, aligned with your momentum going forward. If it's not, correct this and then practise bowling fast. Set aside sessions for just this. Short, sharp sessions – 12 balls with long rest where you practise bowling fast. For these sessions it doesn't matter where the ball goes; we're training speed, not accuracy. This can slowly drip feed into your normal bowling.'
DAVID WILLEY

Whatever pace you bowl seam at, it is vital that you bowl with purpose, attack the crease hard and look to hit the deck hard. Do not try to put the ball there, bowl it there with intent. This intent will get you more accuracy, more pace and, when on offer, more seam movement and more bounce. Even if you are medium-pace seamer who bowls with the wicketkeeper stood up, you should still look to bowl with intent, attack the crease hard and try to make the keeper wince a bit when they have one to take off you!

'To add more pace have a faster, balanced run-up, be more explosive through the crease and channel all your energy towards the target. Balance through the crease is very important, being as upright as possible at the point of delivery. Keep the body moving in straight lines toward the target area for as long as possible.'
BRENDEN FOURIE

In terms of adding pace or bowling fast, a lot comes down to your mindset. You have to want to bowl fast and bowl quicker. Physically this is harder on the body, so you have to be mentally prepared for more effort (and pain) and willing to spend the time training to gain the physical attributes. You will not be a fast bowler for long if you can only sustain for a few balls or a few overs. You need to be physically very fit. This is discussed more in chapter seven. Pakistan's Imran Khan and England great Darren Gough are both bowlers who started out their careers medium-paced, but simply decided they wanted to bowl fast!

There are some technical characteristics or adjustments you can try to gain more pace. Two have been discussed already in this chapter – pulling in hard with your left elbow (and delaying your bowling arm coming over). With this, many bowlers find it can help to go from an open fist and then, as you pull down, clench the fist. The other is adding a flick of the wrist upon ball release – think of it as a wrist snap.

You can also try adjusting your length of run-up. Do you feel quicker if you run in for longer and gain more momentum like Mark Wood or are you more comfortable with a more controlled approach and late acceleration into the crease like India's Jasprit Bumrah. Try some alternatives and see if either helps. A longer run-up can add a psychological affect.

> *'The run-up is always a good starting point when wanting to add pace. How effective is my run-up in getting to a top speed that can be maintained? Is my base solid on release or do I collapse or spend too long on my back leg (areas of strength and technique). Back-foot contact drills help build awareness of transferring from back-foot contact quicker. Also encourage the bowler to push their limits and see what pace they can get to; sometimes sacrificing consistency in the short term and building those in at a later date can help build confidence in a bowler to push their boundaries.'*
> CHRIS LIDDLE

Getting through the crease is important for pace. The more momentum you have towards the target the better, and you will not add pace if you have a high bound and then a back-leg collapse from this. You will lose a lot of momentum this way. The quicker you move from back-foot contact to front-foot contact the better. Get the knees and chest driving in a straight line towards the target. Adding a braced front knee on landing, as in the photo below, can allow the top half of your body to snap over it, generating extra pace.

The former Australian fast bowler Brett Lee is a very good example of a braced front leg aiding bowling fast.

For side-on bowlers, you can definitely try leaning back slightly as you get side-on and even adding a drag to your back foot (not very common these days). However, a lean back can affect length, so timing of release is crucial.

Making sure your chest is going through towards the target and that you maintain a strong upright action are also important aspects of bowling fast, as is delaying the bowling arm coming through. This is only for a split second, but instead of your bowling arm and front arm working together, here your front arm pulls in and you delay the bowling arm coming over as in this photo:

> **Note for players and coaches**
>
> Adding pace can make a bowler more dangerous, but if it is at expense of accuracy and technical skills it will not actually make you a more dangerous bowler to face. The golden egg is adding pace, bowling fast but also being able to put the ball where you want it to go consistently and being able to move the ball laterally. Lateral movement combined with accuracy – with faster pace – is very hard for batters. Ultimately, the most successful bowlers are the most accurate ones who can move the ball. If they can add a few mph, this will make them even harder to face but not at the expense of accuracy and movement.

Picking the Right Ball

We have stressed the importance of lateral movement in this chapter, and in terms of swing the best balls you can pick to play with are ones that generally feel a bit smaller in the hand (spinners also prefer this), the seam not over-pronounced and the red colour is a darker shade – dark cherry is ideal. Of course, picking a ball only happens at certain levels of the game and often you will simply have to make do with the one that the umpire gives you!

THREE
OFF SPIN BOWLING

'Having a strong repeatable action is a huge asset. A spinner can bowl all day – want to bowl – don't go away. Aim to win the war; the odd battle will not go your way.'
GARETH BATTY
Surrey & England
Surrey CCC Head Coach

An off-spinner (or finger spinner as often referred to) is a slower bowler than a seamer who bowls with the wicketkeeper up to the stumps. It is the art of turning the ball from off to leg, or back into the batter as the ball pitches. The art is applying enough revolutions on the ball (spin) to achieve this movement off the pitch as well as deceiving the batter in the flight. There are also ways to vary the amount of turn, and other variations such as the arm ball and the carrom ball. All are discussed in this chapter.

The Grip

'Aim for a comfortable grip, spin the ball as hard as you can. Try and get the feeling of the ball staying on your primary spinning finger as long as possible.'
GARETH BATTY

The ideal grip for an off-spinner is to just use the index and middle finger, with the seam nestled in between the second knuckles and having no other fingers touching the ball:

Note that the seam is in the opposite direction to a seam-up delivery.

If you are young player and are struggling to keep a firm grip on the ball with this grip, then use the thumb and third finger on the ball as well:

Once your hands become big enough, try to revert to just your index and middle finger.

Before attempting a delivery, try spinning the ball by turning the hand clockwise and flicking the ball upwards:

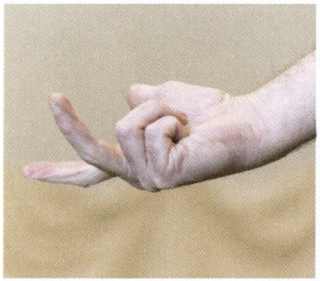

Try to keep the seam straight even though it is rotating. You can imagine that your hand is performing the same turning action as opening a doorknob. You will get more spin off the wicket if the ball hits the seam. Spin is imparted off the side of the index finger.

The Action

As with any style of bowling off-spin can be bowled with a side on, midway or front on action. The vast majority of off-spin bowlers (as well as leg spin bowlers) are side on or midway. England's Moeen Ali is a great example of an orthodox side on action, as is India's Ravichandran Ashwin.

> *'It is good practice to bowl without a batter to concentrate on hip control. Hips are our source of power and will change how the ball arrives.'*
> GARETH BATTY

The reason that this style of action is more widely used is it allows the rotation of the body to gain more turn and drift, as well as what is imparted on the ball by the wrist rotation. This sequence depicts the action from gather to completion:

Note that the feet are aligned towards the target on front-foot landing, and that on release the bowler has come on to the ball of the foot with a straight front leg. This allows body rotation and maximises height on release. The step forward is not as large as that for seam bowling. Try also to avoid a large cross-over of the feet, as in this photo:

The action is similar to that of the seamer – the one major difference is that the body rotates more to complete, and the back leg drive-through can be more circular.

However, you also still need to have momentum going towards where you want the ball to go. The completion should be around 180 degrees. The back foot comes through in line with the front foot. In terms of hand position, most will start with the palm of the hand facing the batter and then rotate it so the back of the hand faces the bowler. The wrist is straight, not bent backwards, so that the seam can remain upright upon release. The bowling arm can be straight or slightly bent throughout the action as long as it does not straighten on delivery.

Note here that the head has remained up and focused on the target. The front arm and bowling arm have completed similarly to an outswing bowler.

In terms of a stock ball, it is a delivery that upon landing on a good length turns from off to leg to hit to the top of off stump. As with any style of bowling top of off stump is goal number one. The line that you bowl will vary depending on how much turn there is in the wicket. If there is a lot of turn you will need to pitch the ball wider to hit top of off. The less turn there is the straighter you will need to be. Simply, you want a delivery that can challenge both edges of the bat. If it turns, you are challenging the inside edge or hoping to miss it and hit the stumps. If the ball does not turn, it brings in the outside edge for a catch to the wicketkeeper or slip.

In terms of the ideal pace, certainly the better batters you bowl to and the higher level you play, the quicker your stock ball will need to be, but ultimately it is finding a pace that the ball turns on the wicket you are playing on. Some bowlers are skilful enough to be able to work this out early in their spells. Other spin bowlers will have a natural pace that they bowl consistently well at.

Your pace and trajectory will also be dictated by your height. Shorter spin bowlers will need to get the ball up and then down (above the batter's eyeline). A tall spinner's bowling arm is already above the batter's eyeline and can therefore have a flatter trajectory towards the target, which also enables more pace but less drift and drop.

In the photo opposite, the bowler is mid-crease, which is a good starting point but it is possible to change angles on the crease – which is discussed later in this chapter.

Note for players and coaches

Before matches and spells in the nets it is good practice to isolate the action with no run-up and bowl from a standing position at the crease. This puts an emphasis on the body's action to impart spin and pace on the ball.

The Front Arm

To help with getting up on to the ball of the foot on release, many spin bowlers unfurl their front arm from a bent position to a straight one. It is easier to show in pictures here:

Once up on the toe, the front arm can drive forwards towards the target, or the elbow can pull into the side of the body. This is a personal preference – use the method that best helps get your line and length consistent. As discussed later in this chapter, a front elbow pull-in can add snap to the action and therefore more revolutions on the ball. As with seam bowling, the arm can also go straight until around waist height and then pull in.

The Run-Up or Approach to the Wicket

'The most important thing in a run-up is momentum to allow your action to be strong and repeatable.'
GARETH BATTY

There are a few spinners who can bowl without a run-up and a few who actually have a run into the crease. Former England spinners Phil Tufnell and Derek Underwood attacked the crease this way. For the majority of spinners, it is an 'approach' to the wicket. For some it is more of an amble (such as Moeen Ali), for others more bustling (Graeme Swann). Have a look at both and experiment with different paces. What works for you?

The pace that you must find is the one that works for you so that you can still keep your action strong and consistent at the crease and provide enough momentum to add pace on the delivery to get it down the other end. It also needs to be one where you feel you can let go of the ball in your own time –

when you are ready. This helps you in seeing whether a batter will be using their feet at you.

To work out where to start your approach, this should be the same as for a seamer aligned in a straight line through the crease to where you want to land the ball. Certainly, a slightly angled approach helps bowlers achieve a side-on action.

Completion

Unlike seam bowlers, you ideally do not want to follow the ball down the wicket. You need to be in a position to be able to field the ball off our own bowling or take a return catch. So, after the back leg comes through, try to bounce out of that position into this one:

The position is very similar to the position a fielder will take up as the batter goes to play an attacking shot. You need to be a strong position with weight on the balls of your feet, with your knees bent so you can move quickly side to side, dive if you need to and get down to the balls hit low back at you. The ball gets hit back towards spinners a lot, and often hard. The better you are at fielding off your own bowling the more runs you will save (you will have better bowling figures) and the more caught and bowled you will get. Both can make a big difference to how your stats look at the end of the season.

Where to Look and How to Respond to a Batter Using Their Feet or Sweeping

'Where you look is very individual – some watch the batter, some look at the keeper's gloves and others look at an area on the pitch. No right or wrong, its individual.'
GARETH BATTY

As for any bowler, start by looking at the spot where you want to land the ball. If bowling fuller than that, look shorter and vice versa. However, a batter using their feet to you is more common when bowling spin so it is also vital that you can detect this movement with your peripheral vision so that you can make last-minute adjustments to your line and/or length should the batter be shaping up to come down the wicket to you. This is also true if the batter has premeditated a sweep shot.

If you detect a batter is going to come down the wicket to you, it is important that you bring your length back so the ball will still land on a good length to where the batter will end up. This makes the ball harder to hit as there is more distance to travel to the bat, giving it more chance of beating the bat and bringing in a stumping opportunity. Another adjustment you can make is that of line. If you are getting some nice drift, but not much turn, then going slightly wider will give you a chance of beating the outside edge. If you are getting a lot of turn, then going straighter (hoping to turn it past the batter on the leg side) is a good option. Both can bring in stumping opportunities. Changing pace subtly here can also deceive the batter – either slower or quicker.

Watch out for the dummy to come down the wicket. After coming down the wicket a few times the batter may fake to come down but then stay in the crease.

For batters shaping to sweep or reverse sweep, it generally helps to go fuller and try to get under the bat. If looking for paddle or fine sweeps, then taking the pace off the ball gives them less pace to work with to score runs from that delivery.

Bowling with Purpose and Spinning the Ball Hard

Although slower through the air, a spinner should not be looking to put the ball where they want it to go but still bowl it there with purpose and intent. As with any style of bowling, the more lateral movement you can get off the pitch the harder it is for the batter to play. To gain this lateral movement you have to spin the ball hard – this requires effort. The harder you spin the ball not only means that it has the best chance of turning upon landing, but also that it behaves differently in the air. A ball with a lot of revolutions applied to it will drift in the air (away from the right-hander) and also dip if a certain amount of overspin is applied (discussed later in this chapter). This movement in the air also creates problems for the batter. A ball that is drifting away from them and then turning back in off the pitch is hard to play, and if you can get dip, that can deceive them in length – they think the ball will be a half-volley to drive but if it dips on to a good length they end up hitting the ball in the air rather than along the ground.

The more you spin the ball the more drift, dip and turn you will get. Thus, the more you spin the ball, the harder it will be for the batter to face. There are things you can try to gain more turn. One has already been discussed – pulling in harder with your front-arm elbow. You can also do this with your bowling-arm elbow into your stomach (but remember the arm needs to be straight on release):

For some, adding more pace to their approach can help. Also, having your bowling hand facing away from your head as it comes through to release allows more wrist rotation and therefore imparts more revolutions on the ball.

Lastly, exaggerating the rotation of the body (the 'snap') can also achieve more spin.

Variations

Variations are important for all types of bowlers and there are so many at an off-spinner's disposal. They can vary the amount of turn, vary their pace, vary their position on the crease, come round the wicket, vary their arm height, as well as bowl alternative deliveries such as an arm ball.

> *'Flight, drop, curve, spin and bounce are all in an off-spinner's armoury. Try to understand how to use against each batter and which is most effective on what surface.'*
> GARETH BATTY

Varying the amount of turn

To generalise, the perfect seam angle is 45 degrees – aiming to where the 45 fielder is. This allows the ball to turn but also bounce because of some overspin.

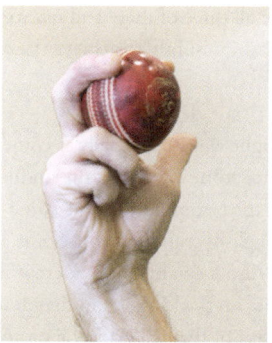

However, on some wickets the ball may not turn enough and you will need the seam more horizontal.

Note from both photos the slight difference in which part of the hand is facing the batter on release. It is also possible to bowl a top-spinner. Here it is the side of the hand that is facing the batter:

It is really difficult to master all three of these and takes great skill and practice to be able to vary your wrist position subtly to achieve the varying amounts of turn.

Arm Height

Every spin bowler's arm height will vary. Ideally it comes from high so that you can get the maximum bounce from the wicket on landing as long as you can still get the required amount of turn from here. Some come slightly lower with their arm to achieve the perfect angle of seam position. Some also come lower with the arm to get more drift away. Also it can help to undercut the ball where it does not pitch on the seam but pitches on the leather and therefore does not turn as much or not at all, and has the effect of the ball skidding on to the batter.

Varying Pace

Varying when the ball arrives to the batter is a useful skill. If every ball is identical in pace, the batter knows when it will arrive, making it easier to line you up for a big hit. If they know that you can vary your pace, then it will make them more wary of lining you up. The art of it is that the changes of pace need to be subtle, with no difference in approach to the wicket – the less cues the batter has the better. As with any variation you can change your pace but still land the ball in the same spot and still impart spin on the ball.

Undercutting the Ball

As mentioned earlier, a lower arm can help undercut the ball, but it is also possible to achieve this with your wrist position. Instead of having a straight wrist on delivery, cock the wrist back as it comes over and then rotate it from there as you release. The seam should now come out more like a flying saucer, meaning the ball will land on the leather, not the seam, and it is more likely to skid straight on rather than turn. Graeme Swann was a master of this delivery. You still need to apply as many revolutions as you can to the ball so that is drifts in air.

Use of the Crease and Coming Round with Wicket

As with any bowling, changing the angle can greatly upset the batter's rhythm. If the ball is turning a lot, coming wider on the crease can help you achieve a line outside off stump more consistently, and likewise, if it is not turning as much, coming tighter to the stumps can aid you bowl more wicket to wicket. But if your stock ball is mid-crease, it is still good practice to bowl some balls in your spell from wider and some tighter to the stumps – both make it harder for the batter to consistently line you up. You still need to be able to hit a good line and length from these different positions on the crease.

As with seam bowlers, you can simply start your run-up straighter or wider, but with spin bowling it is easier to make later adjustments to your run-up and therefore your arrival point at the crease, particularly in tighter to the stumps.

Another variation to change the angle completely is to come round the wicket. This may be simply to do something different to disrupt the batter's rhythm and make it harder for them to score through the off side, or it is often because there is some turn in the wicket and it can bring lbw more into play.

To right-handed batters it helps to start your run-up reasonably straight to help gain the correct alignment at the crease:

You also need to be aware of your follow-through and make sure you do not follow through in front of the umpire.

Cross Seam

A very simple variation is to grip the ball with your index finger completely on the seam so the seam is facing down the wicket to the batter as in the photo:

The index finger is still the finger imparting the spin on the ball. On release the ball will now come out completely scrambled, which means it will only land on the seam occasionally and other times on the leather. This will cause natural variations of turn and bounce and is particularly effective on wickets where there is a good amount of turn on offer. It is also easier to disguise an arm ball as well as subtle variations in turn. It also makes deliveries that turn in the opposite direction harder to pick in the air.

The Arm Ball

The arm ball is effectively the off-spinner's version of an outswinger (although it can also be bowled as an inswinger). Here the grip is the same as the cross-seam delivery above, but instead of rotating the wrist you are going to lock it in place with the aim of the seam staying upright as it goes down the wicket, to allow it to swing in the air. The shiny side should be pointing towards the leg side.

The art of the delivery is to keep the pace the same as your stock ball to make it harder to pick.

The Carrom Ball

This is a delivery that, instead of turning into the batter, turns away from the right-hander. Ravichandran Ashwin is a regular exponent of this delivery. The ball is held between the thumb, the index and the middle finger:

The ball is flicked out by the fingers, rather than any wrist rotation imparted on the ball. It is not a leg spin wrist action – the palm of the hand stays facing the batter. The spin is mainly imparted on the ball by the middle finger, with the thumb also playing a part to squeeze the ball out with leg spin imparted. Strong fingers are required for this delivery and it may not be possible to attempt it until adolescence. As with any variation, try to keep all other aspects of the action the same.

The Pause Delivery

This is easier to bowl the slower your approach is to the wicket. This variation involves stopping completely (pausing) in the gather for a few moments before completing the rest of your action. If you rely on a lot of momentum from your run-up to achieve pace on your delivery, this will be a very hard one for you to bowl well. If, from the gather, you can still get the ball down the other end easily, then this can be a good option. It is particularly useful against batters who pre-meditate their shots a lot, whether this is coming down the wicket or sweeping.

You can vary the amount of the pause to keep the batter guessing exactly when you will release the ball. And, as always, you then need to be able to bowl it well and land it where you want it to go.

Bowling to Left-Handers and Left-Arm Orthodox Spin Bowlers

It is most common for off-spin bowlers to come round the wicket to left-handed batters. The angle (whether you drift the ball much or not) is back in to the batter and the turn is away – which makes the delivery harder to play. It also brings lbw and the stumps more into play.

The challenge is getting the alignment right, and here it is very much what works for you. It is easier to align yourself correctly at the crease (front arm angled towards off stump) if you start your run-up straighter.

However, a lot of spin bowlers prefer to start their run-up on the off side of the stumps and come round the umpire, who is standing close to the stumps, or with the umpire further back to allow the bowler to approach between the stumps and the umpire. These two photos show the difference:

As a bowler, the first port of call is hitting top of off, so which stump you align yourself with will depend on the amount of turn you are getting. Whichever approach you go for is the one that works best for you to achieve a consistent alignment to where you want to bowl. If you are front-on off-spin bowler, then a straighter approach is certainly recommended when coming round the wicket to left-handed batters.

The use of the crease is important. If lining you up well from here, coming wider as a variation is a great option as the angle is so big that it makes it harder to turn the ball. They may leave a ball that goes straight on or they play at a wider one they should let go, bringing the outside edge into play.

If you are struggling to gain good alignment or get much turn from mid-crease, try coming tighter to the stumps. Here a straight approach rather than an angled one will help.

Of course, you can stay over the wicket, or use this as a variation. This would be a good option if you wanted to encourage the batter to hit you into the leg side predominantly and make it harder to access the off side of the ground. You may have a left-arm seamer in the team that has created some rough for you to target, or you simply want to change the angle of attack to disrupt the batter and make them do something differently.

All of the above also applies if you are a left-arm orthodox spin bowler bowling to a right-handed batter. You can still use the variations recommended in this chapter as well using the crease to vary the angle. Just like the off-spinner to a right-hander, aim to challenge both edges of the bat as often as possible.

One thing there is usually more of is rough outside a right-hander's leg stump – making the option to come over the wicket more valuable. Former England left-arm spinner Ashley Giles was an excellent exponent of this, mixing his line so that he pitched on leg stump to hit off but occasionally just clipping the rough created by the right-arm-over seam bowlers. This gains prodigious turn and variation in bounce. This angle can make it harder for batters to use their feet, and for sweeping it brings the top edge into play if it bounces out of the rough. There is also a chance to bowl the batter round their legs. In this photo we have used rolled-up paper to mimic the rough for the left-arm-over bowler to aim at:

Of course, in limited-overs cricket if the ball passes down the leg side it is likely to be called a wide, and if you use this ploy in other forms of the game then you need to be making the batter play for it not to be deemed negative bowling by the umpire.

Due to the chance of more rough as a left-arm orthodox bowler, the skill of bowling over the wicket should be practised regularly so it is an option when conditions suit.

> **Note for coaches**
> When working with any style of bowler on their run-up, to add realism have an umpire in. Some bowlers behave differently in their approach to the wicket when an umpire is there to when they are not. Some also prefer the umpire to stand further away from the stumps than close to them, and they need to work out their preference. If a person is not available to act as an umpire, then a set of stumps, kit bag or another item can be used to replicate the umpire.

Shining the Ball

If you are a good exponent of an arm ball, then keeping the ball shiny is important, but even if it is not one of your variations it is still important for the seam and swing bowlers in your team to look after the ball. You need to think of them as well, and keep working hard on the ball, especially if you mainly bowl with a cross seam.

Bowling with the New Ball

More and more of you are seeing orthodox spinners being asked to open the bowling – particularly in T20 cricket. Despite the fact that they can only have two fielders on the boundary, it is commonly used by teams, mainly because a batter has to add some pace or do something different to create a scoring opportunity. If a spinner can land the new ball consistently in the over and bowl to their field, then it can be an over that rattles by with only a few runs scored. The fielding team get an early 'cheap' over in. It also brings an arm ball variation massively into the game, as the new ball will swing. The normal spinning delivery can also skid on, so behaves slightly differently to an older ball. Or simply it is a big-turning wicket and the captain wants the main wicket-taking threat on as early as possible.

Therefore, you need to have some training sessions where you bowl with a new ball to get the feel for it as well as toughen the fingers for it. Spinning the ball hard off your index finger can rip the skin, which is more likely with a brand-new ball with a hard, pronounced seam – so you need to toughen your fingers to this.

There are not any technical changes you need to make when bowling with a new ball, but to avoid it slipping out you may need to grip the ball tighter. If the ball is skidding on rather than turning, then think about your line and where you bowl the ball from the crease.

FOUR
LEG SPIN BOWLING

'You have to be very fit, physically strong to deliver powerful spin, and aerobically fit to deliver long spells. Mental strength is crucial for confidence and success. Try to take a wicket from ball one and every ball after that. Always remember the next ball is always the most important, whatever happened before.'

IAN SALISBURY

Surrey & England

The art of leg spin has had a resurgence because of T20 cricket. Every team wants a leg-spinner (whether right- or left-handed) because they can usually gain lateral movement no matter how good the wicket is, and they have a plethora of alternative deliveries up their sleeve, in particular a googly. If you can spin the ball both ways and the batter cannot read your delivery, it makes you a lot harder to hit and your wicket-taking threat goes up. England's Adil Rashid has been a mainstay of England's white-ball team for years, winning two World Cups. He is accurate, has a big-turning leg break, a big-turning googly and can also vary his pace. Leg spin can be harder to master and bowl as accurately as off spin, but if you can bowl them well you will be one of the first names on the team sheet. Some of the principles of off spin apply to leg-spinners and are not repeated here, so do read that chapter as well, even if you are already a seasoned leg-spin bowler.

The Grip

Primarily the grip is with the index finger, the middle finger and the third finger:

Again, if you are young with small hands you may need to bring the thumb on to the ball to help stabilise it in your hand.

Spin is imparted primarily by the third finger, this time rotating your wrist anti-clockwise. Most leg-spinners will cock their wrist:

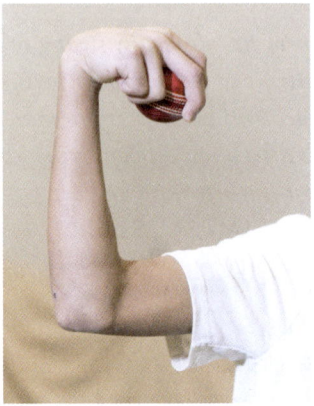

Try spinning a few balls up in the air with your wrist rotating anti-clockwise, trying to keep the seam upright in its rotation:

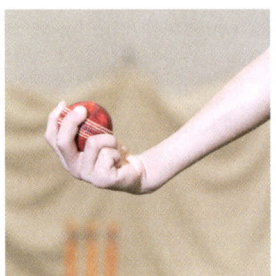 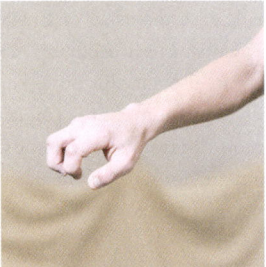

In terms of a stock ball, the leg-spinner is a ball that turns from leg to off, or away from the batter. The hardest part of leg spin is actually the control of release and the use of the wrist. This is why leg-spinners, to generalise, bowl more 'bad' deliveries. On release the wrist goes from a cocked position to a straight, where the palm of your hand should be facing the batter as you let go of the ball.

Try bowling some from the gather to see if you can get the ball turning from leg stump to off stump.

Hopefully, if you have got the wrist action correct, you will also get some drift – this time from off to leg. If you can combine drift in to the batter and turn the ball away from them, you will be harder to play.

The timing of release is even more important for leg-spinners as it will not just affect your length, but also your line, due to the nature of the wrist action. Timed perfectly it will drift nicely on to a good line and length. Too early and it will go full and to the leg side, and too late it will be short and wide of off stump. Often when a leg-spinner releases the ball too late they have to resort to 'putting' the ball and they lose the big spin. Work really hard on the timing of release and bowl plenty of balls from the gather position to work on this.

The Action

A leg-spinner can be side-on, midway or front-on. If you are front-on you will rely on wrist action and arm speed (as well as your approach) to generate turn and pace on your deliveries. If side-on you will also be able to add a lot of body rotation as well to add pace.

To generalise, a leg-spinner has a longer delivery stride than an off-spin bowler – more like a seamer.

You can see here that the front foot is still aligned with the back foot and is driving through towards the target. The head is up and focused on where you want to land the ball. Ideally, from here the leg-spinner comes on to the ball of their foot to aid body rotation and gain height.

As in this photo do not be concerned if the back leg comes out on drive-through as this aids the body rotation, which helps impart more spin on the ball. There is an old school of thought that the back-leg drive-through must be straight, like a seam bowler, but nearly all leg-spinners will have their back leg come out in this way. The main thing to avoid is a large cross-over on front-foot landing. Ensure the back-leg drive-through aligns with the front foot and that there is energy going towards the target.

In terms of the front arm, all the options that applied to the off-spinner apply here as well, as does the completion – where you need to be ready for a return catch.

Stock Ball

As with any style of bowling it is important for a leg-spinner to have a good stock ball: a hard-sprung leg break that you can land on a line and length consistently, again targeting top of off stump. It is so important that you practise this repeatably before trying to master any variations.

The line that you bowl will vary depending on how much turn there is in the wicket. If there is a lot of turn you will need to pitch the ball on or outside leg stump to hit top of off. With less turn you will need to aim for a middle or off stump line.

As with an off-spinner, you need a delivery that can challenge both edges of the bat. If it turns you are challenging the outside for a catch to the wicketkeeper or slips. If it does not turn, then you are challenging the inside edge for a chance of bowled or lbw.

In terms of the ideal pace, certainly the better batters you bowl to and the higher level you play, the quicker your stock ball will be, but ultimately it is finding a pace that the ball turns on the wicket you are playing on. Some bowlers are skilful enough to be able to work this out early in their spells. Others will have a natural pace that they bowl consistently well at.

Note for players & coaches

Before matches and spells in the nets it is good practice to isolate the action with no run-up and bowl from a standing position at the crease. This puts an emphasis on the body's action to impart spin and pace on the ball, as well as focusing on the wrist to impart spin.

As for any bowler, start by looking at the spot where you want to land the ball. If bowling fuller than that, look shorter and vice versa. However, a batter using their feet to you is more common when bowling spin, so it is also vital that you can detect this movement with your peripheral vision so that you can make last-minute adjustments to your line and/or length should the batter be shaping up to come down the wicket to you. This is also true if the batter has premeditated a sweep shot.

If you detect a batter is going to come down the wicket, it is important that you bring your length back so the ball will still land on a good length to where the batter will end up. This makes the ball harder to hit as there is a greater distance to travel to the bat, giving it more chance of beating the bat and bringing a stumping opportunity. Another adjustment you can make is that of line. If you are getting some nice drift but not much turn, then aim on or just outside leg stump. This will give you a chance of a stumping down the leg side. If you are getting a lot of turn, then going wider is a good option to go past the outside edge to bring about a stumping opportunity. Changing pace subtly here can also deceive the batter – either slower or quicker.

Watch out for the dummy to come down the wicket. After coming down the wicket a few times the batter may fake to come down but then stay in the crease.

For batters shaping to sweep or reverse sweep it generally helps to go fuller and try to get under the bat. If looking for paddle or fine sweeps, then taking the pace off the ball gives them less pace to work with to score runs from that delivery.

Run Up or Approach

'You want your run-up to be rhythmical (relaxed + efficient + repeatable) towards your target, body/action aligned, so balanced and powerful at release to impart maximum spin and maximum accuracy.'
IAN SALISBURY

Again, this is so much down to personal preference. The greatest leg-spinner of them all, Shane Warne, had a slow approach and simply accelerated slightly quicker into the crease in his last few strides. On the flip side, the great Indian spinner, Anil Kumble, would bound into the crease. Certainly, if you are a front-on leg-spin bowler, then a faster approach is recommended to help aid pace on the ball. If you are converting from seam bowling you will probably also find that a quicker approach suits you. Leg spin can also put a lot of strain on the shoulder, so you may find that more pace in your approach helps ease this.

Experiment with it to see which approach suits you best. The main thing is getting the alignment correct, not crossing the feet over and having enough momentum from your approach to get a decent pace on the ball.

Bowling with Purpose and Spinning the Ball Hard

Because of the wrist action, bowling leg spin well is difficult to land consistently but do not resort to 'putting' the ball there. The more spin you apply to the ball, the more drift and dip you will also achieve as well as more turn off the wicket. As discussed in the previous chapter, combine this with good accuracy and you will be harder to play.

As with off spin, pulling in harder with the front-arm elbow can help, and added to this you can experiment with a slight delay in bringing your bowling arm over. Imagine that someone is behind you holding your bowling arm and then they suddenly let go and the arm snaps over. Think of it like a catapult effect. It is a very difficult skill to master but can greatly add arm speed and snap.

Another good option for the leg-spinner is exaggerating the wrist cock so that you can apply more wrist action on ball release.

Note here that the ball is held facing you. Adding more pace to your run-up could also help, as can exaggerating the rotation of the body (the 'snap') on release.

Variations

One of the most exciting parts of leg spin is the sheer number of variations on offer to you. However, do not try any of the below until you have mastered the big-turning leg break. The key as always to any variation is that it looks similar to your stock ball, and the pace you bowl should also be the same.

> *'Ultimately spin is imparted by revolutions put on to the ball by the fingers at release. There are different types of spin determined by different positions of wrist at release:*
> *• Side spin (barrel spin) – palm facing target.*
> *• Top spin (over spin) – side of hand towards target.*

• Mixture of side and top spin (seam at different angles)
• Underspin (out the front of hand)
• How the seam hits the wicket, at what pace and amount of revolutions applied by fingers will determine the amount of spin.'
IAN SALISBURY

Seam Angle:

One of the simpler options is changing your wrist angle on release. Earlier we talked about having the palm of your hand facing the batter to achieve leg spin. If you have your hand completely facing the batter, then they should only be able to see one side of the ball, as in this photo:

We will call this the big leg-spinner, where maximum side spin is imparted but no overspin. The ideal, though, is to gain some overspin and having the seam coming down facing where short third man would be fielding:

See here that the wrist has now turned slightly to achieve this seam position. From here you can turn your wrist slightly further so nearly a top-spinner, but not quite. We will call this a little leg-spinner.

Here there is a lot of overspin on the ball but only a small amount of side spin. If you can master these small adjustments, they will help you deceive the batter with barely any change to your action.

The Top Spinner
Now on release you want the side of the hand facing the batter so the seam is pointing straight to them, as in this photo:

This is a really good delivery if you have beaten the bat a few times with your leg break or they are leaving your leg break well. Even if they play it well, it may mean that they start playing at your leg breaks more. It is also a good delivery to get more bounce and perhaps bring in a short-leg catcher.

The Googly

Here the wrist now rotates so that the back of the hand is facing the batter and the ball comes out over your little finger:

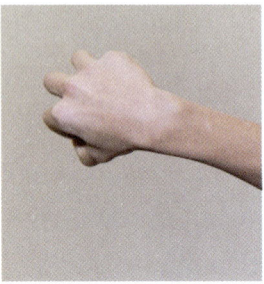

It can help to rotate the bowling shoulder further to help get the wrist round. Adil Rashid bowls this ball particularly well, although generally it is easier to pick. However, even if a batter can pick it, they still have to play it if you can land it well. As this is now effectively an off-spinner, your line may need to change to bring in the stumps, so it is often valuable to bowl a few leg-spinners on a slightly wide line first and then surprise them with this. If they cannot pick it and you bowl it back of a length it is a good one to get the batter bowled, shaping to cut and then the ball comes into the stumps under the bat.

If you are not gaining much turn from your googly, exaggerate the wrist turning further so that the back of your hand is facing the ground rather than the batter.

Note for coaches

Do not add the googly at the expense of a big-turning leg break. We would advise not introducing this until a player is at least 15 years of age and highly competent at the orthodox leg break.

Flipper & Back-Spinner

These deliveries are very difficult to master but provide a very hard-to-play straight-on delivery that is much quicker than your stock ball. They often bring in bowled and lbw opportunities. We would recommend either of these as a more important variation to the googly due to their hard nature to pick and the change of pace element.

> *'The back-spinner is bowled out of the front of the hand (palm facing forward) with back spin/under spin. The flipper is also out of the front, but with the side of the hand pointing forward, and squeezed out between first two fingers and thumb as if clicking your fingers.'*
> IAN SALISBURY

The flipper is similar to the carrom ball – it is flicked out towards the batter by the thumb and fingers. Often it is held more in the tips of the fingers to aid this release. For this delivery the wrist remains cocked, with the palm of the hand facing the floor on release, and then it is flicked out from underneath the hand:

The wrist will flick up slightly on release with some back spin applied – and ideally the seam should be upright to aid the deception. It can help to have a slightly lower arm for this delivery.

Shane Warne, in his pomp, was a master at this delivery, so do watch some video of him bowling it. It is a very difficult ball to bowl and will take hours of practice. Long and strong fingers are important physical attributes to have.

The back-spinner is a similar delivery to the flipper. One that you deliver quicker and flat that skids on and is hopefully not detected by the batter. The grip of the ball remains the same but now you want the back of your hand facing the leg side of the ground – towards mid-wicket. The wrist action applied is that of you impart back spin on the ball as you release (flicking the wrist up).

It is likely that you will still have some leg spin on this delivery, but the skill of it is that it comes out quicker and flatter without much change of action.

Use of the Crease and Coming Round the Wicket

As with any bowling, changing the angle can greatly upset the batter's rhythm. If the ball is turning a lot, coming wider and increasing the angle of approach can help you achieve a leg-stump line to hit top of off more consistently. Likewise, if it is not turning as much, coming tighter to the stumps can aid you bowl more wicket to wicket. But if your stock ball is mid-crease, then it is still good practice to bowl some balls in your spell from wider and some tighter to the stumps – both make it harder for the batter to consistently line you up. You still need to be able to hit a good line and length from these different positions on the crease.

As with seam bowlers you can simply start your run-up straighter or wider, but with spin bowling it is easier to make later adjustments to your run-up and therefore your arrival point at the crease, particularly in tighter to the stumps.

Another variation to change the angle completely is to come round the wicket. This may be simply to do something different and to disrupt the batter's rhythm and make it harder for them to score through the off side. It also allows you to target the rough outside a right-hander's leg stump. Balls pitching in the rough can turn dramatically more, as well as bounce high or skid very low.

To right-handed batters it helps to start your run-up reasonably straight to help gain the correct alignment at the crease:

As with off-spin, make sure you are keeping that ball shiny between deliveries.

> *'I like to use different positions on the crease to create different landing points on the pitch. Set off from different starting points in run up to create this without changing length of run up.*
> - *Front of crease – fuller length*
> - *Mid crease – good length*
> - *Back crease – back of length*
> - *Use width of crease to vary line of ball and angle and think how different seam positions and pace of balls will change what the ball does off the pitch.*
> - *Tactic 1 – if someone likes to sweep good length balls, bowl front of crease and back of crease and use different pace and variations.*
> - *Tactic 2 – if someone is using their feet or has a long reach use mid and back of crease, vary pace and variations.*
> - *Tactic 3 – if someone is playing back, use front and mid crease as well as mixing your pace and other variations.'*
>
> IAN SALISBURY

Arm Height

Many leg-spinners bowl with a slightly lower arm – this is fine. You can experiment to see which works best for you in achieving a consistent hard-spun leg break with a 45-degree-angle seam. However, leg-spinners do have the option to vary the height of their bowling arm as another variation. This can be higher or lower. A higher arm is often helpful for bowling the top-spinner and it aids getting even more bounce. A lower arm can aid the ball's drift and lower bounce, as well as the shoulder rotation required for the googly.

You can even go further and bowl the occasional delivery with a completely horizontal bowling arm:

This changes the angle of the delivery, will do something different off the pitch and again just makes it harder for the batter to line you up for the big hit. As long as you can still land it well of course!

Varying Pace

Varying when the ball arrives to the batter is a useful skill. If every ball is identical in pace, the batter knows when it will arrive, making it easier to line you up for a big hit. If they know that you can vary your pace, it will make them more wary of lining you up. The art of it is that the changes of pace need to be subtle, with no difference in approach to the wicket – the less cues the batter has the better. As with any variation, you can change your pace but still land the ball in the same spot and still impart spin on the ball.

Bowling to Left Handers & The Left Arm Leg-Spinner

When bowling over the wicket to the left-hander the only technical adjustment to make is coming slightly wider in your approach to get your alignment on delivery outside the batter's off stump (with the aim of turning back into off stump).

You still want to be challenging both edges of the bat, as an off spinner would bowling to a right hander. Drifting it away to turn back into the stumps or skidding on upon landing and challenging the outside edge. Staying over the wicket can improve your chances of LBW decisions front and back foot.

However, if the left-hander batter is playing you well from over the wicket then coming round the wicket to him is a good variation. This is mainly because it gives you more chance of targeting the rough outside his off stump (although it is still possible to hit this from over the wicket).

Again, bowlers will vary their approach, either coming between umpire and stumps or behind the umpire stood up to the stumps. To generalise it is easier to achieve good alignment at the crease from coming straighter in your approach:

As with off-spin, if you are front on leg-spin bowler then a straight on approach round the wicket is recommended. A side on leg-spinner may find they still need the angle to get side on.

In this photo you will see that the bowler has landed mid-crease, but use of the crease is still important. If the batter is lining you up well from here, coming wider as a variation is a great option as it makes it even easier to hit the rough and more challenging to get the ball square on the leg-side. Coming tighter to the stumps is a good option if you are finding yourself bowling too wide – especially if you are getting a lot of drift. Here it maybe preferable to keep the angle of attack from over the wicket. It is harder to get tighter to the stumps round the wicket if you have an angled approach or the umpire is close to the stumps. Naturally, you are pushed wider on the crease.

> *'To left-handers practice different alignment and run up at the crease as well as bowling around the wicket. Also work on your variations as often batters like the ball spinning into them, so use top spin, googly and back spin. Make sure you do your homework on how you get left-hand wickets and where you get hit and set appropriate fields. Lastly learn to use rough patches created by the right arm seam bowlers to your advantage.'*
> IAN SALISBURY

All of the above, also applies if you are a left-arm leg-spin bowler bowling to a right-handed batter. You can still use the variations recommend in this chapter as well as using the crease to vary the angle. Just like the leg-spinner to a right-hander aim to challenge both edges of the bat as often as possible.

Bowling with the New Ball

Due to the difficulty of gripping the ball and the wrist action of a leg-spinner it is rarer to see a leg-spinner take the new ball compared with an orthodox spinner. However, there is no harm giving it a go in training. If you can still bowl just as accurately and not rip the skin off your middle finger then it would be an option for the team if format and match situation called for spin to bowl first up in the game.

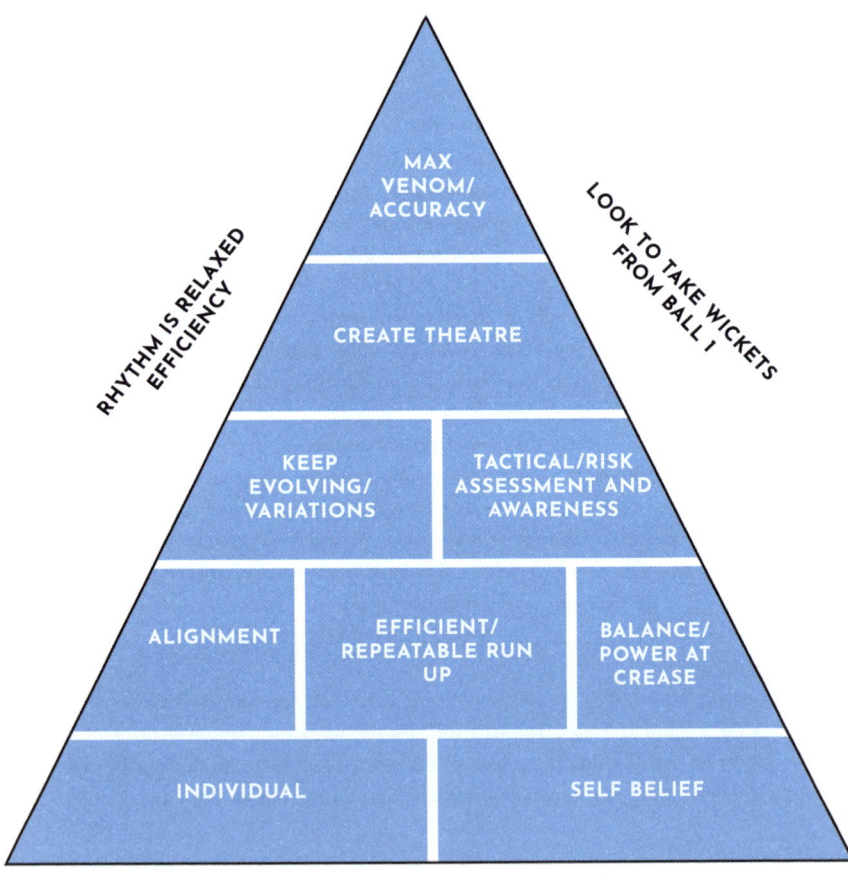

FIVE
BOWLING PRINCIPLES

'The love of bowling is important. Bowling is hard work and if a player is a reluctant bowler, then they will likely have a short career. From a coaching perspective, look out for those who show a love of bowling and work with them!'

PHIL ROWE

Former Northants Bowling Coach

In this chapter we look at some general bowling principles and skills that will improve performance as you become a more seasoned campaigner. These include the power of visualisation, how to adjust to different wickets and conditions, as well as dealing with no-ball issues.

Finding Top of Off

We have talked a lot in the previous chapters about the importance of a repeatable stock ball and hitting top of off stump. However, the length required to hit top of off will change slightly on every wicket that you play on. Generally, if the wicket has bounce, the length will be fuller, and if the wicket is keeping low then the length will be shorter. The bowlers that can adapt the quickest to each wicket they play on will be the most successful.

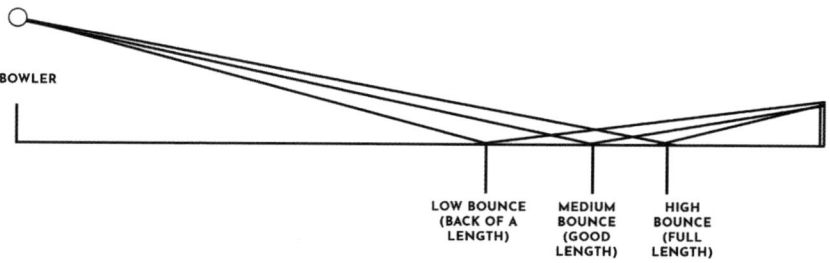

It is an easy trap to fall into that on a wicket that has bounce a seam bowler ends up bowling too short and any movement ends up beating the edge rather than taking the edge. Be brave, get the ball fuller and bring the outside edge and stumps into play.

As the diagram above shows, when playing on a low-bouncing wicket the length must be shorter to still hit top of off. Back of a length, but not short. Here you will be targeting the stumps primarily as the ball is less likely to carry to the slips. If you have a good wicketkeeper they should be up to the stumps so the batter is pinned to the crease, making it harder for the batter to negate the lbw.

It is also true to say that the more movement there is, whether that be swing, seam or spin, the fuller you can risk bowling. You may be driven once or twice, but when a batter is driving and there is movement it also gives you the highest chance of a wicket. Format and match situation will also dictate, but if the remit is taking wickets, you can afford the occasional boundary.

The ideal length is also determined by the size of the batter. Shorter players (like England's Ben Duckett) tend to be strong off the back foot and you need to be slightly fuller. Taller batters often use their reach advantage and get a bigger stride in to the ball, like England's Zac Crawley, so the ideal length is slightly shorter.

> *'The length we bowl to short or tall batters will change. Naturally, shorter batters play more from the crease, meaning we have to push our length slightly fuller; for tall batters who are able to get their stride more down the wicket and closer to the pitch, our length needs to be dragged back slightly. Our aim is to separate the hands from the body to force a false shot or trap them in the crease. This is also the same on wickets that have more bounce than others. As a bowler we need to work out what the most threatening length is on a wicket and try to execute that length with the skill set we have often enough to get a wicket.'*
> CHRIS LIDDLE

Wind & Slope

We would all love to play in perfect conditions all the time but, alas, that is never the reality, especially in the UK! Often there are blustery conditions, high winds and possibly a slope on the pitch as well, or the square is slightly raised. All of these provide challenges that are not often there in training, particularly indoors during the off-season.

In general, if you are bowling into a strong wind or it is coming left or right across the pitch, the important aspect is really attacking the crease hard in your last few strides. Even as a spinner, approach with more purpose. Try to keep your bound low, look to get through the crease to the target. Most importantly, stay strong at the crease and exaggerate the technical aspects of staying upright and compact. This is particularly important when there is a strong wind right to left, which can easily cause you to fall away at the crease and lose your wrist position behind the ball.

Although harder work, if you are a swing bowler or spinner do not shy away from coming into the wind. Usually, bowling into the wind can help you get more swing for the pace bowlers and more drift for the spinners.

When the wind is at your back (nearly all fast bowlers prefer this!) the only thing to watch out for is overstepping the front line because the wind has caused you to increase the size of your strides in your run-up. Make sure you keep a consistent stride pattern and even slow this down if the wind is causing you to bowl no-balls.

Some grounds, of course, have sizeable slopes on them, which could be across the ground (such as Lords) or you will be running up or down a hill as you approach the wicket. The same principles as with wind apply here. If running up a hill to get to the wicket, attack the crease hard in those last few strides, and when the slope is across the crease stay strong at the crease. Focus on the technical aspects so you do not fall away on delivery. Similarly, coming down a slope, be careful not to overstride in your run-up and lose your natural stride pattern.

Bowling with a Wet Ball

Unfortunately, in a typical English summer you will encounter a wet outfield, and indeed play through some rain. It is important that the ball is kept off the ground as much as possible. Throws should be over the top of the stumps from the deep, and the ball should not touch the ground as it makes its way back to you at the top of your mark. You should have a towel to ensure you get the seam as dry as possible for you to grip the ball before starting your run-up. This is particularly important for spin bowlers as a slippery grip means it is very hard to control your line and length. The key message here is do not run in to bowl until you have dried the ball enough to get a good grip of it. A bar towel or tea towel should be an essential component of your kit bag.

The Three Second Rule & the Power of Visualisation

We talked in the previous chapters about looking at the spot where you want to land the ball as a good starting point on where to look when you are bowling, from the time you start your run-up to the second you release the ball, and then even in your follow-through.

However, the few seconds before you run in are also important as to what happens when you let go of the ball. Take some time (up to three seconds) at the top of your mark to get a clear picture of what you want to bowl and visualise this in your head. Get a picture in your mind of the ball coming out of your hand, hitting the line and length you want it to. And then start your run-up. Commit to this plan and do not change it halfway through your run-up.

Taking time at the top of your mark is also a good way to settle some nerves with a couple of deep breaths while you visualise, and it is also a good way of composing yourself if things before this delivery have not gone your way. Perhaps you have been hit for two boundaries on the trot or have just had a catch dropped off your bowling and the frustration is building. Take a few seconds, deep breaths, compose yourself, visualise, then run in.

Should I Bowl with the Wicket Keeper Up or Back?

Sometimes a seam bowler needs to park their ego and invite the wicketkeeper up to the stumps. When to do so depends on how the individual batter is playing you, and the quality of your wicketkeeper, of course.

If a batter is standing outside of the crease or having some success running down the wicket at you, then this would be a good time to invite the wicketkeeper up to the stumps to make the batter stay in their crease. This would be particularly effective on a low-bouncing wicket where you are looking for bowled and lbw as your main option of dismissing a batter as, even if they get a stride forward, they will not be that far from the popping crease. On a low-bouncing wicket the outside edges may not carry to the wicketkeeper if stood back, so coming up to the stumps is the best option.

Another time that you may invite the wicketkeeper up is for shorter-length matches where you want to restrict the batter from advancing down the wicket immediately to take away that scoring option. You may also ask the wicketkeeper to come up simply as a 'variation' if nothing much is happening and you want to force a mistake. It is then simply like changing the field to get inside the batter's head about a perceived flaw, whether this is bluff or not.

If there is movement and a genuine chance of an outside edge being found, and there is good carry in the pitch, then it is nearly always better to have the wicketkeeper stood back so they have a better chance of catching the ball if the edge is found.

Run-Ups & Dealing with No-Ball Problems

Former bowling coach at Northants, Phil Rowe, gave us some excellent advice on developing a good run-up:

> At take-off we want to be as balanced as we can with energy going towards target. A balanced run-up, in particular the last couple of strides, has a big impact on balance. So, assuming we've run up with no cross-overs, we now need to leave the ground, to take off. Look out for the stride before take-off. Some bowlers cross over at this point, trying to get into a bowling position too early. You will see a right-arm bowler's left foot often come across the string line, crossing over, often placed underneath the left shoulder. Look out for that – the left foot underneath left shoulder. Taking off 'square to target' is generally helpful; i.e. not twisting or turning while on the ground. Here I like to use 'knee drives' as a way of thinking about keeping energy going to target. Right knee to target as we leave the ground. This helps the bowler stay 'square' on take-off with maximum energy going towards the target. At this phase and throughout the run-up, I am a fan of arms being close to the body.

At some stage in your bowling career you will have some issues with your run-up. This is very common after a growth spurt. There are a few things you can try to negate the chances of this happening:

• Measure with tape and mark pre-match. Counting a certain number of strides back to your mark will always have some slight variation to it as you cannot guarantee the length of your stride will be the same each match and practice. It is good practice, if you have the resource available, to measure your run-up with a tape measure. This guarantees it is the same each time you play. At the start of every season rework your run-up to see if there is anything different from the year before. Then take a measurement.

• Mark length of first step. We stressed previously the importance of always starting your run-up off the same foot, and it is also important that the length of that first stride is the same each ball. If you always start the same, then it is more likely that the rest of your run-up will be the same as well. It is therefore often worth marking your first step as well, with the aim of making this first step as consistent as possible.

- Mark point of take-off. Similarly to that first step, a lot of bowlers also have a mark they like to hit when it comes to taking off into the bound. They know if they hit this they will be safe on the crease. If they overstep this they know they are like to overstep the front line and can pull out. This marking is less common, simply as it is taking your focus away from where you want to bowl, but if you have had no-ball issues then this is worth a try.

- Umpire – where should they stand? Most umpires like to stand as close to the stumps as possible so they can get a good look at the front line; however, most will come back if asked to. Certainly, if you have had no-ball issues, ask the umpire to go further back. Also, a lot of bowlers find an umpire close to the stumps off-putting and it can force them wider on the crease. You need to work out where you like to have the umpire and use a kit bag or another player to stand in that position when practising. Work out in what position you feel most comfortable running in.

- Lose your run-up – start again. At some stage you will be running in to bowl and it will not feel right. This often happens on the blustery, windy days. If this does happen, do not continue and hope things will be alright. This will drastically increase the chances of bowling a no-ball and there is certainly a very high chance that the delivery will be a poor one. Instead, stop and start your run-up again.

Bowling Principles

- Physically and mentally ready from ball one. It is important in all formats that you start well in your spell. This gives you confidence and it puts the batter under pressure straight away. To be ready to go from ball one of your spell is vital. It is important that you are physically ready (stretched, bowl-throughs to a fielder, had a run up to the crease) and mentally ready with a clear mental picture of your first ball. You do not want to give the batter any freebies early in your spell, and if you are one of the opening bowlers you are setting the tone for the innings.

- Same intensity – first ball to last. Having set this good tone early in your spell, it is important to keep this intensity throughout, with the aim of your last ball of your spell having the same intensity as the first and that you are bowling with purpose throughout.

- Finish off the over. By this we mean do not waste a good start to the over. It can be a mental block that you bowl four or five good balls (perhaps all dots) and then finish the over with a bad ball that goes for a boundary, thus releasing the pressure you have built. Towards the back end of the over, if you need to, take longer at the top of your mark to compose yourself and visualise.
- Pressure on new batter. Whatever format you play it always important to bowl well at the new batter. It is your best chance to get them out before they get their eye in and their feet start working, and it is always a good time to sneak in some dot balls even if you do not get them out. Every batter wants to get off the mark early, get an early boundary and feel the ball in the middle of the bat. Starve them of this if you can. It is quite easy, after the elation of getting a wicket, not to focus as hard for your next ball, but make sure you do. Aim to be all over the batter and put them under pressure the moment they arrive at the crease. Let them know they are in a contest. Even in a T20. A few dot balls and no easy boundary balls early in the innings might be the difference between winning and losing.
- Work as a pair. For six balls it is all about you. The batter can affect the game but, ultimately, where you bowl determines a lot of the outcome. However, you cannot build pressure on your own. Hunt as a pair with the bowler at the other end. Even get a little contest going as to which of you can bowl the most dot balls or take the most wickets and, above all else, plenty of vocal encouragement for each other.
- Limit extras. It is very hard to build pressure if you are bowling lots of extras. No-balls can also lead to free hits in some formats. With all wides and no-balls it is not just the extra run awarded but also the runs that are scored off the extra delivery(s). The more deliveries you have to bowl the more tiring it is, and the more tired you are the greater chance of bowling more poor deliveries. There is also nothing more demoralising than getting a wicket off a no-ball. As a rule of thumb aim for wides to be no more than a fifth of your overs (i.e. no more than two for a ten-over spell). Aim for zero no-balls.
- Back to the stumps, back to your mark. Most of the cricket in the amateur game is played in one day and all runs saved are vital. It is your duty as a bowler to assist in achieving run outs. When the ball is played into the outfield it is

good practice to get back to the stumps at the non-striker's end as quickly as possible so you can affect a run out at that end. This also allows the fielders to focus on the backing-up (therefore, helping to prevent overthrows) rather than covering the stumps with no one behind them.

• Next ball you bowl is always the one that counts. It is so easy for us to beat ourselves up for bowling a bad ball and to let our heads drop, but remember that ball has been and gone. There is nothing you can do to change it – it is in the past. It is the next ball that counts. Take time at the top of your mark, compose yourself, visualise, then run in. You need the belief that the next ball will be one of the best you ever bowled. Honest reflection on your spell can take place once the match is over. In a spell, just focus on the next ball, one ball at a time.

The All-Rounder

With any luck you are also a good batter and have a part to play with both bat and ball. Whether you bat at the top of the order or in the middle, the key element is that you need to be fit (see chapter eight) and you will have to spend more time than others working on both aspects of your game if you want to be equally as good at both disciplines.

It does also give you a chance to perform well with the bat if you have not with the ball, and vice versa, but you mentally want to affect the game with both bat and ball in hand. Just because you have performed well in one skill, do not take your foot off the gas for the other – you still have a job to do for the team. However, be doubly determined if the first half of the game did not go to plan – you can make amends.

Verbals

Lastly, we will talk about verbals in this chapter. Verbals (where the bowler, wicketkeeper or fielders attempt to put the batter off) are common in all levels of the game, and whether you are a player who will get involved is entirely a personal preference and will be influenced by your personality.

Some bowlers need a bit of verbal confirmation to fire themselves up to get into the contest, others might be clever and pick out a technical weakness they hope to exploit to get inside the batter's head. Sometimes just a look and a smile are enough to unsettle.

The overriding consideration here is, whatever you do, it does not affect how well you bowl. You have a much better chance of getting a batter out by bowling well than saying something clever to them. If you are spending a lot of time and energy talking to the batter, it can affect your bowling. If this is the case, say nothing at all. Win the battle by getting the batter out!

Anything said to the batter should never be personal and there should never be a send-off. The batter is out – you have done your job – nothing more needs to be said.

> *'The best way to get inside a batter's head is knowing how they've previously been getting out, then exploring their weakness with field placements or a style of bowling which can play on their ego.'*
> CHRIS LIDDLE

SIX
BOWLING TACTICS

'Having the right field placings is very important. Try to set your own field and take responsibility where you are trying to bowl.'
MARTIN BICKNELL
Surrey & England

In the professional game, the general consensus is that crowds want to see batters score lots of runs, culminating in high team totals. They do not want to see teams bowled out for low scores (time and match revenue issues), so wickets are generally prepared for batters to score runs. Therefore, bowlers need to find a way of taking wickets on batter-friendly surfaces, ten wickets in one-day games, and 20 in County Championship and Test match cricket.

In the shorter formats of cricket there is less chance of the wicket condition deteriorating over the duration of the game. However, in the longer, multi-day format, where there may be ever-changing weather conditions and a lot of wear and tear on the wicket over the game's duration, the wicket condition usually becomes more bowler-friendly. This can mean that the type of bowler emphasis changes as the match progresses.

However, often in one-day club cricket, deterioration of the wicket over the duration of the game is more common, as the resources, time, equipment and options for wicket preparation are far less than in the professional game.

In terms of tactics for multi-format cricket, it is literally the amount of time on offer that dictates how the game is played. Restriction breeds creativity. Shorter-format cricket has brought more creativity to the game, throughout batting, bowling and fielding, and these advancements inevitably find their way into the longer formats as the game of cricket evolves.

The longer the format, batters generally bat in a more conservative manner, and in a more aggressive manner in the shorter-format games. You will still get attacking T20-type periods in a multi-day match when necessary and, conversely, consolidating short periods of play in a T20.

Before any game of cricket takes place the following ground and pitch assessment must be made:
- Wicket condition (new or used, grass or bare)
- Wicket condition (wet and soft, dry and hard, or hard and cracked)
- Wicket characteristics (slow and low or fast and bouncy)
- Wicket slopes and cross-falls
- Typical score at this ground for the format being played
- Batters' or bowlers' wicket
- Location of wicket within the square
- Pitch orientation (north–south or east–west)
- Wind direction (ever-changing)
- Current and predicted weather forecast
- Boundary sizes (short or long)
- Outfield slopes and grass length
- Outfield condition (bumpy or flat)
- Sight screens at both ends? (dark backgrounds if there are no screens)
- Heights of sight screens (tall bowler may release from above the screen)

Careful assessment of the criteria will give essential assistance when deciding whether to bat or bowl first, and clarity for specific bowling and fielding tactics.

Some other things to consider will be:
- Match format being played
- Your own team's strengths, weaknesses and team make-up
- Opposition's strengths, weaknesses and team make-up
- The make-up of your bowling unit
- Does the wicket suit your bowlers?
- Type of ball being used
- Does your team prefer to set or chase?
- Does the opposition prefer to set or chase?
- Which end will the last over be bowled from?
- When is the hottest and coldest part of the day?
- Available time left if rain-affected
- Impact of positive or negative result
- Match result points-scoring system
- Results of games being played elsewhere

General Bowling Tactics that apply to all formats of cricket

The perfect game of cricket for one team is to bowl the opposition out for 0 off 1.4 overs (ten balls), then score off the first ball of their innings to win by ten wickets (11-ball match). This is a dream for one team, a nightmare for the other. To the best of our knowledge this has never happened!

Putting it simply, if you cannot get a batter out, the next best thing is to stop them scoring, then next is to limit their scoring.

It all comes down to the accuracy of where the particular type of bowler (seam or spin) lands the ball, regardless of the speed it arrives there at. Assessing and predicting a batter's intention and movement are very important, as is where the ten fielders are placed. Remember, you cannot set a field for a bad ball.

The bowler's primary aim is to take wickets, and the most common methods of dismissal over the history of Test match cricket have been found to be, in decreasing order: caught 60 per cent (wicketkeeper 20 per cent; fielder 40 per cent); bowled 20 per cent; lbw 10 per cent; run out 6 per cent; stumped 4 per cent.

It is worth noting that generally the best method of taking a wicket is to bowl a good line and length, as at least 50 per cent of wickets are taken that way (i.e. bowled, lbw and caught by the wicketkeeper). The power of a three-in-play delivery! The percentages may change for the different formats of cricket. The results have fluctuated over the years, but are generally correct at the time of writing.

Another survey has shown that many of the T20 games finish with approximately a 15-run differential between the two teams. Further analysis proves that if you remove the top four or five batters cheaply, you have statistically a great chance of winning the match. Having three quality spinners in a team is statistically harder to score off, and also greatly increases your chance of winning.

In addition to doing the basics well, which accounts for the vast majority of a team's success, if the final amount of 'one-percenters' can be increased through diligent assessments and tactics, the team and individual bowlers will experience even more success in the future.

There are so many ever-changing variables affecting bowling tactics in any game of cricket, especially when assessing all the different formats. The score, number of wickets taken, number of overs bowled, length of batting partnership, individual scores, style of scoring, preferred scoring areas, ball condition, type of bowlers available, field placings, weather forecast, etc. are just a few factors to take into account.

Both team are obviously looking to be in control of the game, and that invariably starts with the toss of the coin before the start of play. Factors to assess when deciding whether to bat or bowl first have already been listed, but it is worth briefly discussing some of the points.

Before Play (Deciding Whether to Bat or Bowl First)

The first and most important item to assess is the condition of the match wicket. Is it a new strip or a repaired used pitch? If the pitch is new, regardless of its condition, there will not be any bowling follow-through footmarks on the wicket, so it should play relatively well, particularly in the first innings. By the time the second innings starts, there may be footmarks developing that spin bowlers could take advantage of if the ball were to land on them.

If the match takes place on a used pitch there will already be footmarks on the wicket. These will be in play from ball one. As the game progresses these are likely to degrade substantially, making it potentially more difficult to bat on in the second innings, particularly if facing spinners.

Is there a lot of grass or is it relatively bare? If the wicket has a lot of grass and is relatively green, there is a very good chance that it will move off the seam a lot more for the seam bowlers. Conversely, green wickets do not generally assist the spinners, as the ball does not grip as much as it would on pitches with hardly any grass. If the wicket is bare, or has very little grass on it, the spinners should have the advantage, as the seam of the ball should grip much more. Generally, in these conditions there will be less movement for the seam bowlers.

Is it wet and soft, dry and hard, or hard and cracked? The main influence will be if the wicket has been covered in the lead-up to the match. Generally, if the wicket is wet and soft, the ball will come off the surface slightly slower than the batter is expecting, thus making it harder for them to time their shots. This is because the ball compresses into the surface more, retarding its initial speed. This is quite common in early-season matches in April and May in the UK, as the wickets have not yet had enough sun and warm temperatures on them to harden them up. Team totals at this time of year are noticeably lower than later in the season when the wickets have hardened and are more batter friendly. The bowlers, particularly seamers, have the advantage at this time of the season, as these conditions are ideal for seam movement off the pitch.

A sprinkling of rain on a dry pitch can very often speed the wicket up for a while, as the ball tends to skid off the pitch more. As it eventually starts to dry, it can temporarily produce a two-paced pitch, depending on if the ball lands on a wet or dry contact area. When the wicket has totally dried out it may be easier to bat on. Overnight rain usually gets the ball swinging and seaming early in the match. A team could pick a seam-heavy bowling attack and hunt for early wickets. On a fast wicket with the ball coming through, both third man and fine leg fielders may be a sensible option. On slower pitches, third man could be dispensed with, and fine leg could be moved up into the inner ring.

Bowlers will generally bowl with different field placings on these types of slow wickets, compared to when they bowl on harder, drier wickets. Due to the lack of pace, fielders that may be stationed behind the bat on faster wickets are now positioned in front of the bat in catching positions, as batters have a tendency to chip balls up in the air on the slower-paced wicket.

Generally, if the wicket is dry and hard, the ball will travel through with much less retardation in its initial delivery speed after pitching. The wicket will be faster, and there will be more carry and bounce on the ball. There will still be an amount of seam movement, but the spinners will definitely come more to the fore, as the revolutions imparted on the seam will now grip on the harder surface, causing the ball to spin more. Fast bowlers find that hard wickets are much more rewarding to bowl on as they retain more pace for their physical efforts.

Most batters prefer batting on the harder wickets, as the ball now comes through at a better speed for them to achieve the timing of their shots. Please remember the previous discussion in this book regarding indoor winter training in the UK. Batters and bowlers will have been practising on hard, fast indoor sports hall surfaces for potentially six months, to be suddenly confronted with soft, slower outdoor wickets at the start of the season. The batters have to adapt to the ball not coming on to the bat as quickly, while the bowlers have to re-engage on to fuller bowling lengths, having spent the winter potentially bowling much shorter, with seamers having spent six months probably bowling front-foot no-balls!

If the wicket also possesses cracking in its surface, this will help the bowlers, as any ball pitching on these cracks can potentially bounce up sharply, keep low and deviate laterally. As soon as the cracks start to break up and crumble this persistently worsens the effect for the batter. If the seam bowler's footmarks have degraded the cracked areas too, this opens up the full potential of having an array of spin bowlers in the attack, as allied with the unpredictability of the bounce, the ball will spin even more.

Historical knowledge of how a pitch performs over the course of a match is very important, as is knowledge of what a typical score is at the ground. Is it bowler or batter friendly? Pre-match research may show it is advantageous to bowl first at this ground or bowl second. Does the wicket play well first innings, then keep low in the second? If so, it may be worth batting first, then bowling gun-barrel straight at the stumps in the second innings, with the added scoreboard pressure assisting you. Does this vary at all during the season, April to September? Some bowlers historically bowl well at certain grounds, so they may well be required to bowl an extended spell in this particular match.

Is the current weather hot and sunny, but the forecast is for overcast conditions later, or vice versa? Hot and sunny conditions may favour the spinners but, equally, overcast conditions may favour the seamers. If your team is packed with either seamers or spinners, will this affect your decision? Is it a disadvantage to be out in the field bowling for 50 overs in very hot temperatures in the first innings, or bat first, conserving the team's energy while the opposition sweat out in the heat, potentially exhausting themselves before it is their turn to bat? You are then bowling in potentially cooler conditions as the temperature drops. Is rain forecast later in the day? If so, would your team prefer to be bowling first or second?

Would you prefer to be bowling or batting under the Duckworth Lewis System (DLS) of scoring in a rain-affected match? Lots of teams prefer to bat under the DLS, as it gives them the opportunity to keep an accurate eye on the required run rate at the start of every over. This is fine if they are not losing wickets. However, if the bowling team is taking wickets, the required run rate starts to increase rapidly, and combined with scoreboard pressure mounting, the bowling team then gains the upper hand.

Does your team historically and generally prefer to bowl first or second regardless of conditions? Many teams do keep it that simple, and if they win the toss adopt that strategy. However, with greater assessment of influencing factors, combined with confidence and bravery to take a chance, they may improve their chances of winning more games.

The type and colour of the match ball may affect your decision, as they may have different characteristics regarding the amount and duration of swing, and the general degradation throughout the innings. This may also vary during different times of the day's play. The bowling unit may have been selected purely on the colour/characteristics of the ball being used.

Most cricket grounds have sight screens at both ends, but some do not have any at all. It is worth assessing whether any of your tall bowlers would release the ball from above the screen, as they may prove to be a challenge for the batters trying to sight the ball. This is worth checking at the lower end of a sloping ground.

A ground without sight screens can be a challenge for the batter for obvious reasons. Sometimes the view behind the bowler could be clear sky, but on most occasions there will be some form of visual distraction, such as trees or buildings. It is worth assessing whether a particular bowler in your team could take advantage of the helpful backdrop.

Inspect these areas, and by looking at the current weather and the forecast for the duration of the match, and the make-up of your team, an overall assessment can be made as to whether a team bowls first or second if they win the toss.

Very often it may be very difficult to decide whether to bat or bowl if winning the toss. If you lose the toss you may quote the phrase: 'That was a good toss to lose,' as the ultimate decision was taken out of your hands by the opposition!

Even a simple assessment of a pitch running east to west, rather than the normal north to south, can give a potential advantage to the team bowling second. Batting first, the sun is no problem when batting. Batting second, part of the innings will be spent with the west-facing batter facing directly into the setting sun. Combine that with a spin bowler tossing the ball up, and batting suddenly becomes more of a challenge for 50 per cent of the remaining overs. Some fielders will also experience the challenge!

During Play (General Bowling Tactics for All Formats)
Determine the current wind direction
This is a crucial part of the bowler's tactical decision-making process. By determining the wind direction, a bowler can immediately start to assess which end would be the most favourable for them to bowl from, whether they are a seam or spin bowler. Different countries around the world have different prevailing wind directions. The prevailing wind in the UK is mainly from a south-westerly direction. However, this does not mean it is always from this direction. The wind direction does change regularly, and can change numerous times during the course of a match, even a T20. The bowler should make regular checks to see if the wind has changed its direction.

Modern phone weather forecast apps present accurate wind direction information, both current and predicted.

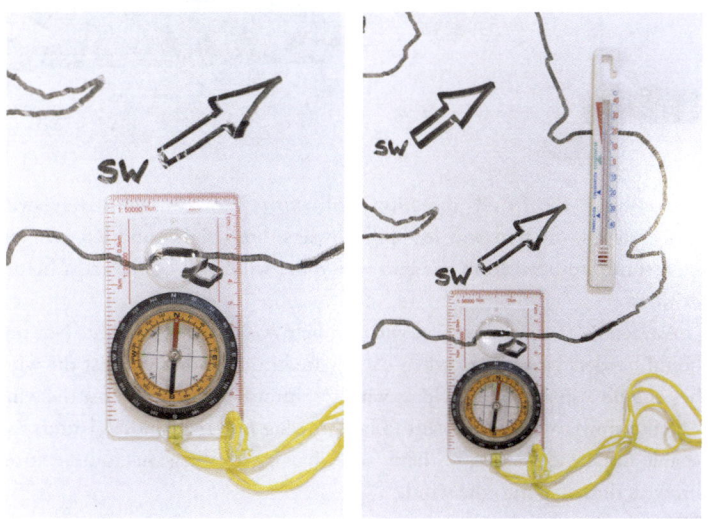

By utilising this information in conjunction with an aerial view of the ground displayed on Google Maps, for example, a bowler can get an idea of which end they are likely to bowl from days in advance. Determining whether the wicket runs in a north–south direction or an east–west one is critical. The vast majority of wickets in the UK run in a north–south direction, so run top to bottom when viewed on the screen. They can possibly also assess short and long boundary distances too. The team's bowling strategy could be drawn up in advance, remembering that the plan must be flexible, as the wind may have changed direction on matchday.

Determining the wind direction will now allow inswing/away-swing seam bowlers, off-spin and leg-spin bowlers, both right- and left-arm, the opportunity to bowl from the end where the wind will be the most helpful for them.

Awareness of wind direction will also help with field placement. Not only should bowlers be aware of when batters are hitting with or against the wind, they should also assess the fielders who are throwing with or against the wind. A weak thrower would not want to be throwing into the wind, as batters may be able to take extra runs to them, so it may be advantageous to have strong throwers throwing into the wind.

Bowlers should always be aware of the situation where a batter is hitting with the wind to a short boundary, as they may have to alter their bowling line accordingly to avoid being regularly hit over the boundary. The positioning of fielders protecting a long boundary when the batter is hitting into the wind is another scenario that needs attention, as runs can be saved with correct field placement.

Which is the Best End to Bowl From?
This decision can be crucial for the outcome of the match and the individual bowler's performance. Generally, swing bowlers bowl with the wind, increasing their natural direction of swing, and spin bowlers bowl with the wind acting on the ball in the opposite direction it will spin.

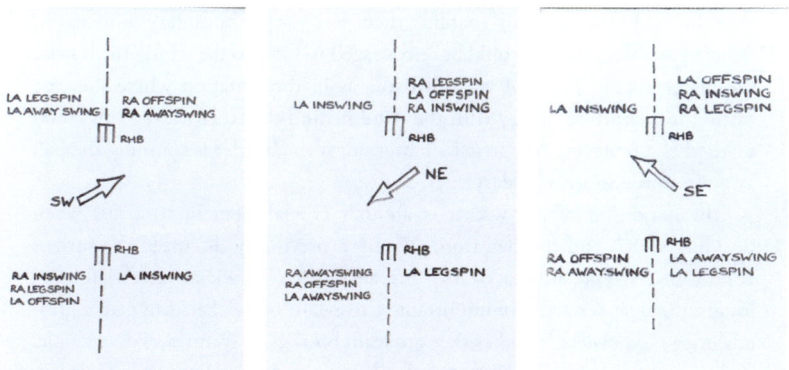

The above whiteboard tactical plans show potentially the best end for certain types of bowler to bowl from, based on wind direction influences.

The wind direction is normally used to increase the amount of swing obtained from the seam bowlers, so an inswing bowler may have to push the ball a lot wider of off stump to ultimately hit the stumps after the bowler's natural swing and the additional wind component have acted upon the ball.

The spin bowler's criteria is totally different, as they want the ball to swing or drift in the wind in the opposite direction to which the ball will spin. This gives the batter the added challenge of a 'double movement' of the ball. For instance, a leg-spin bowler should bowl from the end where the wind drifts the ball into the batter, then turns away from them after pitching. This squares the batter up, as they initially line up a leg-side shot, only to be confronted with the ball spinning away from them off the pitch. The chance of stumpings increases greatly in this situation.

Equally the off-spinner should bowl from the end where the wind drifts the ball away from the batter, only for it to spin back into them after pitching. The chances of being bowled are greatly increased in this situation.

The fastest seam bowler usually bowls with the wind behind, if possible, as the ball gains added speed from the wind, combined with the fact that the bowler's action is not impeded by a headwind, although a tailwind can sometimes cause issues.

A spinner can have an advantage bowling into the wind, as the headwind will hold the ball up, thus drawing an early drive from the batter, potentially popping up a catch. The challenge here is that if the spinner is bowling into the wind, the batter has it behind them, thus enabling them to get it up and over the fielders, potentially enabling them to clear the boundary more easily. Where possible, a batter should be encouraged to hit into the wind. The bowler should be totally aware of when a batter is in the situation where they are hitting to a short boundary with the wind behind them. However, this could be used as a tempting way to get a batter out if the bowler is spinning the ball away from the short boundary!

The condition of the wicket is another crucial element to assess when deciding which end to bowl from. We have previously discussed the surface conditions to take into account, but areas such as wicket cross-falls and longitudinal slopes are very important. Cross-falls on wickets can give a great advantage to bowlers, whether they are seam bowlers or spinners. For example, if the cross-fall is from leg side to off side, this may give extra turn for a leg-spinner, and if the fall is from off side to leg side, this may benefit the off-spin bowler.

Additionally, an inswing seam bowler may wish to bowl with the slope going from leg to off, and the away-swing bowler may want to bowl where the slope goes from off to leg. This combination would give the double movement phenomenon associated with the spinners/wind situation. The swing bowler could opt to bowl with the slope, adding pitch movement to the direction of swing.

Movement off the seam is exacerbated on a pitch with a cross-fall. A great example of this is at Lords, where there is an eight-foot drop from one side of the ground to the other. Many wickets have been taken there utilising the slope on the wicket.

Bowling on a downhill slope will mean the ball could potentially keep lower than normally expected, as it tends to skid off the slope. This situation could lead to more bowled and lbw wickets, particularly if a shorter bowler is operating. Bowling on an uphill slope normally means the ball could potentially bounce a little higher than normally expected, as it impacts on to the ground. This situation could lead to more catches taken behind the wicket, especially if combined with a taller bowler.

Sometimes matches are played on 'used' pitches. These are wickets that have already had a match, or multiple matches played on them. While the wicket itself may be relatively untouched, there will inevitably be footmarks from the previous bowlers' run-ups and follow-throughs. The run-up footmarks can be off-putting for the bowlers, as they may have to realign their own run-ups to avoid them, thus giving them potentially a physical and mental challenge to overcome. However, the footmarks on the follow-throughs should be examined carefully, as they will have a tactical bearing on which end bowlers will bowl from, especially the spinners. There could potentially be follow-through footmarks to all four corners of the wicket, particularly enticing for off-spin and leg-spin bowlers. Generally, the footmarks are usually too wide for the seamers to extract an advantage, but for spinners bowling over and around the wicket, they can become a deadly target.

For example, a leg-spinner may have footmarks to target outside off stump, but unless they bowl googlies these marks are not really a threat. However, if they bowl around the wicket, aiming at the marks outside leg stump, they immediately become a great danger to the batter, as the ball can now potentially turn and bounce prolifically at the batter, threatening both bat and stumps. While an lbw dismissal against the right-handed batter is totally eliminated, being bowled around their pads is a distinct possibility.

The off-spinner bowling over the wicket to a right-handed batter, aiming at the footmarks outside off stump poses an equally deadly proposition. Prodigious turn and bounce is on offer if the footmarks can be exploited. Additionally, lbw is always a potential wicket-taking option, should ball contact with the pad take place in line with the stumps.

Obviously left-arm spinners, both off spin and leg spin, offer the same threat but from different angles. Careful consideration of bowlers should be made if bowling to left-handed batters, or a combination of both right- and left-handed batters.

Wind influence and boundary sizes should always be considered when deciding which end to bowl from.

Finally, having previously discussed boundary sizes, it is worth mentioning bowling to a short boundary. Some bowlers enjoy this challenge, using it as a temptation for the batter to take them on, especially if they are a spinner turning it away from the short side. Consideration should always be made if bowling to a left-handed batter or a combination of both. Many bowlers will alter their line in this instance to protect the boundary, which may be a sensible option, but by doing this, by bowling wide outside off stump, for example, the bowler loses the threat of the lbw and bowled forms of dismissal.

Keep Shining the Ball Throughout the Innings
This is an essential duty and can be carried out by any of the bowlers or the 'designated ball shiner', normally a fielder at either mid-on or mid-off. The ball should be shined throughout the whole innings, as it not only helps the seamers swing the ball but will also help the spinners when they bowl 'arm balls'. The ball will be in the best possible condition for the bowlers.

Coaches, captains and players should ensure this is being carried out at every opportunity.

Never Bowl the Last Over of the Innings with the Batters Hitting to the Shortest Boundary
In any limited-overs game the outcome of the final few overs will be crucial to the ultimate result of the match. Most limited-over games comprise of an even number of overs/balls, equally bowled from either end – T20, the Hundred, or 50 overs, for example.

With this in mind it is vital that the last over of the innings is not bowled from the end that brings the shorter boundary into play. This obviously makes it harder for the batting team to hit a big score from their final over. The decision is usually made assuming that two right-handed batters will be on strike for the last over but, as we all know, this cannot be guaranteed as there is the distinct possibility that they could be left-handed.

Obviously, if this general rule is applied, and the innings forms an even number of overs, the first over of the innings should always be bowled from the short boundary end. If the innings is comprised of an odd number of overs, the first over should be bowled from the opposite end to the short boundary.

Finally, another factor to consider is the wind direction, although this is variable and can be different from the start of the innings to the end. The worst scenario for the bowler is to be bowling the last over at the short boundary end with a heavy wind heading that direction!

> *'Setting the field is very important skill for bowlers to learn ... this comes with experience though. Bowlers who are good at setting their fields will be aware of the different angles fielders need to be as they will be aware of where they get hit to the most. We can also use our field placements to force a batter to hit in a different place to score runs, which may result in finding the edge of the bat, especially if the ball is swinging; squarer field placements if the ball is swinging a lot away from the right-hand batter, forcing the scoring option to be straight and potentially finding the edge; straighter fields if the ball isn't doing anything, forcing the batter to play squarer or across the line, bringing in lbw and bowled. White ball ... where do you want to get hit to? Can you close off one side of the field at the death, and how does that look like in terms of field placements?'*
> CHRIS LIDDLE

Bowling and Fielding Plans when Confronted with Shorter/Longer Boundary Distances

When bowling to a short boundary, the bowler must decide whether they are going to defend to it or use it as a form of attack. Some bowlers enjoy the attacking option, using it as a temptation for the batter to take it on, especially if they are a spinner turning the ball away from the short side. Letting a batter hit with the spin towards a short boundary can be a risky proposition but can also be overly tempting for the batter, who may fail to execute their shot correctly. The bowler needs to be fully aware of when a batter will be hitting to a short boundary with the wind behind them. However, once again this could be used as a tempting way to take the batter's wicket.

Defensive options could be to bowl a left-arm seamer from over the wicket, or a right-arm seamer from around the wicket. This changes the angle the ball is delivered from, making it more of a challenge for the batter to successfully hit the boundary. Many bowlers will alter their line in this instance to protect the boundary, which may be a sensible option, but by doing this, by bowling wide outside off stump, for example, the bowler loses the threat of the lbw and bowled forms of dismissal. Bowling right-arm around the wicket may also remove the threat of lbw unless the ball is swinging back into the right-handed batter.

A useful strategy is to employ tall fielders around the short boundary, as there is more chance of them taking a catch than a shorter fielder. In recent years many catches take place involving two fielders, one initially catching the ball before parrying it to an adjacent fielding partner just before they cross the boundary. Therefore, teams should practise this in training, encouraging two fielders to be near the ball whenever a boundary catch opportunity is presented.

When patrolling long boundaries, the fielders can be pushed in an appropriate distance to stop any additional runs being taken. There may also be more twos run by the batters, as the ground area is now very large, hence there are more gaps to be found. A good idea could be to bring more fielders over to reduce the 'patrolling area' of each fielder. However, this tactic needs very accurate bowling-line control. It is essential that any boundary fielder is quick across the ground and possesses a strong throwing arm.

Very often in junior cricket, relay throws will be seen. This is where the boundary fielder cannot reach the stumps with their throw and another fielder has to rethrow the ball to get the ball back. By careful assessment of the boundary fielders, this can be avoided in adult cricket.

Whenever possible, a batter should always be encouraged to hit into the wind, and please remember never allow the batter to be hitting to the short boundary in the last over of the innings.

Finally, further consideration of boundary sizes and strategy should be upmost in the mind when bowling to a left-handed batter or a combination of both.

Bowling Plans for a Bowler-Friendly Wicket
Bowler-friendly wickets generally have a lot of seam movement or spin, and either bounce or keep low more than would be normally expected. Even more concerning for the batter is if the bounce is totally unpredictable. They can also be very fast, very slow, or two-paced. Used wickets, more often than not, can be termed bowler-friendly. Wickets like these generally appear in the early part of the season, or after wet periods, as the wickets can have a lot of grass and the pace is slow, as the wicket will be potentially soft. Outfields are usually soft and slow too. Careful pre-match inspection can usually, but certainly not always, give the bowler an idea on how the wicket will perform.

If the bounce is unpredictable, a good strategy is to bowl on a good length, straight at middle stump, regardless of the standard of cricket being played. A good-length ball could 'spit' off a length, and a shorter ball could keep low. On a good batting wicket the batter always plays the ball on length, moving either forwards or backwards, thus predicting the height at which the ball will arrive. On this type of wicket they are unable to confidently predict this, so batting is extremely difficult. Generally, individual and team scores are low on a wicket like this. Chasing low scores on such pitches are extremely challenging, as the pitch has probably deteriorated further as the day progresses.

Attacking fields are the norm on wickets like this, with slips, bat-and-pad catchers, and catchers on the drive to the fore. Batters very often decide that if they try to occupy the crease for too long in a defensive mode there will be 'a ball with their name on it'. Therefore, they may start hitting out to collect as many runs as possible before they get the unplayable ball. An experienced bowler may predict this and post a couple of strategically placed boundary fielders.

On wickets that are either seaming or spinning a lot, similar strategies can again be applied. Seam bowlers should mainly bowl straight and on a good length, keeping 'three in play'. Attacking fields are set again, looking to take the outside edge or bat-and-pad chances.

On turning wickets, attacking fields are set according to the type of spinner bowling at the time. The bowler should be looking to have the stumps in play as often as possible, finding the correct pitching line and length to achieve this. Once again, bat-and-pad chances are very likely. Bowling on used pitches, where there may be follow-through footmarks at both ends of the pitch, creates a great opportunity for spin bowlers to maximise their wicket-taking potential.

In all situations the occasional ball pitched up wide of off stump can produce a wicket. The batter may have faced a sustained period of dot balls and then is suddenly presented with a potential boundary-scoring delivery. They are enticed in to driving at the ball, which if not played technically well could result in their downfall. A short ball may well be effective too, as the batter may again see this as a scoring opportunity. Bowlers should always try to be unpredictable.

It goes without saying that the fielding team will be loud and very encouraging to their bowlers, placing further pressure on the opposition batters.

Historical knowledge of how a particular ground's wicket plays can have a major influence on the make-up of the bowling unit selected, as it may be advantageous to pick either a seam- or spin-heavy attack.

Bowling Plans for a Batter-Friendly Wicket

Batter-friendly wickets generally have little or no seam movement or spin. The bounce is true and consistent, and usually there is a bit of pace in them. Wickets like these generally appear in the warmer part of the season as the sun and warm, dry weather act to produce the harder wickets. Outfields are usually hard and fast too. Careful pre-match inspection can usually, but certainly not always, give the bowler an idea on how the wicket will perform.

On a good batting wicket the batter always plays the ball on length, moving either forwards or backwards, thus predicting the height at which the ball will arrive. On this type of wicket they are able to confidently predict this, thus providing the best conditions for batting. Because of the lack of seam movement or spin, the batter can hit through the line of the ball very confidently. Generally, individual and team scores are high on a wicket like this. Chasing down high scores is possible as the pitch is unlikely to have deteriorated as the day progresses, other than for potential follow-through footmarks created in the first innings.

If after an unsuccessful spell of bowling good lines and lengths, with the batting team scoring at a good rate without losing wickets, the bowlers must adopt tactics to stem the flow of runs and hopefully take wickets. More defensive field placings will need to be made, with slips replaced with more inner-ring and boundary-sweeper fielders.

The batters will be very keen to cash in on a wicket like this, knowing that the longer they are at the wicket the more runs they will score. The risk/reward scenario is well in their favour: low-risk shots, high-reward outcome.

The seam bowlers could decide to bowl a different line and length from the 'three in play'. They may decide to 'hide the ball' outside the batter's off stump, bowling there continuously, ball after ball. The off-side field would be set accordingly, possibly as a 6-3, or even 7-2 field. This tactic can stem the flow of runs, potentially frustrating the batter, leading to a loss of composure, ultimately leading to a wicket.

In the 2023 England v Australia Ashes series a similar tactic was used by both teams to stem the flow of runs and take wickets. However, on this occasion the seam bowlers set leg-side fields, both inner-ring and boundary catchers, and persistently bowled short-pitched balls, tempting the batters to mistime a pull or hook and get out caught. This went on for lengthy passages of play.

Even if the bowling team does go on the defensive, on occasions it still may be prudent to keep a slip fielder in position if possible. A tactically placed bat-and-pad catcher could distract a batter enough to play a false shot, even if there is little possibility of a catch being presented.

Seam bowlers should also look to take the pace off the ball by bowling slower balls, and bowl variations such as cutters and yorkers etc. The bowler may need to make slight field changes in these situations, so it would be an advantage to have some sort of bowling sign employed with the fielders.

Similarly to seam bowlers, spinners could bowl a different line; for example, bowling straight at the stumps. They should also bowl variations such as arm balls, quicker and slower balls, and vary their flight. Field placings would need to be set accordingly for all options. The spinners may potentially come back into the game more later in the second innings, as follow-through footmarks may have developed, thus creating a favourable target area.

Once again, a tactically placed bat-and-pad catcher could distract a batter enough to play a false shot, even if there is little possibility of a catch being presented.

In all situations, the occasional ball pitched up wide of off stump can produce a wicket. The batter may have faced a short period of dot balls, become frustrated, and is then suddenly presented with a potential boundary-scoring delivery. They are enticed into driving at the ball, which if not played technically well could result in their downfall. A short ball may well be effective too, as the batter may again see this as a scoring opportunity. Bowlers should always try to be unpredictable.

Rotating the bowlers regularly is an important method of stopping the batter's rhythm. Opening up some tempting scoring areas by removing fielders can also be a useful tactic. The batter may then be conscious of trying to score in that area, only to be dismissed if they fail to execute the shot correctly.

The fielding team may be feeling despondent if the batters are dominating, so it is vital that they lift each other with a good level of encouragement, thus placing some visual, audible, and mental pressure back on to the batters. It is vital that the fielding team stays strong and alert, as any run saved or wicket taken could prove to be the turning point of the game.

Breaks in play can bring wickets, such as drinks, lunch, tea, etc., as the batter has the opportunity to switch off, relax and lose concentration and rhythm. Celebrating batting milestones such as 50 or 100 can also cause a distraction that leads to a dismissal. The fielding team should anticipate wickets at these times.

Historical knowledge of how a particular ground's wicket plays can have a major influence on the make-up of the bowling unit selected, as it may be advantageous to pick either a seam- or spin-heavy attack.

What is the best Length to bowl on this wicket?
This varies, as no two pitches are the same. Even on the same square, wickets can have slightly different characteristics, meaning that the ball can react differently when pitched on identical lengths. Many diagrams give distances measured from the stumps to the 'ideal length' but in addition to the pitch characteristics, the ideal length depends on factors such as the height of the bowlers, height of the batters, type and speed of bowler, length of the pitch, where the batter is standing, age and condition of the ball, etc. With these criteria in mind, it could be argued that the length for a 'good length ball' could be different for many different deliveries.

> *'As play develops you should have assessed the pitch conditions by now, and know what good lengths to bowl are. The state of the match will also determine how you bowl – attacking or defensive.'*
> BRENDEN FOURIE

The normal good length ball pitches on the length that would enable the ball to go on and hit the top of the stumps, ideally top of off stump. It is a length that is generally hard for the batter to score off, and statistically is the best one for taking wickets. This length would be different if bowled on a soft wicket compared to a hard wicket, or one that keeps low when compared with a bouncy wicket. It will also be different when using a hard new ball, as opposed to a soft old one.

The 'three in play' length, generally gives the potential for three different types of dismissal to be taken off a single delivery. These are lbw, caught behind, and bowled. If an imaginary line is drawn from where the ball pitches, to the top of the stumps, this shows how this is achieved. The batter is generally drawn into a semi front-foot position, with the ball hitting around knee roll height on the pad for the 'lbw', and continuing on its path before hitting the top of stump for 'bowled'. The outside edge occurs somewhere on the ball's trajectory.

Putting it simply, if the ball is too short or too wide, the wicket options reduce to one (caught), as lbw and bowled disappear from the equation.

If a straight ball is bowled too full, or is a half-volley or full toss, it is very likely, but by no means certain, that the ball will be hit by the batter. The same applies if it is bowled too short. However, a well-directed yorker is a very difficult ball for the batter to face. It does not matter how a bowler achieves hitting the stumps, but if the ball hits halfway up the stumps after bouncing, it could be said that the batter missed a half-volley.

The aforementioned descriptions effectively apply to a wicket without any batters! As soon as the batters appear, they have their own physical characteristics and tactical game plans that can deter the bowler from bowling the ideal good length. The batter could stand outside the crease to turn the good-length ball into a half-volley or go deep in their crease to get under the ball to hit over the infield or boundary rope. Equally, a good length to a short batter could be a half-volley to a tall one. Batters also move laterally in their crease to create different shots off any length of delivery bowled.

> *'When bowling to shorter batters you can afford to pitch the ball up a bit further, trying to draw them on to the front foot. For taller batters, bowl a bit more back of a length. How the pitch is playing will also influence the length you bowl. For any batter, you want to find a length where they are unsure whether to come forward or play back. Once you create that doubt, you increase your chances of dismissing them.'*
> BRENDEN FOURIE

What is the Best Pace to Bowl on this Wicket?
This varies, as no two pitches are the same. Even on the same square, wickets can have slightly different characteristics, meaning the ball can react differently when bowled at different speeds. In addition to the pitch characteristics, the ideal speed depends on factors such as the height of the bowlers, height of the batters, type and speed of bowler, length of the pitch, where the batter is standing, age and condition of the ball.

Firstly, it is worth highlighting again the role of a bowler. It is basically to take as many wickets as possible for the least amount of runs. Occasionally, both will be achieved together, other times not. We have also discussed that some wickets are inherently fast, some slow, and that they can vary on particular days.

With the new ball, the general pace will be quicker than when the ball is old and soft. The hard new ball will also bounce more, and the older soft one will tend to keep lower.

The bowler should try bowling at slightly different speeds, because they may find the wicket is more responsive when bowling slower than when bowling faster or their normal speed, for example. An experienced fast or seam bowler will know that on some wickets it is an advantage to take the pace off the ball, and they are not afraid to do so, throwing away any pride they may have regarding having to bowl fast. Very often on a slow wicket their extra pace actually makes it easier for the batter, as the ball may then come on to the bat nicely, as opposed to the difficulty of slightly waiting for the ball to come on to the bat when facing a slower delivery.

The field will also need to be changed to suit the different bowling speed, as the ball will be hit to different areas. Not only is accuracy and ball movement important in restricting the batter, but discovering the right pace to bowl on the wicket adds to their challenge. This applies to both seam and spin. If the wicket is keeping low, taking pace off the ball may make it bounce even lower, which is useful when looking for lbw. A quicker ball may make the ball spit off the wicket, giving a surprise catch to one of the fielders.

The bowler should try this at all the batters, because they all possess different strengths and weaknesses regarding shot selection, execution, etc. Variation balls may suddenly become even more effective, as they may expose something in the wicket that had not been seen previously.

Tactics for Bowling at a New Batter
The bowler definitely starts with an advantage when a new batter arrives at the crease, as a wicket has just fallen and they are most probably feeling nervous and a little apprehensive. In this situation the batter's reflexes, hand-eye-foot coordination are not at their best. The fielding team is noisy and full of encouragement for the bowler.

The batter's plan is to get themselves in and get into a batting rhythm. The bowler's plan is to remove this batter as soon as possible, and there are many ways in which this can be achieved from a tactical perspective. In short, the bowler is looking to remove the batter's plan. The bowler wants the batter to hit the ball where the bowler wants it, not where the batter wants it.

The bowler may have a specific individual plan based on their knowledge of the batter's strengths and weaknesses. It might be a 'heads and toes' option, which means bouncers or yorkers. Subtle field changes can be made using bowling signals without the batter knowing, particularly useful when bowling bouncers and yorkers. It may be building pressure by bowling dot balls, or by varying their length, anything to stop the batter settling in and getting into a rhythm.

The bowler should ensure they have an attacking field, with close-in catchers posted for added pressure. It is crucial that the bowler bowls accurately and does not allow the batter to escape the 'chains of pressure'. Stopping strike rotation is essential, so the fielders have a massive part to play.

Bowling the 'three in play' line and length is an important tactic for bowling at a new batter while they are attempting to settle at the crease. The bowler should endeavour to bowl balls that the batter has to play at all times, but it is also essential that the bowler is not predictable. Why not bowl a slower-ball variation the first ball they face?

How Many Consecutive Dot Balls Build Pressure?
There is a phrase in cricket that mentions 'wicket-taking balls and wicket-taking overs'. One describes an individual ball that dismisses a batter, and the other

describes a passage of play that contributes to the dismissal of a batter. Wicket-taking overs effectively describes bowling that creates pressure on the batter by stopping them scoring, leading to frustration, then impatience, and eventually to poor decision-making and execution, ultimately resulting in their dismissal.

> *'The best way to get into a batter's head is to bowl with good accuracy and control. Bowl to your field and force the batter to come after you – change their game plan.'*
> BRENDEN FOURIE

This usually takes place after a period of dot balls, deliveries where a batter does not score a run. The more consecutive dot balls bowled contribute greatly to the pressure put upon the batter. This pressure will usually build much quicker in a T20 match than it would in a multi-day match. All batters have different skill levels and frustration/patience thresholds, but for general guidance for T20 the threshold is two to three balls, 50 overs is four to six balls. It has been found that in u18s boys multi-day cricket the threshold is between 18 and 24 balls.

If the fielding team can apply pressure through sustained dot-ball bowling, backed up with aggressive tight fielding and verbal encouragement, there is a high probability that a play and miss, false shot, run-out opportunity or wicket is quickly approaching.

Try to Avoid Boundaries Off Specific Balls in an Over
While a bowler never wants to be hit for a boundary, there are certain balls within an over that tactically are very important for the bowler and batter. We will look at this from the bowler's viewpoint. Critical balls to avoid conceding a boundary on, if possible, are numbers one and six.

If the bowler concedes a boundary on ball one, the pressure is on them, as there are still five balls to be bowled and the batter is not under pressure. Furthermore, a bowler may have bowled an over where they have delivered five dot balls, putting the batter under pressure, but if the last ball gets hit for a boundary all that pressure is released from the batter.

Another outcome to try to avoid is getting hit for two consecutive boundaries. This obviously puts a lot of pressure on to the bowler and greatly increases the confidence of the batter.

Having well-thought-out bowling plans for the individual batters, reinforced with astute, adaptive field placings, with consistently accurate bowling execution, greatly enhances the bowler's chances of dominating the batters.

Utilising Specific Predetermined Bowling and Fielding Plans for Individual Batters
This should be undertaken before the match starts and is a very important part of any bowling strategy. Assumption is made that the bowlers have previous knowledge of the individual opposition batter's strengths and weaknesses. Examples of some areas to assess are listed below:

- **Front-foot or back-foot strengths and weaknesses.** Do they prefer front-foot or back-foot play? Do they misjudge length? Do they chip the ball up when driving? Can they only defend on the back foot? Do they get squared up? Where are their favourite boundary options off both front and back foot?
- **Off-side or leg-side strengths and weaknesses.** Do they prefer off-side or leg-side play? Do they constantly hit the ball in the air on the off side off the front foot? Do they hit the ball in the air off the back foot? Do they play the sweep shot? Do they play straight or hit across the line? Where are their favourite boundary options on both the off and leg side?
- **Seam- or spin-bowling strengths and weaknesses.** Do they prefer seam or spin? Do they back away from fast bowling? Do they reach for the swinging ball? Do they sweep or use their feet against spin? Do they have unstable bases when driving? Do they have hard hands when defending? Do they always get out to seam bowlers or spin?
- **Batting style. Are they an attacking or a defensive batter?** Do they like to dominate? Are they flexible in their play, or one-dimensional? Do they soak up dot balls, thus pressuring themselves and the other batter? Do they hit over the top tactically? Are they proactive? Do they accelerate their scoring?
- **Comfort level to the short ball.** Are they intimidated by short, fast bowling? Do they attack the ball, or duck and weave? Do they pull and hook in the air or keep the ball down.
- **Does sledging weaken or strengthen their performance?** Are they intimidated or motivated by verbal distractions? Do they employ verbal distractions towards the bowlers.
- **Mental toughness.** Are they affected by verbal distractions. Do they get frustrated if not scoring runs? Are they patient or impatient? How do they react to short, fast bowling? Do they get intimidated? Do they intimidate the bowlers? Are they highly motivated to win? Can they bat under pressure?

- **Running between the wickets.** Are they good at running between the wickets? Are they good at calling, or indecisive? Are they involved in regular run outs? Do they take quick singles and rotate the strike? Do they turn blind? Do they back-up aggressively?
- **Running speed and stamina.** Are they fast or slow runners? Have they got stamina for a long innings, or do they get tired easily?

When setting fields for specific batters, bowlers should focus their mind and ask these questions:

- What ball am I going to try to bowl?
- If I bowl that ball, what shot do I want the batter to play?
- If the batter plays the shot I want, where will I get a wicket?
- What field placing could I use to encourage a higher-risk shot?

The bowler should be continuously assessing their plan, remembering what they have just attempted to bowl and its subsequent outcome.

> *'Setting the correct field is of vital importance. The bowler needs to set the field with the captain, but the most important thing is the bowler needs to have the control and accuracy to be able to bowl to that field.'*
> BRENDEN FOURIE

If the bowlers encounter a batter they have no knowledge of, they have to quickly formulate plans by assessing the batter at the wicket. In addition to watching them bat, a great way of potentially gaining early information is to inspect their batting gloves, rubber handle grip, bat face and edges, and their pads whenever possible. The wicketkeeper is the ideal person to do this, as they are always passing by the two batters at the end of every over. Items to look at are:

- **Gloves.** Lots of cherry marks may indicate they do not like facing the short ball. Try to ascertain which palm has the most wear and tear. If it is the top hand this may indicate they have good top hand control and can play well through the off side. If it is the bottom hand this will indicate they are bottom-handed so may hit across to the leg side a lot. This batter could be a candidate for lbw.
- **Rubber handle grip.** Check the condition to see if there is extra wear and tear at the bottom or top. Assess as per the palms of the batting gloves.

- **Bat face and edges.** Check for cherry marks on the face and both inside and outside edges. Cherry marks high on the outside edge may indicate a struggle against the short ball, and edges lower down may indicate they nick off when driving or playing the front-foot defence. Inside-edge marks may indicate they play on to the stumps regularly.
- **Pads.** Check for cherry marks, particularly on the front pad. This could indicate they play across the line or around their front pad. Once again, this batter could be a candidate for lbw.

Plans for any batter should always be adaptable, as match situations are ever-changing and will need to be taken into account. Field placings should be adjusted when necessary, to take into account the individual batter's strengths and weaknesses.

In simple terms, bowling plans should result in the best bowlers bowling at the best batters. High-strike-rate batters should be counteracted with low-strike-rate bowlers. The bowlers should be bowling at the batter's weakness, in the hope of dismissing them, or at least restricting their scoring.

> *"Use the batter's skill set against them. If they can't sweep, set a field to encourage them to try – all of a sudden the odds stack in your favour. Different pitches and sizes of grounds will dictate what shots are on. Don't be afraid of setting the field where the most traffic is going to go.'*
> GARETH BATTY

Bowling and Batting Match-Ups

Match-ups are really the result of producing bowling plans for the opposition's individual batters. Having produced the batting profile, the bowling team can then determine which of their bowlers would be most suitable for dismissing the batter or restricting their run-scoring capacity. It is literally a battle within the war.

The batter may be weaker against the ball turning away, so a left-arm spinner or right-arm leg-spinner may be employed against them. This tactic should also be employed against a left-handed batter, using a right-arm off-spinner of left-arm leg-spinner. The opposition may have three left-handed batters, so it would be beneficial to have an off-spinner bowling at them. A batter may be destructive against spin, but vulnerable against the short, fast delivery. A seam bowler may be very economical when bowling at the death in a T20. A high-strike-rate batter opening in a T20 will be countered by a low-strike-rate bowler bowling at them.

Having the correct bowling match-up is a critical part of the bowling game plan. Very often the batting team will mix up the batting order to try to disrupt the opposition's bowling plan.

Utilising Bowling Plans When Confronted with Right- and Left-Handed Batters
The bowling team will already have a bowling plan specific for individual batters, whether it is a pre-match or reactive one. When confronted with a right- and left-handed batting combination, the fielding team should ensure that the field-placing changes are done accurately and quickly. If the batters are rotating the strike well, this could happen very regularly.

The bowlers should also be focused on their plan, as they may be switching from bowling over the wicket to around the wicket, and they may need to alter bowling lines as the long boundary to the right-handed batter will now become the short boundary to the left-hander. This will be especially important when it comes to bowling the last over in a limited-over game. The bowling team will have assumed that the last over will be bowled to two right-handers, so will have planned for them to be hitting to the longer boundary. However, if a left-hander is on strike, it becomes the shorter boundary. They may need to really spread the field to give the batter a single to take them off strike. The real challenge comes if two left-handers are batting together!

Does the Bowler Bowl Straight or a Particular Channel? (Field-Placing Changes)
When producing bowling plans for the individual batters, the bowlers will have decided where the best line is to bowl, to either dismiss them or restrict their scoring. These plans must be flexible, as the pitch characteristics or game situation may render the original plans obsolete.

For example, a plan to bowl outside off stump on a good pitch may be changed to bowl directly at the stumps if the wicket is keeping low. The bowler may even deliver the ball from a position closer to the stumps at the bowler's end.

When targeting the stumps it may be prudent to employ a fine leg, because having that fielder will give the bowler security if they happen to stray on to the leg-stump line. Many bowlers often stray outside off stump if a fine leg is not stationed, as they can overcompensate to avoid bowling a leg-side delivery.

Equally, it is beneficial to have a third man if deliberately bowling outside off stump without any slips in play.

Once again, boundary distances may influence the line bowled, as will bowling to right- or left-handed batters.

If the bowler can accurately hold a line consistently, they can reinforce the pressure on the batter by setting attacking fields, dominated in favour of the line bowled. An outswing bowler or leg-spinner may be able to set a 6-3 or even a 7-2 field if attacking the off stump or beyond, and an inswing bowler or off-spinner may be able to do something similar if attacking middle stump, etc.

A spinner may bowl full and wide of off stump if they have been hit over long-on for six when bowling straight, in the hope of getting a stumping.

A signalling system should be employed by the bowler when bowling a particular type of variation, so that subtle field changes can be made without the batter knowing. This should also be undertaken for bouncers and yorkers.

Finally, the bowler is also reminded to be unpredictable, as the batter will be trying to predict the bowler's next delivery, as much as the bowler is trying to predict the batter's next shot.

Does the Bowler Bowl Right Through Their Spell or Save Some Overs for the End?
This is a very flexible area of the bowling responsibilities, and is governed by numerous factors, ranging from the match situation to the bowler's specific skills, fitness and endurance.

Some bowlers like to bowl their overs in one continuous spell, while others like to bowl an initial spell then come back on later in the innings. Some are very good at bowling at the death, and others very good at 'mopping up the tail'. Others are very good bowling to left-handed batters, whiled some are not. A great new-ball bowler may not be as good when the ball is old. It is so important for the captain to know the strengths and weaknesses of their bowling unit, thus employing the most suitable bowlers for dealing with a specific match situation.

It is essential that the bowlers can bowl at any time they are called upon to do so, as the match situation rarely goes exactly to plan throughout the whole innings. They must be adaptable and confident in carrying out the specific task asked of them.

Try to Predict the Batter's Intentions
This is an essential part of a bowler's strategy when attempting to remove or restrict a batter's scoring opportunities. Strong game awareness and the ability to think like a batter will give the bowler considerable help in achieving their goal. The batter will be aiming to settle at the crease and gain batting rhythm, while they will also be aiming to unsettle the bowler's rhythm.

The current match situation can be viewed as the current over situation. Even though the scoreboard indicates the match score, the bowler should be assessing who is winning currently and why. What has the bowler and batter got to do at this current time to win the game? If one decides they are currently losing, what have they got to do to win? For instance, a batting team 35/0 off three overs in a T20 are going to bat differently than if they were 35/4 off six overs. Scoreboard pressure can help the bowler immensely. (It can also help the batter too!) Thinking like a batter will help the bowler with bowling tactics and field placement.

If a batter is soaking up dot balls at a critical period in a run chase, it is clear that a big shot is coming due to the build-up of pressure, so the bowler could rearrange the field and bowl a slower ball, for example. The bowler could also double-bluff the batter. If the bowler knows that this batter likes to come down the pitch, it may be worth bowling full and wide of off stump to potentially get a stumping. Some batters go deep in their crease, others move around laterally.

The bowler should try to predict when it is time for a slower ball or other form of variation, a yorker or bouncer, or even a slower-ball bouncer. An important thing for the bowler to remember is what was the outcome of the last ball they bowled? If it was successful, it may be worth trying it again.

Observing the batter's body language gives a huge indication of their frustrations and hence helps the bowler with their predictions. Look for outward and audible signs of frustration, and twitching feet is a good indication of a big shot coming! Another easy way of predicting batters' intentions is to try to listen to their conversations at the end of each over, and then bowl to thwart those plans. The wicketkeeper is often in the best position to do this while passing by for the next over.

Batters like to score boundaries early and late in an over, thus putting pressure on the bowler. Is the bowler confident enough to bowl a variation ball at these times? If the over has gone well for the bowler, it may be beneficial to drop some fielders out deep for balls five and six just to protect the over.

Once again, the bowler is reminded to be unpredictable, as the batter will be trying to predict their next delivery, as much as the bowler is trying to predict the batter's next shot.

Bowling at the Death
There is great skill in bowling at the death, and bowlers who can do this successfully are worth their weight in gold. Batters are at their most aggressive at this time, looking to clear the boundary with a combination of orthodox and unorthodox shots.

The main skill in bowling at the death is putting the ball where the batter does not want it to be. This comes from much practice, good technical skills and an ability to predict the batter's intentions. More often than not the bowler makes the batter hit the ball where the bowler wants it to go, and very often they do not hit it at all. To counter this, the batting team will try to get the death bowler introduced into the game earlier, so they have fewer overs at the end of the innings. Most death bowlers will bowl a set number of overs earlier in the innings, saving enough for the crucial period at the end.

One of the key technical points of bowling at the death is to bowl a length or pace that stops the batter getting underneath the ball to clear the boundary. A yorker is the best example of this, either bowled straight or wide of off stump. A slower ball, bowled on the correct line or length, is a good option, as is a good bouncer. A death bowler has lots of variations in their armoury.

The bowler should be trying to make the batter play shots that have a minimal backswing. However, in recent years, shots such as the ramp, reverse ramp, etc. have come to the fore; the batter's method of counteracting that form of bowling. This may well make the third man and fine leg essential again, but this then obviously opens up other areas for the batters to exploit.

Confident bowlers often leave tempting gaps in the field, encouraging the batters to hit across the line, both sides of the wicket, increasing their chances of a bowled or lbw dismissal. There is no substitute for bowling straight. They also adjust their length regularly to disrupt the batter's rhythm, this unpredictability making it harder for the batter to produce a clean connection on the ball.

A signalling system should be employed by the bowler when bowling a particular type of variation, so that subtle field changes can be made without the batter knowing, particularly when bowling bouncers and yorkers.

It should be remembered that the batter should not be hitting to the shorter boundary in the final over of the innings, and neither should they be hitting with the wind behind them if at all possible. Obviously the wind can change direction through the innings, so this can be harder to predict.

> *'When considering when to bowl a slower ball, ask yourself, "Where do I want the ball to get hit to and do I have cover in that area?" Another factor is: how is the wicket playing and what slower ball is going to be the most effective on this wicket?'*
> CHRIS LIDDLE

Give the Weaker Batter the Strike?
A usual tactic to employ when a strong batter is joined at the crease by a much weaker batter is to give the weaker batter the strike, thus keeping the stronger batter at the non-striker's end. This gives a greater opportunity for the bowlers to get a wicket, while also potentially slowing down the run rate. It is done by spreading the field as deep as possible when the strong batter is on strike, in the hope that they will then easily score a single. Once the weaker batter is on strike, the field is repositioned to stop singles, effectively keeping them on strike for as many balls as possible. As the end of the over approaches, balls five or six, if the weaker batter is still on strike, the field is dropped back out as deep as possible to allow them to score a single and be on strike at the start of the next over.

Equally, if the stronger batter is on strike as the end of the over approaches, the field should stay in closer to stop them taking a single, which if taken, enables them to be on strike for the start of the next over. This 'in-out' field strategy should always be undertaken as quickly as possible.

Finally, this tactic, if unsuccessful in removing the weaker batter, can actually result in the weaker batter actually playing themselves in and scoring some runs!

Defending or Attacking?
In the shorter formats of the game, while the bowling team is still looking to take wickets, the primary aim is to stop runs. The shorter the format (T20/100), the less time the batters have to bat, so they take more risks to score, and the fielding restrictions encourage this. There is much less chance of bowling a team out in the short timescale available. It does not matter what field is set if the ball is hit for six!

The 50-over game has more of a mixture between the two, while the multi-day format will produce passages that again produce both forms of play, but over longer periods of time.

The number of wickets taken and runs scored will always dictate which team is on the attack and which is playing defensively. As play progresses this may fluctuate regularly until there is a winner. Keeping it simple, the shorter the format, the more attacking the batting team will be. It is all about the risk/reward scenario.

Bowlers will need to decide whether to attack or defend. Attacking may bring wickets but could also bring runs for the batters. Attacking could mean bowling match-ups against certain batters, and also mean bowling attacking lines, such as straight at the stumps. It could also mean setting attacking fields, with catchers in front of and behind the bat.

Defending could be seen as setting defensive fields, such as five on the boundary, or bowling defensive lines and lengths, such as hiding the ball outside off stump, bowling yorkers or bouncers, etc., although these two deliveries are probably seen more as attacking balls. Conversely, bowling wide outside off stump could also invite batters to get their hands through the ball if extra width is given. A defensive length could be one that stops the batter being able to get under the ball, thus enabling them to clear the infield or the boundary. (To hit a six, a batter has to hit the ball on the upswing at the point of contact!)

In a T20 match, for example, if the batting team is three wickets down inside powerplay one, there is a good chance they will consolidate for a few overs, their more conservative batting tactic allowing the bowling team to bowl with a more attacking game plan. A good bowling unit will know when is the best time to attack or defend. Many games, especially the shorter-format ones, are lost when a bowling team attacks for too long, failing to see the necessity to change to a more defensive plan.

In the multi-day format, the only format having a draw as a form of result, there will inevitably be games where the batting team is defensively batting out for this result, while the bowling team is in full attacking mode, going for the win. These games can be equally, if not more exciting than a closely fought T20 match. On the other hand, the batting team could be chasing down a total in a set number of overs remaining, so the bowling team may have to adopt a defensive game plan to stop them achieving this.

Variations, Slower Balls, Cutters, Yorkers, Slower-Ball Bouncers, etc.
The main reason for bowling a variation ball is to disrupt the batter's timing. This is usually carried out by changing the bowling speed, angle of delivery, or both. The slower ball comes as a surprise to the batter if well disguised, whereas changes of direction are obvious, especially when alternating between over and around the wicket. A change in delivery angle can also be made by bowling wider on the crease or closer to the stumps.

> *'A bouncer should be a surprise delivery. Find a spot halfway down the pitch, drop the front shoulder and bang the ball into the pitch as hard as you can. For the yorker find a spot that works for you. This could be*

> *looking at the crease line, the batter's toes, a spot at the base or halfway up the stumps. Stay upright at the crease and drive your head and bowling shoulder towards the target.'*
> BRENDEN FOURIE

It is very important to know when to bowl variations, as they are great tactical balls when used correctly. Bowling at the death is one such occasion, as is when bowling to an aggressive batter, or trying to break a stubborn partnership.

There are many grips for slower-ball deliveries indicated elsewhere in the book, including wide split fingers, knuckle balls, and back of the hand releases, and a good bowler would look to have at least two methods of delivering these. Cutters are also effective, as they combine slower-ball speed with movement off the pitch. It is essential that there is no discernible difference in arm speed when releasing the slower ball.

> *'The purpose of the slower ball is to deceive the batter. A slower ball is often bowled after short-pitched bowling, getting the batter to hang back on the back foot. It is important to keep your bowling action the same. Variations are important to apply pressure on the batter by not allowing them to settle. The types and frequency of the variations will be determined by the match format, pitch conditions, weather conditions and state of the game.'*
> BRENDEN FOURIE

Spinners also have an array of variations, such as arm balls, googlies, top-spinners, doosras and carrom balls, to name but a few.

Bowling off 23 yards is another way of bowling a slightly slower ball, as the ball takes a fraction longer to get to the batter if bowled off a longer distance, and even bowling with a different arm angle on release can be a good variation.

A signalling system should be employed by the bowler when bowling a particular type of variation, so that subtle field changes can be made without the batter knowing, particularly when bowling bouncers and yorkers.

Why wait for a batter to settle, why not bowl a variation first ball! Be unpredictable.

> *'Before bowling a slower ball I'd think about the following:*
> *• Why am I considering a slower ball – am I reacting*

> *to the last ball or am I one step ahead?*
> - *Batter – what are they expecting? What does he want me to bowl and where are they trying to hit me?*
> - *Pitch/ground dimensions – considering the above – what is my best option on this pitch with the ground dimensions – where do I want to get hit?*
> - *Field placement – have I got the right field for the ball I'm bowling at this batter on this pitch/ground?'*
>
> DAVID WILLEY

Attempting to Break a Partnership

An initial question to ask here is: 'Do you need to break this partnership?' It may be that the two batters are batting so slowly that it is in your interests to keep them in, especially if a very destructive batter is next in!

Having good game awareness and insight into how the individual batters bat will help in deciding how the bowler intends to attempt to end the partnership. Think like a batter and try to predict their intentions. Bowling variations and using different angles of attack can be very effective. Rotating bowlers regularly after a couple of overs, or even bowling a 'non-bowler' may be successful. (Bad balls get wickets!)

Pushing the infield slightly closer or even slightly deeper may result in a run out. The bowler could set ultra-attacking fields, leaving gaps to tempt the batter into playing a false shot, or even execute a yorker/bouncer strategy. This is a perfect opportunity to try double-bluffing the batter or placing some bat-and-pad catchers to act as a visual distraction and apply pressure to the batter, both of which may produce a dismissal.

Lots of verbal encouragement should be given to the bowler, as the fielding team may have gone a little flat if the partnership is a long one.

Sustained periods of accurate bowling, coupled with tight field placings is another method of breaking a stubborn partnership. Building pressure by stopping the batters scoring will test their powers of patience and concentration, hopefully leading to a false shot being played, leading to the breakthrough wicket.

> *'The best way of getting inside a batter's head is to bowl with good accuracy and control. Bowl to your field and force the batter to come at you – changing their game plan.'*
>
> BRENDEN FOURIE

The bowler could also hide the ball outside off stump for a period, bowling full and wide (fifth-sixth stump line), with an appropriate off-side field set. This tactic also tests the batter's patience, as they may get bored leaving the ball, so eventually mistime a drive into the eager slip cordon or off-side field. It may also force the batter into poor execution of an inventive shot, resulting in a wicket.

After a drink break or similar break in play, it may be worth bowling gun-barrel straight for a period to see if the batters have lost their concentration, timing or rhythm. Taking the new ball in a multi-day game may be the perfect opportunity for breaking the partnership, as the new hard ball will offer additional pace and bounce. Bringing the wicketkeeper up to the stumps may give a stumping chance off a seam bowler.

In this situation, all bowlers should warm up and be prepared to come on to bowl at very short notice. Finally, the bowler should try to be unpredictable.

Bowl Straight Immediately After a Break in Play?

This can be a very successful way of taking a wicket, either after a drinks break or waiting for a lost ball to be found, for example. A brief pause in play can often cause a batter to lose concentration and rhythm, so bowling a straight line and good-length ball ('three in play') is an intelligent tactic to employ. In the game of cricket it is so often the case that a wicket falls straight after drinks.

In the multi-day format, bowling the 'three in play' line and length can be successful at the start of morning, afternoon and evening sessions, following the lunch and tea intervals. Another opportunity will be when a new ball is taken, as the hard shiny ball will react differently off the pitch compared to what the batter has become used to.

It must be remembered that the batter is most vulnerable on the first ball they face, as they have not received any first-hand experience of the speed, swing, seam movement, spin, dip, bounce of the ball, etc. Additionally, their reactions may not be fully switched on, and their hand-eye-foot coordination is yet to be operating at the maximum.

One of the worst things a bowler can do to a new batter is to bowl a ball that the batter leaves. In just one ball they can gain so much information about the ball and pitch characteristics, without any risk of their wicket being taken. However, an experienced bowler may have just set the batter up for an even quicker inswinging yorker, or a well-disguised googly, top-spinner or arm ball.

Ultimately, at most levels of cricket, there is no substitute for a good line and length delivery, keeping 'three in play'.

Bowling in a DLS Situation

Many years ago, batting second in a rain-affected game gave you an unfair advantage, as the predicted score was only based on the average runs per over of the total score that the team batting first made. Right from the onset, the team batting second knew what rate to score at to win. The total they were chasing did not take into account any variations in run rate caused by the numbers of wickets in hand, or the number of wickets taken – a high scoring rate for no wickets down, and a low scoring rate for many wickets down or when rebuilding partnerships, etc.

Therefore, a set of rules was devised to make the contest between the first and second innings of rain-affected contests more equal. The DLS scoring system was formed. For a full description of the DLS rules, etc., the reader is encouraged to inspect resources outside the scope of this book.

Basically, the calculations are based on the resources available to the second team to score the required number of runs to win the game; that is, the number of overs available, number of runs to score and the number of wickets available. DLS applies to the second innings only. The minimum number overs of first and second innings to constitute a match is five per innings in T20, 20 for 50-over games, and 25 balls for the Hundred. DLS does not apply to multi-day cricket.

If rain is forecast during the day or particularly in the second innings, there may be a strong possibility that DLS will come into play if the second innings is reduced in size. Teams may take this into account when deciding whether to bat or bowl first should they win the toss.

A strong bowling team may choose to bat first in the hope of picking up lots of wickets under DLS, or a strong batting team may choose to bat second, confident in the fact that they will chase down the score without losing many wickets. The strong batting team could equally bat first in the hope of producing a big total out of reach of the team batting second. The strong bowling team could equally bowl first in the hope of bowling out the other team for a low score, then knocking it off before the rain comes at all! When a team is batting first they will always endeavour to score as many runs as they can!

If bowling under DLS conditions, it is important that the bowling team has a clear game plan and bowling tactics.

Lots of teams prefer to bat second in a DLS innings, as they feel they can control their batting pace and keep on top of the score. This only works if they are not losing wickets! If wickets are taken, the total DLS target will increase at the fall of every wicket, so taking wickets is as important as restricting runs.

This ensures the batting team is always under pressure.

Does the bowling team attack (go for wickets) or defend (stop runs)? High-strike-rate batters throughout the second innings should be counteracted by low-strike-rate bowlers. It is crucial that pre-planned match-ups are in place to take a wicket or stop runs. Try to save runs by utilising an in-out field, etc., giving a weaker batter the strike, or rotating right-handed and left-handed batters by allowing singles, so neither are hitting to their shorter boundary option.

If the batting team falls too far behind the DLS score because of slow run rate or the of wickets lost, they will need to attack, which may mean they lose more wickets. The fielding team should be aware that the batters need a good partnership without losing any more wickets, so they may look to rotate the score with low-risk shots at high intensity. Setting a tight field to encourage them to take risks by hitting over the top would be recommended to increase the pressure on the batters. Every wicket lost has a crucial impact on the DLS score.

The batters will try to stay ahead of the run rate in case they lose a wicket. It may be worth setting an attacking field for at least the first ball any batter faces, as the batter is at their most vulnerable at this moment. It is vital to build pressure on the batters. They may be forced to accelerate rapidly if wickets are lost. Pinch hitters may be an option for them, but this style of batting is inherently risky, which could be an advantage to the bowling team.

When bowling in DLS situations, it is inevitable that the outfield will be wet. Therefore, to ensure bowling accuracy and control, the ball must be continuously dried with towels, etc. provided by either the bowling team or the umpires. Sawdust must be applied to the bowler's run-ups, landing and follow-through foot marks, immediately the game resumes.

Laptop software keeps the up-to-date DLS score, as most recreational matches today are scored electronically. This can also be shown on the scoreboard, as most of these are electronically displayed nowadays.

It is critical that all the players know the current DLS score, as it will undoubtedly affect the tactics of both teams.

Try to Get Back to the Stumps for a Run-Out Opportunity

Although this is an obvious statement, it is amazing to see how many times this does not happen. Many run-out opportunities are regularly missed, and while it is easier for a spinner to return to the stumps because of their short follow-through, seam bowlers should actively be encouraged to return to the stumps as often as possible.

By being streetwise, having strong tactical knowledge, a flexible game plan and acute game awareness, when added to their technical skills, a bowler becomes a formidable opponent.

If the bowling team is taking wickets regularly, they will be slowing down the scoring momentum of the batting team. Conversely, if they are not taking wickets, there is a good chance that the batting team is increasing their scoring momentum. If the batting team has wickets in hand, this gives them more options for starting to attack the bowling earlier, but if a lot of wickets are lost, this attack may start later in their innings, as a period of consolidation or rebuilding may have to take place. These scenarios can ebb and flow in favour of both teams during the match, until the final result is reached.

The batter will try to disrupt the bowling plan, and the bowler will try to disrupt the batter's plan.

How Will a Batter try to Counteract the Bowling Plan?

- No dot balls.
- Rotate the strike.
- Build pressure on the bowler.
- Hit boundaries.
- Move around on the crease, both longitudinally and laterally, early or late.
- Fake moves to disrupt the bowler's rhythm.
- Come down the pitch or go deep in the crease.
- Reverse and switch hits.
- Set the field they want by hitting shots over the top to spread the attacking field, then milk singles and twos, etc.
- Look for any visual clues the bowler gives for certain deliveries.
- If the wicketkeeper is standing up, the batter may move to the off side to disrupt the keeper's view of the ball.
- Hit a boundary at the start and finish of the over.
- Hit two consecutive boundaries in an over.
- Hit to the shorter boundary.
- Hit with the wind, not against it.
- Direct verbal distractions towards the bowler (the batter never wins if the bowler gets them out though!).

How Will the Bowler Try to Counteract the Batter's Plan?

- Bowl dot balls.

- Build pressure on the batter.
- Think like a batter.
- The bowler can bowl over or around the wicket.
- Bowl 22/23-yard deliveries.
- Bowl wide of the crease or close to the stumps.
- Vary the bowling length regularly.
- Have the wicketkeeper standing up.
- Bowl slower balls, yorkers, bouncers and an array of variations.
- Ensure astute placement of the fielders.
- Bowl to their field.
- Make field changes to set up a batter.
- Hide the ball outside off stump to test the batter's patience.
- Similarly, bowl continuous short balls with an appropriate field set.
- Look for any visual clues the batter gives for certain shots.
- Bowl a 'bad ball'.
- A bowling pair could be spin one end, seam the other.
- Rotate bowlers to prevent the batter settling.
- Appeal for lbw just to stop batter from taking a leg bye.
- Bowl off a short run-up to unsettle the batter's pre-delivery timing routine.
- Leave gaps in the field on purpose to tempt a batter to play a risky shot.
- Give a batter a single to get them off strike.
- Fielders provide a tight fielding unit.
- Get through the overs quickly.
- Attempt verbal distractions.

Additional Bowling Tactics Relevant to Each Format of Cricket Played

All the previously discussed bowling tactics relative to general cricket match scenarios apply to all the different formats played, so have been omitted for the sake of repetition. Areas only relevant to the format indicated are discussed.

Tactical references are applicable to all levels of cricket. Numerical references are generally applicable to elite-level performers, therefore flexibility in these figures should be made when applied to adult and junior recreational/social cricket.

The following bowling and fielding restriction rules contained within each format apply to men's matches. This may change slightly for women's, girls' and boys' matches.

For the full set of playing rules for T20, the Hundred, 50-over games and multi-day cricket, the reader is advised to inspect resources beyond the scope of this book.

Most recreational adult and junior cricket matches are limited-overs formats.

> *'The skill sets required between red ball and white ball are different.*
> *Red ball – tactically have we got the skill set to expose a batter's weakness or*
> *have we got the attributes required to show wicket taking ability? If we look at*
> *the attributes of a fast bowler we look for PACE, LATERAL MOVEMENT,*
> *BOUNCE, ACCURACY. If as a bowler we are able to possess at least two of*
> *these then we have a good chance of being successful in red ball cricket.*
> *White Ball – the same attributes apply but we now need to add in*
> *a slower ball that has a big drop in pace, a slower ball that can*
> *leave the batter and create a big angle away from them, able to*
> *bowl a yorker from over and around the wicket.*
> *With both red and white ball we need to know what fields we*
> *need to bowl to and clarity in what we are looking to achieve.'*
> CHRIS LIDDLE

> *'In red ball cricket you can set more attacking fields and remain patient,*
> *and in white ball cricket you definitely bowl more variations.'*
> BRENDEN FOURIE

T20 Match (White Ball)

Outline of playing rules:
- Win or Lose
- 20 overs Innings – Max 4 per Bowler, to be bowled at any time.
- Min of 5 bowlers
- Power Play 1 overs 1-6 allows 2 Boundary Fielders
- Power Play 2 overs 7-15 allows 4 Boundary Fielders
- Power Play 3 overs 16-20 allows 5 Boundary Fielders
- Time restriction on length of innings (1hr 15mins per innings)

T20 Bowling Tactics

Because there will be an even number of overs, the final over will always be bowled from the opposite end the innings was started from. This is crucial when taking into account last-over short boundaries or batters hitting into the wind.

T20 is about saving boundaries. This is a very frenetic form of the game, and because of the field restriction powerplays the batters come hard at the bowlers from ball one. They have ten wickets in hand and only 20 overs to bat. With only two fielders allowed outside the 30-yard circle for the first six overs, the batters are encouraged to go over the top, avoiding the two boundary fielders. Generally, there are more boundaries than singles in this passage of play and scores of 50-60 are common in these early overs. Batters will generally go hard at the bowling in the first powerplay until three wickets are lost, then a period of consolidation will take place. If the bowlers can take a cluster of early wickets, removing the most destructive batters, this will have a huge effect on the final innings score. The best way to create pressure on the batting team is to keep taking wickets.

Opening seam bowlers may only bowl two overs at the start of the innings, keeping two back for bowling at the death. If they are bowling well, taking wickets, removing the top order batters, it could be worth bowling them out rather than saving overs for later.

Depending on the level of this match, different balls will be used and some will swing more than others. A new ball swinging may encourage you to have a slip or two early on and to keep going as an opening bowler for longer.

Match-ups are the key to keeping the innings under control. The batting team will always open with very aggressive batters who have very high strike rates, followed by equally attack-minded batters who will also look to rotate and pick up runs in the middle overs. Their aim is for one of the openers to bat deep into the innings at a high strike rate, with a few more hitting high-strike-rate scores of 20- or 30-plus.

While taking wickets is important, a cluster of early wickets should always be striven for, but the main aim of the bowlers is to minimise the score. Counteracting the high-strike-rate batters with low-strike-rate bowlers is essential, as this helps in ensuring the batters do not get off to a flying start. By preparing an individual bowling plan for each batter, including field placings, the bowling team is well prepared to squeeze pressure on to the batters by maximising dot balls and minimising boundaries, so limiting the scoring will inevitably bring wickets. A small cluster of two-plus dot balls often brings a poor or high-risk shot from the batter. Building pressure achieves more wickets than innovative field placings, and bowling the 'three in play' line and length is always a good base to start from.

Taking wickets regularly slows the batting team's momentum and pushes back the moment when they decide to launch a sustained aggressive attack on the bowling near the end of the innings. Not taking wickets increases the batting team's momentum and brings forward the moment when they decide to launch a sustained aggressive attack on the bowling near the end of the innings (they go hard earlier!)

Bowlers should be looking to get batters playing shots they do not want to play, to the fielders they do not want to hit to. Plans such as getting left-arm off-spinners or leg-spinners bowling to right-handed batters is a great plan, as the outside edge is always in play, as is a stumping opportunity. The batter also has to hit against the spin to hit leg-side boundaries. Equally, a right-arm off-spinner or left-arm leg-spinner bowling to a left-handed batter is equally beneficial. This could happen at any time in the innings, even for the opening or last over.

Bowling plans should try to avoid right-arm off-spinners bowling to right-handed batters, and left-arm off-spinners bowling at left-handed batters, as on both occasions the batter is hitting with the spin. The batting team very often rearranges their batting order to take advantage of this potential opportunity for increased boundary scoring by sending in another right- or left-handed batter.

The bowler should not be predictable, so variations are crucial, whether that be slower balls, quicker balls, yorkers, bouncers, changes in flight, different lines and lengths, variations in bowling position at the crease, etc.; even bowling the same ball twice may be an option. Consistent line and length may be beneficial in multi-day cricket, but certainly not in T20.

If batters are struggling to clear the inner-ring fielders it is crucial to avoid giving them singles. T20 cricket is less about the technical side of the game, but more about the tactical side – stopping the batters scoring.

Bowling straight at the stumps may encourage batters to hit across the line – so if they miss, the bowler hits, either lbw or bowled. In the middle overs batters will generally be looking to hit a minimum of one boundary per over, with four to five singles, giving them eight to nine runs an over. They will also have targeted bowlers from whom they can take 15-20 runs in an over, with many of these runs coming from predetermined shots forming part of their predetermined plan. Most shots in T20 cricket are six, four and one.

If the wicketkeeper is standing up, batters may move around on the crease, sometimes attempting to block the keeper's view by standing outside off stump, potentially reducing the possibility of a stumping, and increasing the chances of byes. A tactic that has crept into the game recently is for the wicketkeeper to keep their helmet on when standing back as well as when standing up to the stumps. Normally when standing back, the keeper's helmet is placed on the ground directly behind them, a few yards back, but if the ball hits the helmet at any time the batting team receives five runs. Although this is not a common occurrence, it is worth wearing the helmet to completely remove the possibility of giving the opposition five runs. It also saves time between overs, as there are penalties if the overs are bowled outside the allotted time period.

Another useful tactic during the middle overs is to 'bowl dry', or hide the ball outside off stump. This is particularly prudent if the ball has stopped swinging or the shine has gone off the ball, and if backed up by an off-side-dominant field can be a great way of stemming runs. The batters are literally forced to hit one side of the wicket, and if frustration builds a wicket may be forthcoming. This tactic could also be used at the start or end of an innings. T20 bowlers are quite used to going for six to eight runs per over.

If the batting team has wickets in hand they may opt to send in lower-order pinch hitters whose role is to simply hit boundaries. With nothing really to lose, this is a popular batting tactic. Once again the bowler has to decide the best method of stopping runs or dismissing the batter.

It is important to keep the bowling momentum going into the death overs, and in most cases this involves trying to keep the runs down to the bare minimum, including not giving away any extras at all, as is the case throughout the whole innings. Remember, no extras, as any additional balls bowled can prove costly for the bowling team.

In T20 matches, scoring 90-plus runs off the last ten overs is a common occurrence, so it is very important to have overs remaining from the bowlers skilled at bowling at the death. These bowlers are very adept at stopping batters cutting loose to score heavily at this crucial period. They have many varieties of delivery, usually backed up with good yorkers and bouncers if they are a seam bowler. They tend to bowl a length that does not allow the batter to get under the ball, thus potentially clearing the boundary rope!

Again, as with any over bowled, it is essential that the bowler has 'over-awareness', particularly for the first, fifth and sixth balls of the over. Start the over well, and if the over has been a good one, close the over out well. It is so important that the bowler stays in control. Bowling spells may be short in T20 games, due to match-up strategies, saving overs for the death, or not allowing the batter to settle, etc., so it is important that the bowler always stays loose and mentally prepared.

Finally, as we have discussed previously on a few occasions, try to ensure that the batters are hitting to the longest boundary or into the wind for the last over of the innings.

Some points and questions to be asked before and during play:
- What is the time of the match? Day, night or both?
- Spin to open? Spin to finish?
- Think like a batter. How many wickets do they go hard for in the powerplay?
- How long do they consolidate for?
- How do they consolidate?
- All boundary riders to be fast and have strong throws throughout the innings.
- Slower, less mobile fielders to be left in the ring, saving one.
- Set fields quickly!
- What to bowl on a 'free hit'.
- Zero extras.
- Avoid giving a boundary first or last ball of the over.
- Avoid giving two consecutive boundaries in an over.
- Allow singles to get the much stronger batter off strike.
- Once the shine has left the ball, throw bounce throws to the keeper to soften the ball.
- Backing-up throws – boundary fielders to sprint in off the boundary.
- Bowlers to try to get back to the stumps for a run out.

The Hundred (White Ball)

Outline of playing rules:
- Win or lose
- 100 balls (20 five-ball overs) innings – maximum 20 balls per bowler
- Bowler bowls either five or ten consecutive balls
- Minimum of five bowlers
- One 25-ball powerplay on the first 25 balls (two fielders allowed outside 30-yard circle)
- Remaining 75 balls – maximum of five fielders outside 30-yard circle (maximum of five on the leg side)
- No more than five fielders on the leg side at any time in the innings
- Fielding team changes ends after every ten balls
- Batters do not change ends at the end of the five-ball over
- Strategic 90-second time-out any time after the first 25 balls (coach discussion)
- Time restriction on length of innings (1hr 5mins per innings) – time penalties

The Hundred Bowling Tactics

The Hundred was introduced in 2021 as an initiative designed to bring younger people in to watch cricket. There are both men's and women's teams, with both matches taking place on the same day, the women's match taking place before the men's game commences. It is only played in the UK. Bowling tactics for this new format are very similar to the established T20 format, but because of the different rules applied, there are subtle differences. For the sake of repetition, only tactics specific to the Hundred will be discussed, therefore the reader is asked to review the general tactics outlined in the T20 assessment.

The game is compressed into 100 balls rather than the normal 120 balls of a T20, and the rules on bowling and field placements give new challenges to both bowlers and batters. Because there will be an even number of five-ball overs, the final over will always be bowled from the opposite end the innings was started from, which is crucial when taking into account last-over short boundaries or batters hitting into the wind.

The only powerplay in the innings is for the first 25 balls, where a maximum of two fielders are allowed outside the inner fielding ring. Aggressive batting, hitting over the top, etc. will be the norm. Because of the flexibility in the bowling limits – five or ten consecutive deliveries – the batters do not know how many balls the bowler will deliver. It could be five or ten. The success of the first five balls or bowling match-up plans may influence this decision.

The bowling team will be looking to control this situation, while the batters will be doing their utmost to disrupt the bowling plans. The batters will always be looking to target certain bowlers, attempting to engineer them on to the shorter boundary if one exists. Hitting with the wind will always be a batting tactic, so the bowlers must always be aware when the wind is in play for the batters.

If an aggressive batter is scoring freely it is wise to get them off strike as soon as possible, as they could potentially sit on strike for ten consecutive balls! The bowling team should be aware of, and try to avoid, any tactical advantage the batters are trying to exploit.

Tactically, one of your considerations as a bowler is whether to extend five balls to ten. A good first five balls may encourage you to bowl another five, but will the batter be used to you and have lined you up? Is a change better? Are you fit enough to bowl ten balls on the trot with the same intensity? Further, you are more likely to be asked by the captain to bowl at both ends in the Hundred format, so you need to be more flexible in this format and have practised bowling at both ends pre-match.

Some points and questions to be asked before and during play:
- What is the time of the match? Day, night or both?
- The men's game is played on a used wicket as the women's game has been played before.
- Work out which end the last ten balls will be bowled from.
- Spin to open? Spin to finish?
- Think like a batter. How many wickets do they go hard for in the powerplay?
- How long do they consolidate for?
- How do they consolidate?
- All boundary riders to be fast and have strong throws throughout the innings.
- Slower, less mobile fielders to be left in the ring, saving one.
- Set fields quickly!
- What to bowl on a 'free hit'.
- Zero extras.
- Avoid giving a boundary first or last ball of the over.
- Avoid giving two consecutive boundaries in an over.
- Allow singles to get a much stronger batter off strike.
- Once the shine has left the ball, throw bounce throws to the keeper to soften the ball.
- Backing-up throws – boundary fielders to sprint in off the boundary.
- Bowlers to try to get back to the stumps for a run out.

50-Over Match (White Ball)

Outline of playing rules:
- Win or lose
- 50 overs per innings – maximum ten per bowler, bowled at any time
- Minimum of five bowlers
- One formal drinks break
- Powerplay one – overs 1-10 allows two boundary fielders
- Powerplay two – overs 11-40 allows four boundary fielders
- Powerplay three – overs 41-50 allows five boundary fielders
- Time restriction on length of innings (3hrs 15mins)

50-Over Bowling Tactics

For the sake of repetition, only tactics specific to 50-over games will be discussed, therefore the reader is asked to review the general tactics outlined in the T20 assessment.

Because there will be an even number of overs, the final over will always be bowled from the opposite end the innings was started from. This is crucial when taking into account last-over short boundaries or batters hitting into the wind.

50-over games, or ODIs (One-Day Internationals), are the longest form of limited-overs matches. At the elite level, a different ball is used from both ends, meaning there are two balls, each being bowled for 25 overs. This is because after 30-40 overs a single white ball becomes dirty and difficult to see, therefore using two balls with a maximum of 25 overs use leaves the ball in a good condition to see and play with.

Balls vary greatly so you will need assess each match as to how much swing is on offer and for how long it will keep swinging. Usually, a white ball will swing early in the innings but it is harder to maintain this swing throughout a full 50 overs, whereas a red ball may keep its shine throughout.

The pace of a 50-over game is generally less frantic when compared with the shorter formats. There is much more time for the bowling team to bowl the batting team out, therefore batters need to ensure they bat the full 50 overs. They do not take as many risks as they would in a compressed T20 game. Aggressive batting generally takes place in the first powerplay (overs 1-10), and then as the innings goes into the latter phase. Generally, if the bowlers can bowl four to six consecutive dot balls, the pressure starts to build on the batters. There is no substitute for dot balls and wickets to build pressure and control the batters' momentum. If the bowlers can take three wickets in the first powerplay they are definitely in control of the game at that period.

If the opening bowlers are bowling well and taking wickets, it may be worth keeping them on longer than planned, especially if the climatic conditions are suiting them – perhaps the ball is swinging and seaming around a lot. Generally in this format, an opening bowler may bowl six to seven overs straight off, then come back for their final three to four overs at the death. There are many factors to assess here, as they may or may not be a good death bowler or may or may not bowl as well with the older ball.

Remember, although you are a bowler, it is essential that you think like a batter. The bowler's plan is to always do exactly the opposite to the batter's plan. The batter's plan is to go through the second powerplay (overs 11-40) accumulating runs and not losing wickets, then be in a position to attack the last ten overs (powerplay three, overs 41-50). It is the bowler's responsibility to try to predict the batter's next intention and bowl an appropriate delivery to counter this and claim their wicket.

Batting teams generally look to double their 30-over score by the end of the 50 overs (if not more than three wickets down). So, 150/3 at 30 overs would look to be around 300 at 50 overs. Another rule of thumb is for them to be no more than four wickets down going into the last ten overs, with two batters well set. If two batters are well set this gives the opportunity to bat aggressively off the last 60 balls, knowing they have wickets in hand to do so. Again, a general batting rule of thumb is to try to score 80-100 runs off the last ten overs. This can only really be done if they have wickets in hand. Removing the set batter is essential, as their presence at the wicket gives the opportunity for the other batters to play with freedom. Wickets in hand always gives the batters the option to go hard earlier, although, from the bowling point of view, if they have taken wickets, seven down for example, the batting team can really only go hard much later in the innings.

In any form of cricket, often a bowler may be confronted with a lower-order batter who just throws the bat at every ball bowled. This could be that they think they now have nothing to lose, so the risk is worth taking, or they have no faith in their remaining batting partner's ability. Either way these batters can be extremely dangerous, potentially taking a score from 150/7 to 250-plus, for example. The bowlers should have a method of removing these batters as soon as possible, as coming off the field needing to chase down an extra 100 runs can leave the team feeling very despondent and in a poor mindset prior to batting themselves. Variations and bowling 'three in play' line and lengths are vital here.

The longer length of these innings can lead to very different bowling and batting conditions when comparing the first and second innings. It is essential that the weather forecast is confirmed, as this may well affect whether a team bowls first or second should they win the toss. Batting first could mean the opposition are fielding in the heat at the hottest part of the day, which could have an adverse effect on their batting. The day could become very overcast and humid later, which could be an advantage to a team with strong swing bowlers, for example.

There is also more chance of the match being rain-affected because of its time span, seven hours or longer. Therefore, there may be a chance that the DLS scoring system could apply in the second innings, which once again could affect the decision to bowl first or second.

Additionally, if bowling second, the pitch has already received 50 overs of play on it, so the spin bowlers could take advantage of bowlers' footmarks, which only increase as the day wears on. The wicket could be very difficult to bat on after 75-plus overs, so if a team has three or four spinners it may be worth bowling second.

There is always a formal drinks break in each innings at 25 overs in this format, and there may be more than one drinks break in amateur cricket – breaks at 17 and 34 overs if it is a particularly hot day. The time directly after drinks breaks often brings a wicket, as the batters' concentration and rhythm have been disrupted. So a good tactic is to bowl straight at the stumps or bowl a variation for a period of time. Getting a wicket here gives a big lift to the fielding team, particularly if it is hot and they were watching a strong batting partnership developing!

Some points and questions to be asked before and during play:
- What is the time of the match? Day, night, or both?
- Work out which end the last over will be bowled from.
- Think like a batter. How many wickets do they go hard for in the powerplay?
- How long do they consolidate for?
- How do they consolidate?
- All boundary riders to be fast and have strong throws throughout the innings.
- Slower, less mobile fielders to be left in the ring, saving one.
- Set fields quickly!
- What to bowl on a 'free hit'.
- Zero extras.
- Avoid giving a boundary first or last ball of the over.
- Avoid giving two consecutive boundaries in an over.
- Allow singles to get a much stronger batter off strike.
- Once the shine has left the ball, throw bounce throws to the keeper to soften the ball.
- Backing-up throws – boundary fielders to sprint in off the boundary.
- Bowlers to try to get back to the stumps for a run out.

Multi-Day Matches (Red Ball, Pink in Day/Night Test Matches)
Outline of playing rules:
- Win, lose or draw

- Potentially two innings per team in the longer formats
- Only format with a draw to be potentially played for
- Generally around 100 overs play per day
- New ball available if required at 80 overs
- Three sessions of play per day, approximately two hours each (morning, afternoon and evening)
- Lunch and tea breaks, with drinks breaks halfway through each session
- No restrictions or minimum number of bowlers allowed to bowl
- No limit on number of overs a bowler can bowl in a day, except if an u18 player
- Bowling workload restrictions for u18 bowler
- No fielding restrictions, except for u18 players
- No DLS scoring system

Multi-Day Bowling Tactics

For the sake of repetition, only tactics specific to multi-day games will be discussed, therefore the reader is asked to review the general tactics outlined in the T20 assessment.

The multi-day formats of cricket, particularly the four-day games and five-day Tests, are viewed by many as the purist's pinnacle of the sport. A five-day Test match draws together all the ever-changing elements and nuances of the pitch, weather, time, the toss, the ball condition, bowling and batting tactics, a win, lose or draw result, and the mental and physical demands placed on the players.

The lengthy time duration is the overriding factor in these games, which produces ever-changing tactics from both bowlers and batters, with three results possible unless rain intervenes. Because of this, the longest version of the game is tactically the most interesting to watch and assess. Wicket conditions will change over the course of five days, so a damp seamer's wicket on day one could have been transformed into a hard dry track by day five, either by hot sunny weather conditions or general deterioration of the wicket. This will suit the spinners more.

Teams are selected with an array of different bowlers, including fast, seamers and spinners, hoping to cover all the potential changes in the wicket condition.

There are no field-placing restrictions applied to this playing format, other than the safe minimum proximity distances from the batter applied to u18s fielders.

Patience is a huge factor needed by both bowlers and batters in the multi-day game, and this is severely tested in Test match cricket. Both bowlers and batters need the discipline to hold a good line and length, or not give their wicket away, for very long periods of time.

Surveys have indicated that if a bowling unit can bowl between 18 and 24 consecutive dot balls, batters start to become impatient to score. This can be regularly seen, as incidents such as false shots, play and misses, mishits, miscalled runs, run-out chances, and dismissals, etc. all start to appear around this time. Therefore, the bowling and fielding unit should be aware and prepare for the opportunity with an appropriate game plan.

In the past, Tests would generally go into the fifth day, with a draw being a common result. Since the introduction of the T20 competitions across the world, batters in particular have become far more positive in their scoring intent in all formats of the game. This has filtered into Test cricket, with the batters now scoring at higher run rates. This style of batting comes with more risk, so that innings scores are produced in less time, but at the expense of teams being bowled out more quickly. The team totals may still be similar to that of earlier years; however, this often means that the whole match may now be over in four days or less.

In recent years the England Test team has brought a new dimension to their batting, with a very aggressive dominating approach pursued by the head coach, Brendon McCullum. The tactic of not allowing the bowler to settle into a rhythm has worked on many occasions but, as an increased element of risk is always present, sometimes they are bowled out for low scores.

The media have labelled this style of play 'Bazball', and it could revolutionise the way Test matches are played in the future. While this is an exciting way of playing, players should always be aware of the game situation and adapt accordingly. The bowler should always be looking for the best way to dismiss the batter in any situation within the match.

Within Test match cricket, there is nothing more exciting than holding out for a long period of play to achieve a draw, chasing down a large total to win a game, or bowling out the opposition to win a closely fought nail-biting contest.

Because the duration of play could be up to five days, it is vital that the weather forecast is assessed, as this could affect the team selection concerning the make-up of the bowling unit, and the decision of whether to bat or bowl first should the team win the toss. The conditions may be changeable over the five days or they may not. For example, the forecast may be overcast on the first day so a strong seam-bowling unit may wish to bowl first, and if hot conditions are predicted, batting first may be the best option. Checking the five-day forecast will give the bowling unit the best chance of making use of the conditions at particular times should they win the toss, especially if they need to win that particular match.

Generally, multi-day cricket has a slower rhythm than limited-over cricket because there is a lot more time to take ten wickets, and an unknown length of time to bat. Batters are more cautious, not taking as many risks as they would in the shorter formats. Scoring and running between the wickets are much less aggressive on the whole, although there are passages of play where very positive, high-scoring batting is required, and equally where defensive, slow-scoring batting is necessary. The bowlers should be aware of this, and either attack or defend accordingly.

To win a multi-day four innings match, the winning team has to take 20 wickets. Over the course of a five-day Test, bowlers' follow-through footmarks will develop over the four corners of the pitch if there has been a mixture of right- and left-arm bowlers, bowling both over and around the wicket, at both ends of the pitch. With this in mind, it is essential that the bowling unit consists of spin bowlers capable of taking advantage of these footmarks, particularly on day five.

Additionally, the first opportunity to change the match ball is at 80 overs, so because the ball is old there is a good chance that it may start to reverse swing from around 50 overs, a condition that is very rare in 50-over games, and is unlikely to ever happen in T20, etc.

An item of tactical play unique to multi-day, multi-innings cricket is the declaration. This is when the batting team decides to stop their innings, either first or second innings, and allow the other team to start either their first or second innings. This can be done at any time during the innings, no matter what the score is or how many wickets are down.

For example, if a strong team A is batting first and has scored 470/7, they may declare in the hope that they can bowl the opposition team B out twice for less than 469 runs to win by an innings. If B's first innings ends up more than 150 runs behind, say 300 all out, they can be asked to bat again. If B's total is less than 150 runs behind, for example 369 all out, they will not bat again until Team A has had their second innings. While being a good strategy, team A must be aware that their bowlers and fielders will be in the field for two consecutive innings, which is fine if they bowl out their opponents very cheaply twice, bit not so good if they fail to bowl them out twice and face a big run deficit after being in the field for two or three days.

Team A may decide not to enforce the follow-on if team B is all out for 300. They already have a lead of 170, and if the weather forecast is good they may decide to give their bowlers a rest by having another bat, scoring another 200 runs, then declaring again, with their total score being 670, giving them a lead of 370, with a group of fresh rejuvenated bowlers ready to perform!

There are so many permutations for making a declaration, for example runs scored, overs and time available, size of lead (or deficit can be an option), following on or batting again, strength of bowling unit, etc. All need to be considered before making the decision.

A team could set a large total to be chased down in a lot of overs, or a smaller total via a tempting declaration. Either way, the bowling unit will have a game plan set for how they will attempt to achieve victory. Inspecting the average runs per over throughout the match so far will give a good indication of the size of the declaration score to keep the game alive for both teams, should that be the declaring team's aim.

Sometimes in developmental non-competitive elite junior/professional pre-season warm-up matches, declarations can be agreed and fabricated between the two teams to create games where both teams are under pressure in the final innings. An example could be that team A bowls declaration overs to team B (weaker bowling to enable B to score 100 runs in ten overs). Team A then has to chase down 300 runs in 50 overs, at a run rate of six an over. Both teams have to play well to win the game!

Bowlers will often come up against teams settling for a draw by playing very defensively in an attempt to avoid being bowled out. The bowling team can set ultra-attacking fields if run protection is not required. Slips and close catchers in front of the bat are essential. Bowling an array of variations is recommended, as are yorkers and bouncers. Once again, there is nothing better than a 'three in play' line and length. It is often quite a challenge to bowl a team out when they are set on total defence, so the bowlers' technical, tactical, physical and mental skills are once again tested to the full.

In addition to the stoppages at the lunch and tea breaks, there are formal drinks breaks at the halfway point of each session. The time directly after drinks breaks often brings a wicket, as the batters' concentration and rhythm have been disrupted. So a good tactic is to bowl straight at the stumps or bowl a variation for a period of time. Getting a wicket here gives a big lift to the fielding team, particularly if it is hot and they were watching a strong batting partnership developing! This means there are six opportunities in a day's play to take advantage of a batter's potential lack of or drop in concentration and rhythm.

Some points and questions to be asked before and during play:
- Zero extras.
- Have bowling plans for a bowler-friendly wicket.
- Have bowling plans for a batter-friendly wicket.
- Bowl straight, or a particular channel? Associated field placings?
- Which length to bowl?
- Pace to bowl on the wicket?
- Seam or spin?
- Bowling/batting match-ups.
- Specific fielding plans for individual batters.
- Think like a batter.
- Spinners to hit the follow-through footmarks.
- Taking wickets slows the batters' momentum.
- Wickets down means batters go hard later in their innings.
- Not taking wickets increases the batters' momentum.
- Wickets in hand means batters can go hard earlier in their innings.
- Wicket-taking balls or wicket-taking overs.
- When to attack and when to defend?
- Variations, pace off, slower balls, cutters, yorkers, slower-ball bouncers, etc.
- Allowing singles to get stronger batter off strike.
- Once the shine has left the ball, throw bounce throws to the keeper to soften it.

Field Placings Can Be Used as a Guide for Both Adult and Junior Cricket

Please remember, the bowler's accuracy is crucial – you cannot set fields for bad balls. Some factors that can affect field placings are suggested below
- Amount of swing, seam, or spin
- Powerplay fielding restrictions in limited-over formats
- Batter's favoured shots and specific hitting areas
- Young players tend to be bottom-handed, so can be leg-side dominant
- Wicketkeeper standing up
- Match scenario (variable)
- Number of wickets taken or not taken
- Bowling different lines
- Bowling over or around the wicket

- Right- or left-arm bowlers
- Right- or left-handed batters
- Giving weaker batter the strike
- Getting stronger batter off strike
- Wind direction
- Short or long boundary dimensions
- Slower-ball variations may mean temporary changes
- Double-bluffing fake changes
- Age restrictions

There are a very large number of potential scenarios possible in any cricket match due to the different match-up situations between bowler and batter, and the ever-changing match situation. Here are some variables to assess:
- Fast, seam or spin bowler
- Right-arm or left-arm bowler
- Right-handed or left-handed batter
- Over or around the wicket
- Attacking or defensive field

Based on the above listed variables, there are potentially 80-plus scenarios that could be assessed in any one game.

SEVEN
THE MENTAL ASPECTS OF BOWLING

'Mentally you have to be very resilient and learn how to deal with bad days as well as good. You'll have more bad days than good!'
MARTIN BICKNELL
Surrey & England

So far we have looked at the technical and tactical aspects of bowling. However, bowling does not just consist of these two components, as the physical and mental elements are equally important. In this chapter we take an investigative look at the mental aspects of bowling, from concentration and confidence to fear of failure and resilience.

While continually searching to develop technical and tactical skills, the same attention should be given to strengthening a bowler's mental skills.

It has often been said that sport at the elite level, is 10 per cent ability and 90 per cent what is going on inside the head. We discussed earlier the elements that contribute to the bowler's overall ability and skill levels: technical, tactical, physical, mental and lifestyle. Bowlers will generally spend a lot of time working on the first three elements in their training programmes, but spend little or no time on the mental side of bowling. If the 10:90 ratio is commonly agreed to be true, then why is this? If the bowler was to invest as much time on this as the other areas, imagine how much their level of performance may increase.

Here are some examples of areas of concern you as a bowler may have:
- General fear of failure
- Letting the team down
- Embarrassing yourself
- Tensing up
- Bowling wides or no-balls
- Getting hit for six

- Going for a lot of runs off a small number of overs
- Not taking wickets
- Fear of bowling in a match rather than nets
- Releasing pressure off the batters
- Defensive rather than attack-minded
- It is not your type of wicket
- Bowling from an unfavoured end
- Bowling in different formats
- Getting injured, naturally or by the ball
- Lack of confidence
- Poor body language

Some positive things you as a bowler may forget during your bowling spell:
- Your team-mates are fully behind you, succeed or fail
- Nerves are totally normal, normalise the experience
- Bad balls get wickets
- You can bowl another ball, no matter what has just happened
- You have put in a lot of practice to get to where you are today
- The pitch may help you
- You can rest then come back on later
- You can adjust the field placings
- Batters can lose concentration
- Batters can make poor decisions
- Batters can play bad shots
- A fielder can pull off an amazing catch
- Form is temporary, class is permanent
- 'A man who never made a mistake never made anything'
- It is safe to fail
- Nobody fails on purpose
- Relaxing will help
- The power of the mind
- It is always the next ball that counts; you cannot change what has gone before – it is in the past, move on and look forward

> *'Mental strength is crucial for confidence and success. Try to take a wicket from ball one and every ball after and always remember the next ball is always the most important whatever happened before.'*
> IAN SALISBURY

In the forthcoming pages we will deal with some of these negative thoughts and concerns, and provide proven action plans for removing these thoughts, as well as providing coping strategies should they return. Please remember how much time a bowler devotes to the technical, tactical and physical elements of their bowling, so why not invest a similar amount of time improving your mental skills. You will be amazed how attention to this area will further improve the other three!

Mental Toughness

> *'I think the most important mental attribute is resilience – you're likely going to be faced with many challenges as a bowler, whether it be poor performances or injury. It's the ability to not only manage those times but come back from them and be able to perform. Also, in a shorter time period, the ability to come back from a bad first ball or first spell in a game. Finally, you have all the external factors at the higher level, the media, being left out of teams and of course, the devil – social media and the trolling on there.'*
> DAVID WILLEY

Mental toughness is a phrase that is heard regularly in all sports and is very often associated with the highest elite performers. Very often it is the distinguishing feature that sets an athlete ahead of the opposition. Bowlers are no exception. A good description of a mentally tough bowler is a person who possesses mental skills that enable them to prevent negative and distracting thoughts from detracting from their physical bowling performance, caused by uncontrollable and controllable influences.

These bowlers are mentally tough in both competitive matches and training environments. (Training can be boring and tiring at times.) They are not negatively affected by things such as success or failure, errors, inconsistency, bad luck, umpiring decisions, frustrations, nerves and anxiety, fear of failure, lack of confidence, disappointment, anger, tiredness, and injury, to name but a few.

They also possess a very strong will to succeed, a high level of self-belief and a very high commitment to the task. They stay positive under pressure situations, are very resilient, only aim to control the controllable and have a balanced attitude and perspective. These bowlers do not get distracted by errors and they also have a propensity for staying focused at critical moments when under pressure. Additionally, they have very good control of their emotions, using them in a positive, motivating way, rather than letting their emotions get the better (worse) of them. A good phrase that encompasses a highly motivated bowler under complete control such as this is: 'Heart in the oven, head in the freezer!'

Take a moment to think of an elite international bowler you admire. There is a very good chance that mental toughness is one of the traits they are famous for. Additionally, how do they look on the field, how do they carry themselves, what does mental toughness look like?

Positive body language normally accompanies mentally tough bowlers, such as strong upright posture, walking authoritatively, with lots of verbal encouragement and hand-clapping, as opposed to a slumped posture, head down and quiet demeanour more associated with poor body language.

A very important area to discuss here briefly is fear of failure. Mentally tough bowlers do not have a fear of failure, as they are not afraid of playing to win as opposed to playing not to lose. These bowlers do not like to lose but are not afraid to. They seek out challenges and they want to bowl in pressure situations.

For example, an opposition batter could be scoring heavily against the current bowlers. The mentally tough bowler is then asked to bowl. Instead of shying away or having a fear of failure attitude, they grab the ball, calmly set their field, and with a positive mental attitude proceed to confidently bowl to a plan to remove the batter. They will attempt to execute their plan. If it fails, although possibly disappointed for a while, they will not respond in a negative manner, but will move on until the next opportunity to perform arrives.

Finally, an important mental toughness point to clarify is this: while a positive mindset is essential, positive thinking will not make you a better bowler than your physical capacity allows you to be! However, it does allow a bowler to get as close to that potential as possible.

Motivations

There are many elements involved in producing a mentally strong bowler, no matter what type of bowler they happen to be. Elite-level bowlers have continuous access to sports psychologists, providing support and helping strengthen any mental weaknesses they are deemed to have. These experts not only strengthen a bowler's weaknesses, but also work on reaffirming their strengths. As the work progresses, the bowlers realise the huge benefits of dealing with the mental side of their game. However, within grass roots cricket in particular, there is little if any access to strengthen the mental side of a bowler's overall capacity and potential.

It is therefore beneficial for these bowlers to have some form of access to sports psychology, and hopefully this chapter goes some way to alleviating this shortfall by dealing with some of the issues bowlers may have, thus revealing the positive power of the mind.

Before a bowler can decide where they need to work on their mental side of the game, it is important that they honestly and carefully analyse all the aspects of their bowling package – the technical, tactical, physical, mental and lifestyle elements. This is called 'performance profiling'. There are many charts and tables available for recording this information and they are extremely useful, as they provide the bowler with a current self-assessed status level for all the areas surveyed.

Areas looked at could be, for example:
- Technical – control of line and length and type of ball delivered
- Tactical – bowling to attacking batters at the death overs
- Physical – bowling into the wind for six consecutive overs
- Mental – being hit for three boundaries in one over
- Lifestyle – lack of sleep the night before the match

On many occasions the five areas will probably be linked in some way. We will look at the mental area. The bowler would rate themselves on the following performance levels:

- Ideal Level (normally rated 10 out of 10)
- Current Level (latest performance)
- Discrepancy Level (difference between Ideal and Current)

The bowler would be assessing areas such as control under pressure, emotional control, confidence, fear of failure, concentration, resilience, etc. They simply then take the Current Level score away from the Ideal Level score to give the Discrepancy Level score for each subject area assessed. The bowler can then prioritise in numerical order the areas that need attention and come up with a suitable method of improving the weaker areas. This is exactly what a bowler would do if working on technical or tactical issues.

It is very easy to fully focus on the negative results, which are obviously areas that need improvement, but it is also vital that the bowler takes note of positive improvements from previous tests carried out. These rewards go a long way to improving the confidence of the bowler.

Another method of rating a bowler's mental strengths and weaknesses is to complete a mental skills questionnaire. Once again, there are many charts and tables available for recording this information. They are extremely useful, as they provide the bowler with a current self-assessed status level for all the areas surveyed.

Subjects covered, for example, are:
- Mental imagery ability
- Mental preparation
- Self-confidence
- Anxiety management
- Concentration ability
- Relaxation ability
- Motivation

Again, a scoring system exists, so the bowler will be able to determine their weak and stronger areas, thus enabling them to ascertain a method for improving said areas.

As was stated earlier, it is very easy to fully focus on the negative results, which are obviously areas that need improvement, but it is also vital that the bowler takes note of positive improvements from previous tests carried out. These rewards go a long way to improving the confidence of the bowler.

Cricket is a game played by millions of people worldwide, with bowlers coming from different age groups, genders, abilities and backgrounds. A few will play at the elite level, while the majority will not. Some will play professionally, while most will play in amateur/social cricket. Each category of bowler will have different motivations and goals for playing. Some will be looking to progress to professional levels, while some will enjoy the social side of the game. Others will play to keep fit or be with friends. It is important that the bowler identifies their motivation and goals, as this will determine their level of playing and training commitments.

When setting targets and goals there is a useful acronym to remember: SMART:
- **S**pecific
- **M**easurable
- **A**chievable
- **R**ealistic
- **T**ime-based

Specific

In terms of goal-setting, it is essential that this area is very specific. If a bowler just says they want to be mentally tougher, then what exactly does that mean? That comment encompasses many elements of mental training, so a specific area needs to be chosen. For instance, a fast bowler may struggle with losing their line and length if hit for a couple of boundaries. Their 'specific' could be working on emotional control after disappointment, clear thinking plans and the use of deep-breathing relaxation.

Measurable

Any goal set should have a clear way of being measured and recorded so that the bowler and coach can determine whether progress is being made or not. Using performance profiling and the mental skills questionnaire are two ways of achieving this. While the data recorded is based upon the subjective bowler's feel for a situation, it does provide an accurate record of the bowler's progress at a certain point in time.

Achievable

Any goals agreed upon between the bowler and coach should be achievable. For example, a suggested goal for an amateur adult third-team social player could be that they aim to be playing for their country next season! While this indicates admirable ambition, the truth is that it is unachievable. The bowler should be more realistic and aim to be the best bowler in their team first, then aim to bowl regularly in the second team, become the second-team's best bowler, etc.

In addition to a goal being achievable, there also needs to be an element of adjustment incorporated into it, due to the potential for quick progress, or fast regress.

Like any form of training or remodelling, working on a bowler's mental technique takes time and effort. Mental toughness means that the bowler will not give up when things are difficult, very much like they would when remodelling their bowling action, etc. Even areas such as this can be recorded on the mental skills questionnaire and performance profile sheets.

Realistic

While goals should always be challenging, they should also be realistic, as shown in the previous example of the third-team bowler aiming to play international cricket next season. This clearly is an unrealistic goal. In terms of their physical cricket ability, there is clearly a gap between current ability and the ability to play international cricket. It is doubtful that their mental ability is the reason for them not playing for their country.

Mentally, a more realistic goal could be that they work on their resilience in training, so they do not give up as easily when things are not going well. This may then take them through a level of regular performance threshold that elevates them into the second team.

Time-based

For motivational purposes it is essential that every goal has a specific time period assigned to it. We have already discussed that making changes, whether it be technical or mental, takes time. These changes cannot be made instantaneously, so require a time investment from both bowler and coach.

Generally, there are three types of time period goals: short, medium and long term. By completing the short-term goals the bowler arrives at the medium-term goal. By completing further short-term goals they eventually arrive at the long-term goal. Therefore, they have completed their aim. The specific times involved should be challenging, specific and achievable.

For example, a fast bowler's performance, control and body language may deteriorate quickly if they get hit for a couple of boundaries. The long-term goal may be to remove this drop in performance, control their execution of line and length, and promote a positive-looking body language. The short-term goals may start with completing profile questionnaires to determine the ongoing plan of remedial action. The mental exercises can be introduced, both at training and at home, and the outcomes can then be observed in net situations, for example. Over a period of time the medium-term goal is reached, and a progress review made.

The bowler could then be filmed in both net and match situations, with specific match scenarios staged to test the bowler. Further mental-training techniques are implemented at training and at home, including visualisation, etc. Further questionnaires may be completed to assess progress.

The long-term goal is reached when, confronted with a similar match situation, the bowler deals with it with a positive mental attitude, displaying all the attributes of a mentally tough competitor.

Finally, all goals should be within the total control of the bowler. Goals are normally split into two forms: outcome-based and process-based.

Outcome goals are usually defined by results, statistics, numbers, etc., and are not entirely under the bowler's control. The danger of outcome goals is that the bowler becomes overly disappointed if they do not attain their target. For example, this could be a bowler setting a target of taking 100 wickets in a season, or having five six-wicket spells in the first month. While this is a good aim in many ways, it is actually totally out of the bowler's control. Variables such as weather, pitch condition, opposition batters, injury, rained-off games, for example, all come into play. If the initial outcome goal is not attained, this could have a detrimental effect on the bowler, particularly if they are lacking in mental toughness. Using outcome goals intermittently can be a great point of focus and often leads to the bowler striving to be the best in the team, league, country or world.

Process goals usually define 'the process' of bowling. This includes all the technical, tactical, physical, mental and lifestyle elements. Numbers and statistics do not normally form part of the process, although the process itself is totally under the control of the bowler.

Examples would be the bowler keeping their non-bowling front arm active when attempting to achieve greater accuracy, bowling good variations when bowling at the death, bowling a continuous ten-over spell showing good stamina, etc. Finally, the bowler may have bowled well under verbal pressure from the batters, and managed to get eight hours' sleep the night before the game.

It is quite common for outcome goals to be achieved when a bowler focuses on a challenging process goal. Very often, executing the process well leads to better technique, performance and results in all of the five areas forming the complete bowler.

Confidence

To perform at the highest level at whatever level of cricket a bowler plays, it is essential that they believe they are capable of overcoming any of the challenges the match situation ahead presents to them. This could be bowling at the death in a T20 with only eight needed off the last over, coming on to bowl to a batter who has just hit 25 off two overs, or needing one wicket to win the league with only one over left in the season. The bowler must believe they are capable of achieving the desired outcome. If they have prepared sufficiently well in training, are strong in the technical, tactical, physical, mental and lifestyle areas, they are in the best position possible. While they may have some amount of nerves, they will be in a confident frame of mind.

Lack of self-confidence and self-doubt is extremely common in all sports, and cricket is no exception. It is a game where literally everything is recorded, and every name will have a number next to it, whether batting or bowling. Everyone has stats and averages. Bowlers even have no-balls and wides assigned to them. Just by looking at the scorecard, it is clear to see who has played well and who has not! It is a team game, but unlike football or rugby, every individual is numerically accountable!

Bowlers can be equally affected by not taking wickets or going for lots of runs, just as much as batters are when they are on a run of low scores. Therefore, cricket is unique in the fact that it is probably the team sport in most need of a structured mental training programme!

To have a lack of self-confidence means that, for whatever reasons, the bowler has told themselves, either by thought or word, that they are not up to successfully dealing with the task ahead of them. We discussed earlier that there is a direct correlation between negative thoughts and negative performance, as opposed to positive thoughts and positive performance. Therefore, the bowler must tell themselves that they are up to this task. This is called self-talk.

The bowler can be more committed to this self-talk if they are happy they have prepared well in all the other areas of their training programme. However, this is still not enough for some bowlers, so other types of confidence boost methods are needed. This involves writing out personal affirmations and bowling achievement lists. These are evidence of a bowler's general abilities, and specific performances when they achieved great success. They are very powerful reminders when bowlers are down on confidence.

Examples of personal affirmations are:
- I can bowl well in tough pressure situations

- I feel physically strong
- I can bowl really well at both right and left-handed batters
- I am confident bowling my variations
- I bowl well at the death
- I am mentally tough
- I control myself emotionally

Examples of Bowling Achievements are:
- I won the player of the match award in the county final
- I took a hat-trick against the league winners
- I took seven five-wicket hauls last year
- I was selected for the League XI this year
- I won the bowler of the tournament award at this year's festival
- I have been top of my clubs bowling averages for the past three years
- I have been selected for my counties Academy training this winter

These lists should be read and updated regularly, especially at times when self-confidence is being tested. A lot of bowlers keep these lists in their kit bags, in case they need to refer to them during a match or at training.

If the self-talk a bowler uses is negative, it goes without saying that this needs to be changed to a positive form of motivation. Here are some examples of negative self-talk, reconstructed to sound more positive.

Negative Self-Talk
- This batter is going to smash me all over the place
- I cannot bowl on this wicket
- I cannot seem to bowl line and length today
- I cannot bowl straight – I bowled two wides in the last over
- I cannot bowl the last over of the innings
- I am worried about bowling to the left-hander

Reconstructed Positive Self-Talk
- I know how to bowl at a batter playing like this
- I can bowl on this wicket if I alter my normal line and length
- I just need to focus on the target area
- If I get my front arm up, the ball will go where I want it to
- I have all the skills and variations to bowl this last over

- I have trained a lot on bowling to left-handers, so I will be fine

Bowlers can confidently approach these challenges if they have prepared properly in training, with additional mental preparation taking place elsewhere away from the cricket environment.

A common distraction with many bowlers is the hunt for the elusive 'perfection'. Similar to batters wanting to score the perfect 100, bowlers very often start to deteriorate if they bowl a bad ball. Very often a bowler may have bowled well, but in their eyes they have not if they get hit for four. A couple of bad balls are remembered more than the other seven overs where they bowled economically, for example. A bowler like this is always going to be disappointed, so will probably be limiting their effectiveness as a bowler. Bowlers will make mistakes, as perfection does not exist in the cricket world. If a bowler just focuses on performing the basics well, their performances will be consistently good. Very often it is about getting the job done; it does not matter how or what it looks like!

Many bowlers like to review and record their bowling performances, both from training and matchday environments. This is a good idea and can be a comfort when facing challenges. Similarly to the other performance review sheets discussed, they are most useful for ascertaining current performance levels, which then help with planning for further development and upcoming games and training sessions. Both successful and development points should be listed. Be encouraged by the successful points list, but do not be discouraged by the development points list. In fact, the development points list could be classed as a successful points list, because once these are dealt with the bowler will be an even better performer than they already are. They will be given the opportunity to become even better. Remember the acronym FAIL – First Attempt In Learning.

> *'For a bowler it is important mentality to be able to know, under pressure, what your best options are and how to deploy them.'*
> CHRIS LIDDLE

Some examples of successful and development points lists:

Successful List
- Held good control of line and length for five out of eight overs
- Bowled well to left- and right-handed batters

- Very pleased with my off-cutter slower ball
- Run-up felt very smooth
- Started and finished well for five out of eight overs
- Felt physically strong throughout

Development List
- Got frustrated at many play and misses
- Lost control of line and length for the last three overs
- Failed to apply pressure on the batters for the last three overs

Analysis of the two lists indicates that the bowler was bowling well for the first five overs of their spell. Technical, tactical, physical and mental areas were well until the start of the sixth over. Unfortunately, because of the frustration at not taking a wicket with the swinging and seaming ball, the bowler appears to have let their negative emotions take over, causing a breakdown in their overall performance. This probably manifested itself in anger and frustration, causing a loss of line and length, subsequently causing the release of pressure from the batters.

This loss of emotional control (mental) caused the deterioration of the technical and tactical elements of the bowler's quality. Some form of mental technique development would be required to improve the bowler's frustration/patience/control threshold levels.

Bowlers can also keep record sheets of times when they encountered great challenges to any of the five development areas (technical, tactical, physical, mental and lifestyle) and successfully overcame them. This is a very powerful confidence-booster and is just as important as their bowling achievement list.

Finally, it is worth mentioning the power that enjoyment has on confidence. It is much easier to be confident if the bowler is enjoying their bowling. This could be the enjoyment of taking wickets and bowling well, opening the bowling, seeing the ball swing or spin ferociously, or the actual enjoyment of the challenge itself. Bowlers also find enjoyment in positive match results, whether that be the team or individual. Even better if both occur in the same game!

It is amazing to see how easy bowling appears to be when the bowler is really bowling well and on a confidence roll. Everything looks in unison, complemented by powerful body language. The two seem to feed off each other.

Please remember, positive thinking is a skill that may need practising on a very regular basis, so as with any technical skill, the more a bowler practises it, the better they become.

Visualisation or Mental Imagery

Visualisation, or mental imagery as it is sometimes called, is a very powerful way of training the mind to mentally rehearse the technical, tactical, physical and mental components of bowling. It can be done during matches, at training and more often away from the cricket environment totally.

It is probably best to carry out performing visualisation at a quiet time of day in a peaceful location, such as in bed, for example, but it could also be done while travelling on a bus, train or plane. Before visualising the specific subject matter, it is worth mentally warming up, as you would do before an intense physical session. This should be finding a place where you will not be disturbed, and then go through a series of deep-breathing exercises aimed at clearing the mind and relaxing the body. Visualisation is literally putting on your own pair of virtual reality goggles.

It takes time and effort, but once mastered it is an extremely important training tool, as essential as the technical, tactical and physical training elements of a bowler's development programme.

Visualisation is used extensively in sports psychology nowadays and there is no reason for it not to be used with younger bowlers as well as adults. It can be used specifically for seeing, feeling and even smelling any situation that may develop before, during or after a bowling spell.

For example, a bowler may rehearse bowling a yorker, imagining the balance, timing and release point of the bowling action, then watching the ball travel down the pitch to its contact point, bouncing up slightly to hit the stumps at a very low level. They may even see the batter moving their feet abruptly away from the ball, avoiding the potential toe-crushing impact. Finally, they may see and hear the impact of the ball on the stumps, and their team-mates cheering and rushing towards them to congratulate a successful outcome.

A tactical scenario could be imagined where the fast bowler decides to change their field by putting a short square leg in to take a catch off a poorly played short ball, fended off straight into the hands of the fielder. The bowler can see and hear themselves making the fielding change, then imagine their run-up and delivery, again seeing and feeling the release point, watching the short ball bounce up off the pitch. They see the batter take their eye off the ball, take their bottom hand off the bat, turn their head away, get completely out of shape, before fending off the ball straight into the hands of short square leg. Again, they see and hear the celebrations and congratulations of their team-mates.

The seam bowler could also imagine bowling their ninth consecutive over on a hot, tiring, sunny day. They can imagine the tired, hot feeling, out of breath, pounding in. They are bowling very well but are tired. They can hear the fielders shouting encouragement as the overs go by. They can feel the tired body, but imagine the basic technical points they need to keep repeating to bowl well. They see the batters becoming frustrated at the number of dot balls piling up. They imagine bowling the last ball of their spell and the congratulations and pats on the back from the fielders.

Finally, a leg-spin bowler may imagine a mental success situation, such as coming on to bowl at a very aggressive batter who has just hit both the previous bowlers out of the attack. The bowler starts very confidently with an attacking field. Bowling orthodox leg spin, the batter plays a series of dot balls to full-length deliveries. A play and miss occurs when the ball turns away from the batter. On the last ball of the over, the bowler puts the ball a little wider of off stump, the batter shapes to hit through the off side, buts it is a googly, the ball spins back in and hits the off stump. The bowler sees the batter's error and sees and hears the ball hit the stump. They then see and hear the congratulations from the fielders.

In the four examples given, the bowler is imagining a successful outcome. While visualising, the bowler is calm and relaxed, a situation they may not have experienced in reality. This imaging reminds the mind of its current relaxed state, and if repeated enough times can have a massive influence on the scenario when it becomes reality. The bowler is mentally preparing themself for a situation. They see and feel it.

When a bowler is in a negative frame of mind, they may initially visualise a negative outcome. Perhaps the leg-spin bowler bowls full tosses and gets hits for sixes, for example! Therefore, it is essential that while they may still imagine the nervousness of the initial moments of the scenario, they see and feel the successful outcome. They also associate the feeling of nervousness one moment, followed by the mental realisation that they conquered the situation and vanquished their demon.

There are two forms of visualisation: internal and external.

Internal visualisation means that you see and feel the experience as if you are actually doing it in reality – you see and feel from inside yourself. It is seen in full colour. This method is great for practising technical skills such as run-ups, back-foot and front-foot contacts, delivering the ball, follow-throughs, grips and releases, yorkers, bouncers, googlies, etc. A positive outcome should always be visualising a game situation. For the best results, visualisation should be done at normal speed, particularly for technical and match-play scenarios. This allows the visualiser to see and feel the natural body components and shapes working together in real time. However, slow-motion imagery is found useful by many for technical remedial work.

External visualisation means that the bowler sees themselves from the viewpoint of a spectator, or someone recording them on video. This could be from anywhere, side-on, front-on, in the crowd, etc. External visualisation is particularly useful for tactical and match-play scenarios. Again it is seen in full colour. Some bowlers find this method useful for the technical side also, as there are no hard and fast rules concerning either method. As we discussed in other chapters, everyone is different and has different learning styles and methods. It is about what works successfully for the individual.

Through repeatedly performing the skills through visualisation, work can be carried out away from the bowling environment, as was discussed earlier in this section. Not only is the bowler increasing their chances of success, but they are also accomplishing this without the inevitable tiredness associated with extensive physical repetition. The more you imagine and see success, the more successful you will be.

Another method of gaining more confidence through mental imagery is to visualise past successful performances. Imagine the feeling of movement and sound as the batter's off stump cartwheels back towards the keeper when dismissing them earlier in the season; imagine the movement and feeling experienced when the spinner's delivery pitched on the leg-stump line, only to spin away and clip the top of off stump, removing the best batter in the team, prior to winning the cup final.

Why not visualise your list of bowling achievements or even your list of personal affirmations to revisit a time when you displayed great resilience when coming back in a second spell to take five wickets, after an expensive wicketless first bowling spell.

Bowling in a relaxed, yet fully tuned-in state of mind is essential when coming on to bowl. Some bowlers may initially try to imagine they are in an environment associated with feelings of being happy and relaxed. Some imagine they are on holiday, on a beach, sitting by a river, in their garden, etc.

This is a proven way of lowering anxiety and increasing confidence. Remember, if your mind is relaxed, your body will be too.

Finally, when using imagery as a bowling performance enhancer, it is essential that the overriding function should be quality, not quantity. It is so much better to have lots of short high-quality sessions rather than a long low-quality one. If during the session the bowler gets tired, bored or distracted, they should stop immediately and return at another time. If they continue, negative thought patterns enter the visualisation, which then defeat the object of the exercise.

Persevere with mental imagery, as it takes time to master, but once achieved the effects can be dramatic. Please remember, for everything you currently do in your life, there was a time when you had never done it. Examples such as breathing and coughing happen naturally, but there was still a time before you did either of them.

Other examples, such as reading, writing, walking, running, riding a bike, driving a car, playing cricket, etc., all took time and practice. While there were many mistakes and disappointments along the way, eventually, through perseverance and determination, you achieved your goal, to a point where these things are now almost done subconsciously. This result can also be achieved with mental training, whichever form it takes.

Concentration

A dictionary definition of 'concentration' is: 'the action or power of focusing all ones attention'.

There are numerous ways that concentration can deteriorate, this loss of focus being caused by becoming distracted, boredom, over-excitement, repetition, difficulty or ease of task, loss of emotional control, tiredness, anxiety, fear of failure, to name but a few. Bowling, whether in a training or game-play environment, will inevitably come under threat from loss of concentration at some point in time. The more a bowler can keep their concentration, particularly at critical moments, the better, because this could make the difference between winning or losing a match.

> *'Staying focused mentally helps with being able to execute skills under pressure.'*
> BRENDEN FOURIE

It is essential that a bowler knows when these critical moments occur. This could be when they decide what ball they are going to bowl next, and turn to start their run-up. It will definitely be when they are delivering the ball, watching how the batter reacts, and the subsequent action until the ball becomes dead again. This may include taking a catch, throwing down a run out or getting back to the stumps to receive a throw prior to completing the run out themselves.

Being able to analyse a batter's strengths and weaknesses, and even assessing the outcome of their last delivery, require good levels of concentration.

Concentration is a skill. Some people have high concentration levels, others do not. Therefore, we will look at some of the causes of loss of concentration and ways in which concentration levels can be improved.

In simple terms, any loss of concentration is caused by a distraction. There are two forms of distractions referenced in sports psychology circles: external and internal distractions.

External distractions are things that are not specifically linked to the execution of the bowling skill at hand, for example:
- Crowd or spectator movement
- Talking to spectators when fielding on the boundary
- Verbal intimidation by the opposition
- Cars passing the ground, or aircraft flying over it
- Looking out and waiting for certain spectators
- Peripheral vision movement
- Watching players practising in the nets
- Watching another match on an adjacent pitch
- Balls rolling on to the pitch from other areas
- Scoreboard displaying the wrong score
- No sawdust available on a wet day

The bowler must not be distracted by any of these examples.

Internal distractions are negative thoughts related to current match or training incidents, which mentally distract the bowler away from the critical moments discussed earlier. These could be, for example:
- Anger at being hit for boundaries
- Anger at perceived poor umpiring decisions
- Frustration at bowling poorly
- Fear of failure

- Previous errors
- Dropped catches
- Bowling wides
- Incorrect field placings
- Game scenario pressure

Good concentration management and training techniques will lessen the impact of any of these examples taking the bowler away from their ideal performance state (IPS), that successful state of mind and performance where everything just seems to happen naturally.

Two other areas can have a considerable effect on a bowler's concentration: fatigue and anxiety. It is a well-known fact that physical fatigue causes mental fatigue. This is why it is so important for the bowler to be as physically fit as they can be, irrespective of the level of cricket they are playing at. Obviously, the faster a bowler tires, the faster their performance levels drop, so if the bowler is a key player in a 50-over game where they will be required to bowl ten overs, it is very disappointing if they bowl a good first six overs then deliver a poor final four overs because they have physically and mentally deteriorated.

Take a look at the final stages of any sport and you will see that most errors occur within this period when players are tiring. Cricket and bowling, in particular, are no exception. Physical bowling fitness is discussed in the next chapter.

The other area to discuss is anxiety. In addition to physically tensing up, anxiety can induce forms of negative tunnel vision, where the bowler becomes almost oblivious to their surroundings and tactical assessments of the game situation. For example, a bowler may be so focused on bowling a good line and length that they have failed to notice that the batter is taking guard outside their crease, thereby turning every good-length ball into a half-volley, which is then repeatedly hit to the boundary. The bowler is so focused on the length of ball that they fail to adapt to the batter's set-up position. Equally, a similar outcome is reached if the batter takes guard on the crease, but continually advances down the pitch as the bowler bowls.

When the bowler is overly anxious they could fail to spot advantageous tactical opportunities such as a batter who continuously hits the ball over the leg-side field when the ball is bowled straight. The continuous hitting of boundaries causes the bowler to become even more anxious. If they were to notice that when they bowled outside off stump they bowled dot balls because the batter missed every one, this would improve their performance and help alleviate their anxiety levels.

It is important that a form of concentration record sheet be kept when trying to improve concentration levels. While subjective in nature, it will give the bowler a feel for assessing and acknowledging their progress. Similarly to other performance profile sheets discussed earlier, general questions asked could be, for example:

- What are the critical moments when executing your bowling?
- What is your current level of concentration at these moments? (Mark out of 10)
- At what point do you feel your concentration start to drop?
- How many overs were bowled when this happened?
- What was the game situation at this time? (Scores at start and end of spell)
- What caused your concentration to deteriorate?
- Were you bowling to right-handed or left-handed batters, right end or wrong end, etc?

It is important that the concentration performance profile record sheet is SMART and designed for the individual bowler, as they may be working on some specific areas of concentration.

A very successful way of focusing concentration is to be able to intensify then reduce the levels when appropriate. This is essential, because it is very tiring attempting to concentrate continually for long periods. This intensifying then reducing is achieved by the use of 'concentration cues'. These will be totally individual to a specific bowler, and generally take three forms: verbal, visual and physical. Some bowlers may use all three, others may only need one.

Before each delivery, the bowler activates the concentration cue, then after the ball is bowled and ensuing action completed, returns back to the more relaxed state until they are ready to bowl again, once again activating the concentration cue. Some examples of the switching on, switching off process are listed below:

Verbal Cue
- 'Relax'
- 'Focus'
- 'In my time'
- 'Rhythm'

Visual Cue
- Staring at the bowling mark
- Looking at the ball
- Checking your grip
- Waiting for the batter

Physical Cue
- Taking a deep breath
- Closing and opening your eyes
- Shining the ball in a repetitive manner
- Making a particular body movement

A bowler could also use a form of cue if a match situation develops into a certain scenario they have been practising for, whether it be a technical, tactical, physical or mental one. Once again, these mental skills take a lot of practice, but are definitely worth it in the end.

A natural progression from concentration cues is a component called a 'performance routine'. These are very common in all sports and help the bowler to avoid distractions that might otherwise affect their concentration and subsequent performance.

Top-level elite bowlers who utilise performance routines consistently execute their skill levels higher than lesser bowlers who do not employ a similar routine. Performance routines help the bowler eradicate any distractions by giving an alternative focus in what could potentially be an anxious situation, and in turn act as a relaxant, with the familiarity of the procedure. By continually repeating this routine, consistency is increased in both familiarity and performance, which subsequently increases confidence.

The routine should be incorporated into every delivery bowled, regardless of the match situation. On this occasion familiarity does not breed contempt!

A combination of the verbal, visual and physical cues may be present in a bowler's relaxing, familiarising, focusing and executing pre-delivery routine. It is essential that the routine is practised in training situations, especially net and middle practice, as the bowler will associate a less pressured environment reminder every time they repeat it in matches.

It is worth repeating that the bowler initiates every piece of action in a game of cricket, as nothing can happen until the bowler delivers the ball. The batter has to react to that delivery. Therefore, if the bowler wants to deliver the best ball possible, it is essential they are in a relaxed, balanced and focused state of mind.

The fear of failure and making mistakes is a very common reason for losing concentration, particularly at critical moments of a match. We have already discussed how mistakes always happen in cricket, so it is crucial that bowling errors are forgotten immediately, otherwise the bowler starts to heap undue self-inflicted pressure upon themselves. To help avoid this and focus in on total concentration, a method of removing the mistake from the mind, either verbally or imaginary, can be used. Here are some examples:

- Imagine throwing them in a bin.
- Imagine setting fire to them.
- Imagine throwing them into the sea.
- Imagine throwing them over the boundary rope.
- Imagine a little demon sitting on your shoulder, laughing, and you say, 'Go away.'
- Imagine a red traffic light stopping you from dwelling on the mistake.
- Shout 'rubbish' loudly or 'for collection' softly.
- Say to yourself, 'I'm not falling for that.'
- Just forget them!

Another way of honing concentration skills is to have net training and middle practice scenarios simulated in some way to replicate potential distractions inherent in a game situation. These simulations could range from:

- Noise distractions – bowler runs in with people talking and moving in peripheral vision.
- Visual – bowler runs in and everyone just moves close and stares at the bowler.
- Verbal – sledging takes place before, during and after the bowler has bowled.
- Poor umpiring – umpire turns down every appeal or calls imaginary wides and no-balls.
- Physical forfeit – if bowler bowls outside a certain channel they have a forfeit.

All these simulations could upset the bowler's concentration and emotional composure even in the training environment, so that would prove how easy is it to lose focus, thus showing how essential the need for concentration training and distraction management is! The results could be recorded statistically in some way on bowling distraction profile sheets and reassessed at an appropriate time interval to gauge progress.

Bowlers should try to incorporate some form of matchday distraction training into their visualisation sessions. Imagine bowling at a batter who regularly pulls away from their guard as you are in your run-up, or has 'accidently' run into you while running a two! They have followed that up with verbal intimidation tactics. Visualise all your anger and distraction removal imagery and cues kicking in, then visualise bowling a couple of totally focused, patient, emotionally controlled maidens, before finally bowling them with a slower-ball yorker as they attempt to smash you over deep mid-wicket for six!

Anxiety Control

A certain amount of nervousness is good for the bowler, as this is important for preparing them for the task ahead and can be very motivating. However, too much nervousness can cause deterioration in performance, as the nerves descend into anxiety, which can in turn become very demotivating.

Managing and reducing this anxious state of mind is essential if the bowler wishes to produce a good performance and bowl in their IPS. The IPS is reached when the bowler is fully psyched up and ready to bowl. This takes mental skill, as it is not always easy to be appropriately ready to bowl. This state is also often referred to as 'being in the zone', a state of mind and performance where everything just seems to happen naturally and effortlessly.

A bowler may be overly anxious, so needs to reduce their anxiety levels, while another may feel insufficiently psyched up, so an increased arousal condition may be sought after. All bowlers and individuals are different – some need to be highly charged before bowling, while others need to be calm and relaxed, so it is important that the individual knows what best works for them.

Generally, it is thought that if a bowler is either above or below this IPS level, their performance will start to deteriorate in some way. Usually when a bowler experiences heightened levels of anxiety, it is for the following three reasons:

1. They worry about the demands of the situation.
2. They worry about their capability to cope with those situational demands.
3. They worry about the consequences of not meeting those demands.

Mental anxiety is nearly always a hindrance to performance, hence it needs to be reduced, as it will cause the body to tense up and not bowl as naturally and as smoothly when compared to bowling in a relaxed and confident frame of mind, in net practice, for example. Strategies for controlling both the mental and the physical effects of anxiety need to be used. It is generally accepted that there is a direct correlation between positive thinking and positive performance, and negative thinking with negative performance.

The use of positive self-talk is essential here. Turning every negative thought into a positive one is crucial. For example, the bowler could be asked to come on to bowl at a highly aggressive batter who has just hit both of the previous bowlers out of the attack. The bowler's negative thoughts could be:

- They worry about the demands of the situation: 'This batter is great, and is hitting runs for fun!'
- They worry about their capability to cope with those demands: 'This batter is going to smash me all over the park!'
- They worry about the consequences of not meeting those demands: 'The opposition will win and it will be my fault!'

The bowler should restructure their negative thoughts to become positive self-talk, such as:

- They do not worry about the demands of the situation: 'This batter is hitting across the line a lot and in the air!'
- They do not worry about their capability to cope with those demands: 'I have been practising all my variations, I can bowl straight, and have a great yorker!'
- They do not worry about the consequences of not meeting those demands: 'I can win this game for us by getting this batter out!'

The situation now reads and sounds completely different!

Through technical and tactical bowling practice, and preparing well, the bowler has put themselves in a position where they are mentally in a strong position to perform well. A bowler can mentally rehearse these situations, imagining different scenarios. Through this mental imagery, the bowler can then analyse whether they have the particular bowling skills to deal with the imagined scenario, and then incorporate them into their training if they do not. Subsequently, if the scenario becomes reality in a match, they have the technical, tactical, physical and mental abilities to perform well.

Mental imagery should be practised regularly, whether it be replaying a past experience of a good performance or imagining a new untested bowling situation. With any new situation, it is crucial that the bowler sees a successful outcome.

Remember, you are training your mind to think positively. Preparing for as many situations as possible is the key. 'Fail to prepare, prepare to fail.'

An almost instantaneous method of reducing anxiety is to take a few deep breaths, trying to feel the toes and fingertips relaxing. This can be done at the start of the run-up or when walking back to the bowling mark. Try to inhale deeply in through the nose, counting to five, then exhale more slowly to the count of eight. This should also be practised away from the game situation, in training or in bed, for example, so that you are familiar with the calming effects of the exercise.

Removing the physical feelings of anxiety can often be a challenge to remove immediately. However, if the bowler reinterprets these positively, by telling themselves that these feelings are a sign of excitement, anticipation, readiness and eagerness to perform, there is a much greater chance of a positive performance. The bowler should view these signs of anxiety as useful and a precursor to a good bowling spell. When physically delivered, the bowler may have gained another opportunity to remember an anxious situation they conquered successfully.

The use of motivational music in changing rooms, warm-ups, or individually through headphones is a very common way of both energising and relaxing bowlers prior to play commencing. It is a personal choice, particularly for playing through headphones, and more of a collective selection for use in the changing room environment. If it gets the bowlers to the IPS, then it is worth doing.

The warm-up session prior to start of play not only acts as a physical activator but should also act as a mental stimulator. Not only will the heart rate and breathing rate rise, but the brain will start to think of the job ahead, leading to technical, tactical, physical and mental focal points.

Act like a Professional

What does a professional bowler look like or sound like? How do they act and portray themselves? These are very important questions to ask, as the answers given may lead the young or adult bowler, amateur or current professional, to assess their own overall bowling package when comparing to the perceived qualities of the great professionals. When answering, it is important to assess the following areas:

- Training (How do they train?)
- Matches (How do they play?)

- Technical, tactical, physical, mental and lifestyle elements (What are their strengths/weaknesses?)
- Body language (How do they look?)
- Personality and character (Are they a role model?)

Think of bowlers you admire. Why do you admire them? Do they influence the way you play? Do you try to copy any of their traits? Do you notice any common themes between them?

Genuinely great bowlers commonly share similar characteristics. The following show a few examples.

Training

They train regularly, with purpose and intensity. They have structured sessions, working on specific areas determined from their performances in match situations, which may be reinforcing strengths or strengthening weaknesses. Working on new game-play scenarios will also be worked on. There will be short-, medium- and long-term goal-setting in place. They will be regularly reviewing their performances in the technical, tactical, physical, mental and lifestyle areas of their training programme.

There will be a recording system in place regarding these goals, such as performance profile sheets, etc., regularly updated to monitor progress. These bowlers will probably be first to arrive and last to leave the sessions. They are highly driven and very competitive in every aspect of their training.

Matches

Great bowlers will normally be the first out for the warm-up on matchdays and will warm up with purpose, clarity and specifically in areas where they need to as individuals. They are totally in tune with what their body and mind requires to perform to its best capability.

They will be highly competitive and confident in their ability and will look for challenges to help the team. They are generally great team players who always give 100 per cent. Even when tired they will give their best both physically and mentally and will always want to bowl. These bowlers are mentally tough competitors who do not get intimidated. These great bowlers will make their emotions work for them rather than against them.

While they are playing in an extremely competitive environment, these bowlers generally have respect for the umpires, laws, opposition, team-mates, themselves and the game of cricket.

There have been some bowlers over the years who had great stats and were match-winners but unfortunately are remembered more for their lifestyle, bad behaviour, bad reputations and bad conduct on the field.

Technical, Tactical, Physical, Mental and Lifestyle

These bowlers will be strong in all these areas, whether it be from natural ability or hard work.

Technically they will be continuously working on their bowling action in some way to improve even further, such as grips, accuracy, swing, spin, variations, etc. They will be bowling a lot to right-handed and left-handed batters, bowling over and around the wicket, rehearsing different scenarios, etc. They will also use simulation practices for bowling in unfavourable conditions, such as into or across headwinds, on wickets not offering assistance for their type of bowling.

Tactically, bowlers such as this will be training regularly for different bowling scenarios, assessing and experimenting with field placings, while also researching the strengths and weaknesses of opposition batters and their team tactics, etc. They will be practising for potential match-ups and researching the ground characteristics of the venue they will be playing at. Time will be spent working on bowling at different times of the innings, with new and old balls, looking to bowl their variations at the appropriate times in an over or as the match situation dictates.

> *'The best way of getting inside a batter's head is to bowl with good accuracy and control. Bowl to your field and force the batter to come at you, ie, changing their game plan.'*
> BRENDEN FOURIE

These bowlers will be physically very fit, able to perform their bowling duties without a fall in performance levels. They will have spent a lot of time in the gym and training naturally by bowling the correct amount of overs in training. This workload will be recorded to ensure the bowler does not over-train. They will also have good flexibility, strength, speed, endurance, resilience and stamina, and will also be vigilant in their stretching, recovery and remedial work. Great bowlers seem to have a propensity for not being injured very often.

Bowlers such as these will be mentally tough, either naturally or through training techniques, such as visualisation, anxiety and concentration management, and emotional control. They will display all the qualities associated with mentally tough bowlers, such as concentration, control, confidence and commitment. To reconfirm, great bowlers make their emotions work for them rather than against them. They will have found ways to ignore fear of failure and will back themselves to deliver at all times. They know the things that are in their control and the things that are not. Finally, they will display very positive body language at all times, rather than negative body language.

Lifestyle

The final reason these bowlers rise to the 'great' status, is that they apply the same discipline to their lifestyle as they do to the other four areas that make up the bowler's profile. They understand that the five areas are interlinked, so invest equal amounts of energy in managing them well. They invest time into the benefits of a good diet, hydration, quality sleep patterns, relaxation, for example, and avoid bad habits such as a bad diet, dehydration, too many late nights, drinking alcohol excessively, smoking, etc.

These bowlers are proactive in many ways, have great time management skills, are organised and are generally in control of everything they do through good planning. They also make regular reviews and action plans of all aspects of their development. A powerful phrase to remember here is: 'fail to prepare, prepare to fail'.

Check to see whether the bowler you selected displays these qualities? Even at junior and amateur levels, bowlers who are strong in most of these areas will enjoy high levels of success. If they identify weaker areas, after sustained development work (copying their idols) they will achieve even greater success, enjoyment and confidence.

Any bowler serious about bowling consistently well and achieving their full potential should have a professional attitude. Everything they do should help maximise their chances of success.

One final point, which is crucially important, whatever the age or playing level of the bowler is: enjoyment is the key. Without that everything else is virtually impossible to achieve.

Dealing with injury

Unfortunately, due to the unnatural body movements inherent in bowling, injuries can be quite common, particularly with high-impact seam bowlers. Injury areas range across the whole body, with the more serious areas for concern being back problems, knee joints, side strains, shin splits, shoulder and arm issues. Impact injuries are also common, especially when the ball is hit back to the bowler, or thrown in for a run-out attempt by a fielder, with fingers being the obvious point of risk.

The physical injury will be treated by doctors, surgeons and physiotherapists. However, there is a growing trend, particularly in the professional game, for bowlers with short-, medium- and long-term injuries to attend to the potential mental implications of a lay-off. This could be useful for bowlers in amateur and junior cricket too, to differing degrees.

Mental training skills could prove very useful when dealing with initial emotions, maintaining recovery practices, keeping a positive attitude, and patience. After the initial shock of the injury, then receiving the formal diagnosis and treatment plan, the bowler may go through a period of mixed feelings such as anger and frustration, which, if left untreated, may develop into a level of depression. Once the injury is mentally accepted, the road to recovery can be seen more positively.

There are a few components of the mental skills package already discussed that will be useful in the recovery of the bowler. There is a growing opinion that not only will these skills help the bowler mentally, they may also help in reducing the physical recovery time span. Mental skills such as positive self-talk and visualisation are essential. Goal-setting and recovery assessment records will also help, as these will provide encouragement as time and physical mobility progress.

Impatience can be a huge distracter in an injured bowler's recovery phase. Being out of action for any length of time can be very frustrating, but if the bowler is impatient and attempts to come back too soon before full recovery is made, they risk reinjuring the original damaged area, or injuring an associated connected muscle. This happens when the bowler may run or bowl in a way that attempts to protect a muscle injury, for example, and by doing so actually overloads another connected muscle group.

It is critical that the injured bowler's rehabilitation programme stays in total accordance with the physiotherapist's instructions. Regular sessions will ensure the bowler is fully committed to the programme and the recovery process can be regularly monitored.

The bowler should also be vigilant when it comes to nutrition, because if they continue to take on board a high calorie count needed for bowling when they are fit, this may have adverse effects on their body composition, especially if laid-off for a long period. Nutritional advice may also need confirming.

The use of positive self-talk is invaluable to the injured bowler at this challenging time. They should try to look upon the time out of action as an opportunity to rest, and to advance in tactical areas, such as thinking about field placing for different match scenarios. They could also think about field changing for left-handed batters, bowling at the death, etc. It is also a great opportunity to watch live or televised cricket, to enable them to see and gain tactical and technical knowledge from listening to the commentators. The bowler could also watch online footage, DVDs, or even read books on bowling!

Positive self-talk will be invaluable when the lay-off may cause the bowler to become frustrated and despondent. The bowler has to tell themself that they will be even better when they return to action, having had the opportunity to rest and discover so many things that will take them to greater performances. They can also imagine the injury recovery progressing through to the point when they make a successful return to action. Additionally, it gives them the time to practise positive self-talk and potentially recover more quickly.

Visualisation imagery is another crucial component to call upon at this time, as the bowler can recall past successful performances to keep their rehabilitation motivations moving forward to the return date. They can also view themselves achieving their goal, with a fully recovered and strong body. Another good area to visualise is seeing a successful outcome to a tactical area discovered during their time of incapacitation. For example, bowling a wicket-taking over in a manner learned from a TV commentator, heard during a match they watched. Visualising back to their early days of recovery can be powerful, especially when compared to where they have progressed to now. The realisation of progress is a great motivator.

The mind is a very powerful motivator, or demotivator, so it is critical that the images seen are positive and successful.

Dealing with Non-Selection

Most bowlers at some stage in their bowling career will have experienced non-selection. This could be for many reasons, such as loss of form, returning from injury, the balance of the team's batting and bowling units, the pitch condition, ability level, disciplinary reasons. Non-selection could take place for matches, trials, winter training squads, but whenever it occurs it is painful mentally. Initially, disappointment, anger and frustration are the main emotions, the depth of these probably determined by the time span until the next opportunity to show the bowler's suitability for selection.

If non-selection is based purely on lack of form or ability level and the bowler has received reasons from the captain or coach, the bowler's subsequent mental and physical responses are crucial. Some bowlers may look at the situation totally negatively, while others will look at it positively after the initial disappointment has faded. Similar to being injured, it is an opportunity to become a better bowler, especially if the bowler has been given reasons why. This knock to the bowler's pride may motivate them immediately to prove the captain and coach wrong, so approach training and other matches with a highly motivated condition. It is an opportunity to become a better bowler, as they know why they were not selected, so can go away and work on those points and come back even stronger. By doing this they become more selectable.

In addition to working on any technical or tactical points, there may be an area that falls into the mental side of the game, such as bowling under pressure, for example. The bowler could look at areas such as fear of failure, confidence, concentration, and distraction management. With the use of visualisation imagery and positive self-talk, the bowler can use this initial disappointment to their advantage. It is good to remember that 'to use a springboard you have to go down first!'

The Role of the Coach in the Bowler's Mental Development

The coach plays a massive role in developing the mental strength of both young and adult bowlers.

Everyone experiences an amount of nerves, worry and anxiety in their lives, but the threshold causing these concerns is different for every individual. An area of concern and insecurity for one bowler may be a motivator to overcome the challenge for another. Each bowler has their own worry activation threshold and their own methods of reacting to it.

We discussed earlier how fear of failure or lack of self-confidence can affect the physical, technical and tactical elements of the bowler's overall performance. Therefore, we must remind ourselves once again of the importance of mental toughness, and the coach's role and duty in achieving this for their bowlers.

With young bowlers, fun and enjoyable training and playing environments are essential for encouraging self-confidence and good levels of success. The technical and tactical areas of development are the primary drivers here, with physical development accompanying them. Highlighting the mental side of bowling to young bowlers is less of an issue at this stage, although many young bowlers will show varying degrees of disappointment should they bowl badly, and great excitement when they bowl well, particularly when taking a wicket. A young bowler may be very nervous when coming on to bowl, especially if they have just started bowling or bowled poorly in their last spell, whether that be in practice or a match.

Therefore, there are opportunities for the coach to offer both support and encouragement for bowlers suffering disappointment, and congratulations with further encouragement for those experiencing success. As we know in cricket, there are usually as many failures as there are successes, so the young bowlers will experience these ups and downs regularly, especially when they are learning new skills. Even the action of bowling is unnatural, so takes lots of time investment from both bowler and coach.

Similar practice environments are essential for adult players to develop confidence, as, despite their higher age range, all have anxiety thresholds that affect their bowling performance in some way. With this in mind it is recommended that the coach treats both adult and junior bowlers essentially the same, as they have the same nerves, fear of failure and lack of confidence issues.

An important point to remember here is that essentially every individual wants to be liked, be popular and successful. When learning how to bowl or perform any skill, the individual can be overcome by the fear of failure and embarrassing themselves, thus threatening the state of being liked, popular and successful. Therefore, the coach has a duty to encourage a positive coaching environment through lots of praise and encouragement. Any disappointments or perceived failures should be framed in a positive manner so that the bowler realises that making mistakes is part of their development. Every obstacle in the way of a bowler's development should be viewed as a stepping stone rather than a boulder! 'Fail safe' means 'it is safe to fail'. Praise the process as well as the outcome.

The coach needs to be honest with their bowlers at all times, so, for example, if there is a problem with a bowling action or the bowler suffers from self-confidence issues, these must be confronted in the appropriate, positively encouraging manner. It is essential that the coach builds a positive coach/bowler relationship based on trust, honesty and encouragement, particularly

when dealing with the mental development side of the player. For example, this can be established by thinking about the following areas:
- Getting to know your bowler
- The use of 'open-ended' questions
- Listening intently to the answers
- Reacting to answers with appropriate thoughtful responses
- Use of funnelling questions to self-empower the bowler
- Ensuring a positive learning environment

Getting to Know your Bowler

This takes time and involves not only getting to know them as a bowler but as a person too. Once the coach achieves this they are able to cater their coaching to the needs of the individual bowler, particularly when working on any mental development areas. The coach can also ascertain the bowler's preferred learning style and determine whether they are a 'fixed' or 'open' mindset learner.

Briefly and very simplistically, bowlers with a fixed mindset can find change and trying new things challenging, as they can be very reluctant to come out of their comfort zone. It is a challenge for the coach to encourage them to achieve their full potential but, with the right methods, encouragement and trust, this can be achieved. Bowlers with an open mindset are literally the opposite of the fixed type. They openly welcome change, are willing to try new things and do not feel frightened to leave their comfort zone. A common phrase associated with these types of bowlers is: 'They are very coachable.' For further information on open and fixed mindsets, the reader is encouraged to investigate resources beyond the scope of this book.

It is so easy to dive straight into technical and tactical coaching, getting active as soon as possible. Very often an opportunity is missed to ask the bowler how they are, how school or work went this week, how their match went at the weekend, what they learned from that experience. Remembering previous conversations – such as asking how an exam went, whether they got that promotion, how they got on opening the bowling for the first time last week – all go to show that you take an interest in them, while promoting the positive learning environment.

It is crucial that you take every opportunity to talk/chat with your bowler, as they may have something to tell you that may influence the content of the forthcoming coaching session. Taking time to recap the last session and compliment them on their progress is invaluable to the player, as again it shows that you care about their development.

The Use of Open-Ended Questions

This is an extremely powerful method of both getting to know your bowler and empowering them simultaneously. There are two methods of questioning, open or closed. Closed questions are those that literally encourage one-word answers, such as yes or no. They are almost 'closed' answers! An example would be, 'Did you feel your bowling arm wasn't vertical when you bowled the ball down the leg side?' A better 'open' question alternative could be, 'What did you feel happened to your bowling arm when you bowled the ball down the leg side?' In the closed question, the answer will probably be yes or no. In the open question answer, the bowler has to answer with an opinion based on what they actually felt. With careful listening to their reply, the coach can then start a conversation full of open questions, which promotes self-thinking and empowers the bowler to answer them honestly and confidently.

Think about your own coaching style. Do you 'push' answers into your bowler or 'pull' answers out of them?

Listening Intently to the Answers

Listening is an incredibly important skill to have. Very often, coaches switch off quite early in a bowler's reply, as they probably already have their next question lined up. If a coach is inattentive to the bowler's reply, they may miss an opportunity to ask a really powerful question that could really accelerate the player's development.

It is important to let the bowler do as much talking as possible, potentially more than the coach. On many occasions less is more. Coaches should always remember: we have been given two eyes, two ears and one mouth, so let us use them in those proportions! By the coach listening intently, the bowler may reveal something that leads the coach down a completely different line of questioning, thus enabling them to gain better understanding of the bowler they are working with. A coach should never blankly ask a question that has nothing to do with the answer the bowler has just given. This shows a lack of listening skills and respect for the person they are working with. If possible, the coach should only plan one question, and then respond to the subsequent answers the bowler gives, and see where the conversation leads to.

For further information on listening skills the reader is encouraged to investigate resources beyond the scope of this book.

Reacting to the Answers with Appropriate Thoughtful Responses
We have just highlighted the importance of listening intently. With this in mind it is vital that the coach takes time before replying immediately. It is vital to not only assess 'what' the bowler just said, but also to assess 'how' it was said. Was it said in a confident manner, or was it said from an anxious standpoint? Did the bowler answer with an emphasis on the technical, tactical, physical or mental aspect of the question?

Once again, spotting any underlying concerns over a part of the bowler's game can accelerate their development. The bowler's body language can also betray any confidence issues they may be trying to overcome. Therefore, the coach can change or recompose the question they have asked. Careful, thoughtful and encouraging responses can be powerful for the bowler, as they know that the coach is fully committed to their development.

Use of Funnelling Questions to Self-Empower the Bowler
This involves practice and confidence to perform regularly but is one of the best ways to teach a bowler to think on their feet, thus empowering themselves.

Having asked open questions, listened intently to the answers and reacted with appropriate responses, the coach can apply funnelling to their next questions. This involves the coach knowing what the answer to a particular problem is, but instead of telling the bowler the answer, the coach asks appropriate questions to draw the answer out of the bowler themselves. In this situation the bowler has worked out the answer themselves rather than the coach telling them. The bowler can then take the credit and responsibility for their own development, which is an extremely powerful way of learning. This provides great encouragement for the bowler, additionally lifting their confidence and self-esteem.

Here is an example of funnelling, referring back to the bowler bowling down the leg side:

Coach – What did you feel happened to your bowling arm on that last ball?

Bowler – It felt like it wasn't vertical when I released the ball.

Coach – You're right. So why do you think having a vertical arm will help you?

Bowler – Because if I do, there's a very good chance the ball will go straight.

Coach – Yes, I agree. So what do you think is causing your arm not to be vertical?

Bowler – I think I am falling to the off side as I bowl the ball.

Coach – Brilliant. What will help you stop doing that then?

Bowler – I need to try to keep my momentum going straight and keep myself upright.

Coach – Yes, that's right. How can you do that, and what's causing it to happen?

Bowler – I need to get my non-bowling arm up higher, as it's too low at the moment.

Coach – Yes, true, but why is that going to help you?

Bowler – Because my front arm will lead my body towards the target and improve my balance.

Coach – That sounds perfect, well done. Come on then, let's see you do it. I'm sure you will.

The coach knew what the problem was but, instead of diving in and telling the bowler to get their front arm up higher, by a series of funnelling questions they were able to get the bowler to work it out for themself. This is a far more positive learning environment than just being told. A point to remember here is that time constraints can have an impact on how much funnelling can take place. In 1-2-1 coaching situations there is more time for it to take place, but in a group bowling session it may be necessary to 'tell' the bowlers. However, this should be avoided wherever possible.

Ensuring a Positive Learning Environment

By ensuring the aforementioned points are included, the bowler and coach should experience a positive, enjoyable session. In any training environment, an element of fun, competition and progression should always be present. This can be undertaken through group target bowling competitions, for example, or bowling competitions between coach and bowler.

Another potent form of competition between bowler and coach is to have a form of point-scoring game, where only the bowler bowls, with successful outcomes scoring points for the bowler, but unsuccessful outcomes scoring points for the coach. That becomes a very powerful, competitive and positive learning environment for the bowler in our experience.

With regards to the bowler's mental development, both winning and losing present the coach with an opportunity to see how the bowler reacts to each situation, giving an insight in to how their development can be nurtured from a mental perspective.

Finally, the coach should tailor every session to include progression and success. This could again be in a group or individual session, and should apply to all bowlers. This could mean that in a junior group session, for example, success should be achieved in some way for both experienced and beginner bowlers. Initially this may mean seeding players into teams, or having different point-scoring systems operating. However, a danger may be that the beginner's ability is affected by the strong performance of the experienced bowlers, causing them to become disheartened, or, on the other hand, the experienced bowler's performance drops because they become bored at the ease of the task set with the beginner bowler in mind.

The beginner may need to learn the basic skills slowly from scratch, whereas the experienced bowler may need to be pushed a little more in a more competitive environment. This is always a challenge for a coach in junior group sessions.

Games and point-scoring systems can be applied to any age or ability of bowler, irrespective of which technical, tactical, physical or mental element is being assessed.

Dealing with a Bowler's Non-Selection

This subject was discussed in the previous section, mainly referring to the mental strategies for dealing with this predicament. It is very important to remember, as a coach, that the way a player is told they are not selected can have a huge impact on them mentally. They will be feeling they have been rejected, are not good enough, and suffering from very low self-esteem. We have all been there, so appreciate how that feels.

While this is important at all ages and ability levels, it is vitally important when dealing with young players. It is essential that the bowler has the reasons explained to them, so they can go away and work on those points, giving them encouragement that they can return in the future. Everything is relevant, as the decision was made at a particular point in time, at a particular point in a bowler's experience, learning and ability, at a particular point when they were compared to others.

It is crucial that the bowler has this explained to them and that they understand this. For example, bowler A may be considered a lesser player than bowler B at the winter trials for next year's county U14s squad, so they are not selected. The coach relays this disappointing news to the parents and bowler in an honest, positive, sensitive and encouraging manner, suggesting areas for improvement that may help them become a better bowler, capable of trialling and selection the following year.

Bowler A goes away and for that winter and throughout the following summer puts everything into practice, has a great summer, goes to the winter trials, and is selected for the next summer. Bowler A replaces bowler B this time.

It is important to remember that if a bowler does not get in one year they definitely have a chance the next if they have a plan and commitment to do so. It is never over. (Not until the umpire says so!)

The worst thing that can happen is that no reasons are provided. This can cause a huge drop in confidence and self-esteem, and even result in a bowler giving up and totally rejecting cricket. Therefore, it is absolutely critical that any non-selection matters are explained clearly, and an action plan is provided to enable the bowler to potentially return to the team.

Summary

We have discussed the crucial importance of the 'mental' component of the technical, tactical, physical and lifestyle elements of a bowler's make-up. Worry, anxiety, fear and lack of confidence is the brain telling an individual they are not up to the task presented to them. The top international players have been there too, but have practiced and experienced ways of dealing with, if not overcoming these feelings. The key is to find a way to embrace your concerns, meaning you rule them, not them ruling you. Remember, a level of uncertainty + a level of importance = anxiety.

Do not be too concerned about nerves – try to change the narrative. They are a good motivator and prepare you for the task ahead. A bowler can perform well when nervous, and it is unrealistic to think you have to be totally relaxed. For example, the worries and nerves of the night before suddenly disappear when the moment actually arrives to perform on many occasions. Ultimately, it is about the actions rather than how you are feeling. However, the faster and more relaxed a bowler is, the better they will perform.

Bowlers are all individuals, so what works for one may not work for another. It is vital that the bowler understands how their own mind works, determining which situations motivate them and which ones demotivate them. Prioritising the bowling concerns with real-life events will put the concerns into perspective and reduce, if not remove, their negative effects. For example, comparisons such as the sun will always rise tomorrow, or my pet will still love me always help.

It is important to remember that a bowler can only control the controllables. It is impossible to try to control the uncontrollables. It is therefore critical that the bowler identifies the difference between the two. On many occasions the bowler may only be able to control their response to a certain situation or control the process rather than the outcome.

Dwelling on any negative events from the past or worrying about events in the future will have a detrimental effect on the bowler, so it is important to just concentrate on staying in the moment. Having clarity in any bowling situation keeps things simple and manageable.

Good preparation is the key for giving the bowler the best chance of success – control the controllables. Remember the phrases: 'Poor planning promotes poor performance'; 'Fail to prepare, prepare to fail'; and the PRIDE acronym – 'Personal Responsibility in Developing Excellence'.

Good practice leads to improved bowling confidence = better individual bowling performances = greater enjoyment = improved team performances = even greater enjoyment = even better individual bowling performances.

While bowling, the bowler should never be worrying about a technical aspect of their game, as this will be a distraction. If they have practised correctly the bowler should feel confident about the technical aspect of their technique, thus allowing them to simply bowl the ball, trusting in their instincts.

Great personal performances or winning games for your team are not the only areas of bowling that are enjoyable; there is also the satisfaction achieved from giving your best even if it did not work out. Equally, if some aspect of bowling is not working, do not give up after the first attempt. There is no silver bullet or fairy dust to throw over the bowler – it is all about hard work and not giving up. True resilience is also about putting your inner pride to one side, not being concerned about what you look like, just get the job done. Persistently persist! Psychological and emotional management is crucial in determining the amount of success a bowler will experience.

It is worth remembering this: some days it is your day, other days it is not! It is all about how you respond to each of these days.

What follows is a comprehensive list of examples that may affect your success or influence your effectiveness as a bowler. These may help with assessing any areas where a bowler can gain additional percentage performance gains. The bowler may have additional points to add themselves. Please assess which category each item falls into: technical, tactical, physical, mental or lifestyle.

Natural ability
Eyesight
Hearing
Judging bowling length
Reactions
Hand-eye-foot coordination
Technique
Run-up
Balance/head position
Foot alignment
Strong delivery base
Release wrist position
Follow-through
Amount of swing
Amount of seam movement
Amount of spin
Amount of dip
Bowling variations
Preparation
Organisation
Warm-up
Cool-down
Footwear (missing studs?)
Forgotten equipment
Borrowed equipment
Attitude
Clarity of purpose
Clarity of thought
Confidence level
Perfectionist

Positive mindset
Fixed or growth mindset
Patience
Enjoyment
Relaxation levels
Mental strength
Nerves
Fear of failure
Dealing with failure
Visualisation
Positive self-talk
Body language
Resilience
Perseverance
Pride
Arrogance
Fear of injury
Injury prevention
Injury management
Past experiences
Playing experience
Bowler's strengths
Bowler's weaknesses
Batter's strengths
Batter's weaknesses
Length of bowling spell
Number of bowling spells
Confidence
Concentration
Control

- Commitment
- Distractions
- Sledging
- Breaks in play
- Motivations
- Training/work ethic
- Self-responsibility
- Honesty
- Learning style
- Coaches
- Team-mates
- Controllables
- Uncontrollables
- Physical fitness
- Speed and power
- Endurance
- Tiredness
- Physical impairments
- Targets (short-term)
- Targets (long-term)
- Current and past form
- Match format
- Fielding first or second
- Match situation
- Bowling plan
- Know your role
- Tactical awareness
- Situational awareness
- First spell outcome
- Second spell outcome
- New ball outcome
- Older ball outcome
- Top order outcome
- Lower-order outcome
- Scoreboard pressure
- Knowledge of lbw law
- Batter's reputation

- Batter's current form
- Gender of batter
- Level being played at
- Opposition
- Field placings
- Fielders' strengths
- Fielders' weaknesses
- Batters rotating strike
- Right-handed batters
- Left-handed batters
- Over the wicket
- Around the wicket
- Keeper up or back
- Bowling partnerships
- Batting partnerships
- Assessment of batters
- Batters' plans
- Assessment of fielders
- Ball condition/age/type
- Pitch condition/gradients
- Pitch assessment
- New/used pitch
- Bowlers' footmarks
- Outfield condition
- Outfield slopes
- Boundary distances
- Lack of sightscreens

- Available bowling time
- Innings time of day
- Weather
- Temperature
- Sun protection
- Sun in batter's eyes
- Westerly sun height
- Reduced light levels
- Wind direction/strength

Position in bowling order	**Sufficient sleep**
Wickets in hand	**Nutrition**
Number of overs left	**Dehydration**
Declarations	**Energy levels**
Putting opposition back In	**Rest and down time**
Communication	**Recovery**
Run outs	**Waiting to bowl**
Practice/Preparation	**Superstitions/routines**
Prehab or Rehab	**Development plan**
Lifestyle	**Availability**

For further references on sports psychology subjects the reader is encouraged to investigate resources outside the scope of this book.

EIGHT
LOOKING AFTER YOURSELF
(PRE-MATCH PREPARATION, FITNESS, NUTRITION, SLEEP & EQUIPMENT)

'You need to be robust – bowling is not easy! I'm a big believer in "all-round" fitness as it gives you that robustness. I believe that more recent generations who have spent more time in academies, in the gym and sat behind computers are more likely to become injured. I think the S&C in cricket has almost done a full circle now and so there's more belief that to get fit for bowling – you need to bowl.'
DAVID WILLEY
Northants & England

Pre-Match Preparation

'Always be ready to bowl, mentally and physically. Lots of mental game plans and having an understanding of how to bowl in certain periods of the match.'
MARTIN BICKNELL

The most important aspect of any pre-match preparation is to feel physically and mentally prepared for the task ahead, commencing the match feeling confident about your bowling. Similar to a batter hitting the ball out of the middle of the bat via throw-down practice, to feel confident about their game a bowler needs to feel their rhythm and timing through the run-up, bound, delivery release and follow-through.

How much preparation you can do before the start of play will depend on the level you are currently playing, and when teams arrive before play is due to start. You may also be relying on your parents to get you to the match on time!

Primarily, depending on the player's age and ability, pre-match preparation is the player's responsibility, although you need an understanding of how the coach and captain can help facilitate that. Pre-match is not the time for hard-core fitness routines and drills, as you do not want to be physically tired going into the day's play. It is about good time management, knowing what you need to do and for how long to give you the best opportunity to deliver the bowling spell in a confident state of mind.

Pre-match Bowling Warm-Up Routines

The pre-match bowling warm-up could actually be viewed as starting with the matchday breakfast. Nutrition for cricket is specifically discussed after this section but, briefly, a good breakfast will consist of food types such as cereals, porridge, fruit, fruit juices, jams, carbohydrates and proteins. Supplements such as protein shakes, energy bars, glucose tablets and salt tablets can also be taken. Fluids should also start to be taken on board at this time.

Upon arrival at the ground and after changing into the weather-appropriate warm-up clothing, the individual bowler can start their own specific personal pre-team warm-up routine. This may be anything from using foam rollers to ease out any stiffness, to resistance bands, and weighted ball slams specifically used to warm up muscle groups or areas of the body susceptible to potential injury. This may take a period of approximately 10–15 minutes. This could also be an opportunity to perform any mental warm-up routines needed by the bowler.

The bowler needs to ensure they have adequate water with them during the full warm-up period.

All warm-ups should satisfy the RAMP acronym, (Raise, Activate, Mobilise, Potentiate)

After this has been completed there will usually be a general team' warm-up period. This may start, for example, with a short, ten-minute game of football – 'Pig' – followed by a ten-minute game of six-a-side non-contact football. A dynamic jogging, running, sprinting, multi-directional movement stretching period then takes place for approximately 10–15 minutes, ensuring hips, knees, ankles, T-spine (thoracic spine) and shoulders are worked on (Raise).

A-skips, B-skips, and straight-leg bounds are great for promoting efficient running mechanics during sprinting. When performing A-skips it is important to keep the hips tall, knees up, with the feet striking under the COM (centre of mass). On B-skips, running/gait cycling action, leg snaps down beneath COM. Finally, on straight- leg bounds it is important that the hamstrings and glutes apply force to the ground (Activate and Mobilise). At the end of this section of the warm-up some full sprints and races can be incorporated (Potentiate).

There may be a team fielding warm-up incorporated into the overall team warm-up, but once this has been completed a period for the bowlers to have a bowling warm-up takes place. This will normally take place with the bowlers bowling to the wicketkeeper and coach(es). These warm-ups should be done from both ends if possible, so an individual acclimatises themselves with the end they anticipate they will be bowling from. These warm-ups always take place off the square, parallel to the wicket.

The seam bowlers should ensure they do not go straight into bowling at full speed off their full run-up, but gradually arrive at that point having done some gentle jog-through deliveries off a short run beforehand. Bowling-target cones can be placed appropriately on the pitch between the stumps, at length, back of a length, and yorker length, if preferred by some bowlers. The bowler could also bowl a few balls from around the wicket if they feel it necessary.

Many bowlers like to gently bowl a few full toss deliveries into the coach's mitt as part of their initial pre-match bowling warm-up, with the coach standing approximately half a pitch length away. This can also be done in indoor winter training sessions, or an alternative could be bowling full toss deliveries into the side of a net from approximately three metres away. (The coach can hold the net tightly, thus causing tension in the net, which returns the ball back to the bowler.)

Sometimes, more often seen in junior cricket, the seam bowlers will warm up on one wicket and the spinners on another, both groups of bowlers bowling from the same end. This is fine, but potentially means that some bowlers will not be warming up from the end they are likely to bowl from.

The whole warm-up period should be a maximum of 45 minutes for adult cricket, and less for junior cricket (age appropriate).

Upon returning to the pavilion to prepare for bowling, the bowlers may need another session with a foam roller, change from warm-up kit to playing kit, apply sun screen, take on more fluids and have some final snacks for the bowling ahead. In the professional game this may be the time for a final pre-bowling massage from the physio.

If the playing conditions are hot, it is a good time to start taking electrolyte drinks, which should be taken throughout the day, as the body's natural levels can become severely depleted through sweating during hot weather. Otherwise, if playing in more comfortable temperatures, water is fine on its own.

It is important that the bowler has good time management and preparation skills to eliminate any last-minute distractions before entering the field of play.

If playing a one-day match, there will be drink breaks normally at the mid-point of the innings, or an additional break may be included if it is a hot day. Additionally, there is an extended tea interval between innings. In all these situations the bowler should take the opportunity to replenish both fluids and food, including all supplements such as protein shakes, energy bars, glucose tablets, salt tablets and electrolytes.

'Pre-match I would do a generic warm-up, but then, for me, bowling is the best way to get ready to bowl. I'll start with a few paces and build it up until I'm close to match intensity. During the game I aim to keep moving, especially high-speed movement will keep you ready to bowl.'
DAVID WILLEY

Post-Match Bowling Cool-Down Routines

At the end of the match or end of the day's play, it is important that bowlers have a routine and a process for managing this time period. This is especially important if playing in a multi-day match, or perhaps on a cricket tour, where playing continuously day after day is a distinct possibility. In these two cases there is potential for injury and tiredness, so it is crucial that the bowler has a plan in place to help avoid this. This should be used at any time of the playing season, even after a strenuous training session, irrespective of the weather, whether the temperature is hot or cold.

A shower close to the end of play is essential, although the time of year may dictate whether it is a hot or cold one. A hot one is beneficial if it is cold outside, and a cooler one is great if it has been a very hot day. Both serve a purpose of helping the body to avoid potential injuries from each specific temperature condition. Hot baths and cold/ice baths serve the same purpose, cooling or warming the body appropriately.

The use of ice baths is very common within the professional cricket environment. They are thought to reduce any post-exercise inflammation, reduce muscle soreness and reinvigorate mental alertness. During an ice bath, the very cold temperature narrows the blood vessels, which decreases the blood flow to the muscles, reducing inflammation and swelling. After an ice bath the body temperature rises, causing blood flow to return to the body tissues.

A cool-down routine of stretching is most beneficial if carried out close to the end of play and after a hot shower or bath. A gentle jogging session combined with some simple dynamic movements will also raise the muscle temperature sufficiently to perform some post-match/post-training stretching.

This time period is another opportunity to replace both fluids and food, including all supplements such as protein shakes, energy bars, glucose tablets, salt tablets and electrolytes. Foam rollers may be used to remove any stiffness, and a massage given if that option is available.

The evening meal is a great opportunity to refuel, especially with protein and carbohydrates. This should be done as soon as possible, and not left until later, as eating a big meal too late at night will adversely affect the bowler's sleep. A minimum of eight hours' sleep should be aimed for (advice on sleeping is given in the appropriate 'Sleep' section).

Weekly Workload Record Sheets (Summer Matches and Training)
During the summer matches and training season it is prudent to keep a weekly workload record sheet. This is essential at the professional level, as it enables the bowler, coaches, strength and conditioning (S&C) coaches, and physiotherapists to manage the bowler's workload, reduce or increase training levels, and potentially predict when risk of injury is high.

By continually monitoring the number, length and regularity of bowling spells in both matches and training, combined with gym work records, the professional bowler has the best chance of staying on the pitch bowling. If a potential spike in workload is spotted or anticipated after assessing the weekly workload record sheet, the bowler can then be rested or bowled less frequently to ensure overload is not breached. This can affect team selection, so it is an area that is monitored continuously.

This should also be used in a lesser form by serious amateur bowlers, whether they are adult or junior players. Junior players up to the age of 18 are governed by a set of age-dependent bowling restriction rules. These are listed below, and are applicable at the time of writing:

ECB Fast Bowling Match Directives

Age	Max. overs per spell	Max. overs per day
Up to 13	**4** overs per spell	**8** overs per day
U14, U15	**5** overs per spell	**10** overs per day
U16, U17	**6** overs per spell	**18** overs per day
U19	**7** overs per spell	**21** overs per day

In general terms, a good formula to remember is the bowling figure 7-4-2 (seven for two). This means in a seven-day period a bowler can only bowl four times, on a maximum of two consecutive days.

Rehabilitation Work Routines

If a bowler sustains an injury, either short-, medium- or long-term, there is always the temptation to try to recommence bowling too early, before the injury has totally healed. This is fraught with danger, as there is a distinct possibility that reinjury to the original damaged area can occur, or a new injury to an associated area is a possibility, leaving the bowler with an even longer rehabilitation period.

The bowler should always consult a doctor or physiotherapist should the injury be severe enough, and follow all rehabilitation work and timings as instructed. Investing in a week or two's patience will pay off in the long run, as there is little chance of an injury reoccurring. A slow recovery build-up is essential, and the bowler should ease gently back into bowling, starting at a low intensity and duration, slowly progressing through to normal bowling over the prescribed rehabilitation period. The bowler should never go against the physiotherapist's advice; please remember, they are the experts in this area.

When starting to bowl again it is essential that the bowler warms up correctly prior to working the previously injured component.

During the recovery period it is a good idea to keep a weekly rehabilitation record sheet. This is particularly important at the professional level, as it enables the bowler, coaches, S&C coaches and physiotherapists to manage the bowler's recovery, ensuring that they return to action 100 per cent fit to bowl. This attitude should also apply to amateur and junior players alike.

Strength and Conditioning (S&C) Work

The following text provides a general outline on the subject of S&C. For more expansive knowledge the reader should consult literature beyond the scope of this book.

In the modern professional game, all teams across the world employ backroom staff consisting of S&C coaches, along with physiotherapists, sports psychologists, nutritionists and performance analysts. The S&C coaches are primarily assigned to improve the overall fitness of the bowlers, with a view to keeping them injury-free and on the pitch, bowling as regularly as possible.

While bowling support staff are provided in the professional game, at amateur and junior level this will not be the case in most situations. Therefore, it is important that these bowlers have information available regarding body S&C.

Performance components that the S&C coach looks to continually develop and attain in the bowler are generally high levels of:
- Power
- Strength
- Speed
- Stamina
- Endurance
- Flexibility
- Agility

As we know, there are two types of bowler: seamers and spinners. One imparts a large impact and bracing loads through their body, the other substantially less. One imparts high rotations through their body, the other less so. One bowler may bowl in short spells of sharp bursts of high intensity, while the other may bowl longer spells of low intensity. Therefore, each type of bowler requires slightly different physical body and performance component characteristics. This can be found in their individually different training programmes.

For example, imagine the bowling run-up and action of a fast bowler compared to that of the spinner. The fast bowler needs to be very strong in all the major muscle groups, such as:
- Lower legs

- Upper legs
- Glutes
- Lower and upper back
- Core
- Sides
- Chest
- Shoulders
- Arms
- Wrist

Gym work should be suitably designed so the bowler works on all these components. Additionally, the fast bowler needs to have extra-strong ankles, knees and hips, as approximately six times their body weight can be transferred through the body on the impact of back-foot and front-foot contact. Strength through the foot/calf/ankle complex is crucial, since the lower extremities form a kinetic chain, so anything that affects the ankle is thought to affect the knee and hip similarly.

For example, the lower leg gastrocnemius produces approximately three times the body weight of force during sprinting, so exercises such as standing calf raises are beneficial. The lower leg soleus can produce up to eight times body weight of force during high-speed running, so bent-knee work such as seated calf raises are beneficial. Strengthening the Achilles tendon will store and release energy more quickly and with more force, like comparing a thick elastic band with a thin stretchy one. This will generate more energy between back-foot and front-foot contact. Plyometric work (training using speed and force of different movements to build muscle power), such as pogo jumps, ankling, and drop jumps are very good ways of achieving this. Strengthening these areas of the kinetic chain are crucial in providing stability and support for trunk rotation and trunk flexion.

The spin bowler will not generate anywhere near the impact forces generated by the fast bowler, but they will be looking for improvements in rotational strength, mainly through the shoulders and hips, as well as working on all the core components listed earlier. Shoulder capacity and strength work are vital, as are exercises for internal and external shoulder rotations. Hip and wrist rotation strengthening work is also required, as improving these three areas will produce more dip and drift on the ball.

The majority of any S&C work is carried out in the gym, supplemented by different formats of running and sprinting, undertaken in sports halls or outside. Bowlers can be given individual gym programmes for body strengthening and development, regularly assessed and updated as they progress. Additionally, running and endurance tests such as the bleep test or yoyo test provide other methods of recording progress.

In addition to gym work, bowlers can use more bowling-specific methods to strengthen themselves, such as bowling weighted cricket balls from a kneeling position, bowling while resistance is applied by a bungee rope around the waist, and bowling while traversing over gym or crash mats, for example.

A form of circuit training could be incorporated into the bowler's training regime, such as the example detailed below:
- Straight plank (on elbows)
- Press-ups and squats (change at 90 seconds)
- Exercise bike
- Crash mat running (knee lifts)
- Rope raising
- Side plank on elbow (change sides at 90 seconds)

Six stations are set up as shown. The bowler does three minutes on each station, separated by one minute recovery between stations. Total time is approximately 23 minutes. The circuit can be amended regularly, as there are numerous options for exercises at each station.

Working with a weighted (medicine) ball is another method of working on core stability and strength. Here are some examples:

- Sit-ups catching/throwing (coach throws and catches medicine ball)
- High hurdles, ball held over head, hip raises/step overs
- Line of stumps, ball held above head, hip raises over stumps
- Jog in, two-handed overhead slam
- Catch and overhead slam (coach-fed)

Immediately after any training session the bowler should try to have a hot shower or bath, as this will help keep the body warm, relax the muscles and help prevent injury. The appropriate intake of food should also be made, as highlighted in previous text.

Finally, the bowler should manage their time equally between training and rest, an appropriate mix being one day on, one day off. It is vital that the body has enough time to rest and recover between sessions, whether that be training, playing matches or S&C gym work.

Weekly Workload Record Sheets
(Winter Training and Body Conditioning)

After a suitable length of rest and recovery time, winter training and body conditioning usually takes the form of indoor net training, gym work and potentially playing other sports. The bowler should remember that any net training will be carried out in indoor training facilities, so they should be aware of the potential increase in impact injury occurrence when running and bowling on indoor sports hall floors.

During this time it is again prudent to keep a weekly workload record sheet. This is essential at the professional level, as it enables the bowler, coaches, S&C coaches and physiotherapists to manage the bowler's workload, reduce or increase training levels and potentially predict when risk of injury is high.

It is now common for professional bowlers who stay in the UK for winter training to have a break from bowling from the end of the season until the New Year. In this three-month period, seam bowlers may do a little technical work by bowling with walk-throughs, and may not bowl at full speed until January. They take the opportunity to give their bodies a complete rest for a prolonged period.

By continually monitoring the number, length and regularity of bowling spells in training, combined with gym work and other winter sports records, the bowler has the best chance of staying injury-free throughout the winter period, while allowing their bodies to rest, recover and restrengthen before the following season.

This should also be used in a lesser form by serious amateur bowlers, whether they are adult or junior players. Junior players up to the age of 18 are governed by a set of age-dependent bowling restriction rules, and these should still be adhered to during the winter training period.

Fitness

The following text provides a general outline on the subject of fitness. For more expansive knowledge the reader should consult literature beyond the scope of this book.

The challenges of bowling surround the length of the bowler's spells and the number and frequency of them. Depending on the type of bowler – seam or spin – the fitness characteristics will vary. For example, the seamer will be running in off a longer run than the spinner, exerting far more stresses through the body with jumping, back-foot contact, front-foot contact, delivering the ball and decelerating in the follow-through. Great strength and stamina are required to achieve this.

The spinner will exert less force through their body, as their action is less aggressive due to their shorter approach, lower bound and very short, if negligible follow-through. However, the spin bowler will exert a high level of rotational forces through their body action, through the feet, hips and shoulders, as they try to achieve 180-degree body rotation.

The seam bowler will generally bowl short sharp spells, while the spinner is likely to bowl long spells.

To ensure high performance levels the bowlers need to have great levels of stamina and endurance. Additionally, bowlers obviously also have to field for the duration of the opposition innings, and potentially may also be batters. Remember that a high level of physical fitness will also aid concentration and the ability to maintain a sharp focus throughout the bowling spells and the long periods of fielding. High fitness levels also reduce the risk of injury. Without a strong, fit physique, eventually over a prolonged period of a day's play, your bowling technique will start to disintegrate. Finally, you will also need to have good levels of agility and flexibility. A good level of all-round fitness is essential to be a successful bowler.

Remember that cricket is a game generally played in sunny warm/hot temperatures, so being as fit as possible is essential when being faced with the challenges of playing in these conditions.

Do not focus on one area more than another; they are all equally important. Focus excessively on lifting weights to build strength and power and you will bulk up too much to move quickly, which will be detrimental to your energy levels for a full day's play.

> *'Being a fast bowler is hard work, so physical strength,*
> *flexibility, and cardiovascular endurance is important.'*
> BRENDEN FOURIE

Playing multiple sports is a great way to improve your overall fitness, and is also important for developing your hand-eye-foot coordination and reaction times. Games like squash, badminton and tennis are perfect for this. Basketball is a great sport for sprinting combined with endurance; it is really punishing playing four 15-minute quarters with very little rest during play.

A strong core is very important to complement the upper- and lower-body power positions required, in addition to the general range of movement needed to be a bowler. Great core stability, coupled with a strong lower back are essential elements for a bowler. Weights can be used to add upper-body strength, but rowing and swimming are also great alternatives. They are excellent ways to enhance the leanness of your upper body, also providing a high-intensity cardio workout.

For stamina there is nothing better than getting miles in your legs. Unless you have knee, back or ankle issues, running is the best way to build your stamina and endurance. You could use a slow, long-distance run as the initial part of your workout routine prior to commencing your weights. Make sure you do a long stretch after your run as this will help your flexibility. It is also important to keep stretching in breaks between sets when doing your weights routine.

Cycling and swimming are also great ways of increasing your stamina and endurance, and sprint shuttles are a highly effective way of increasing speed, power and stamina.

To improve balance and agility it is important to do exercises that get you moving in multiple directions. Ladders and cone work are the most common, and any drills that involve speed of movement will help you. There are some great examples you can use in the next chapter.

Depending on the format of the game played, each match will offer different physical challenges to the bowler. While the bowler's physical effort will still be intense when bowling, the duration of bowling spells and time fielding will obviously vary. For instance, in a Hundred match a bowler will only be required to bowl a maximum of 20 balls, while in a T20 it will be a maximum of four overs, and in a 50-over game it will increase up to a maximum of ten overs.

In contrast, if you have progressed to a level of multi-day cricket, the intensity of play will be less, but it will take place over a much longer period, around 100 overs in a day's play. In addition to the overs bowled by each individual bowler, they will be fielding for the full length of the innings or day's play. There will be times of intensity, but generally the pace is less frenetic. There are also drinks breaks every hour, and a lunch and tea interval available for a period of rest and refuelling, both on a nutritional and rehydrating theme.

A good training drill that can be used for a group or individual sessions is called 'Run a hundred'. While the title appears to refer more to batters, it can be used for bowlers and is great for increasing endurance. It is similar to the bleep or yoyo tests. It should be carried out on a full-size pitch, and can be done indoors or outdoors, with or without the players carrying their bat. It can be carried out wearing minimal training clothing, or with players fully padded up. The test procedure is shown below:

14	Time	18	Time	13	Time	16	Time	18	Time	21	Time
3	0	2	0	1	0	1	0	3	0	3	0
2	25	2	15	2	25	4	10	3	20	1	25
1	40	1	30	1	40	2	35	2	45	4	35
2	50	3	40	3	50	1	1:00	3	60	2	1:10
3	1:15	1	1:10	1	1:15	2	1:10	1	1:10	3	1:30
1	1:40	4	1:20	1	1:25	1	1:30	1	1:20	3	1:55
1	1:55	3	1:50	2	1:40	3	1:40	2	1:40	2	2:20
1	2:10	2	2:15	2	2:00	2	2:00	3	2:00	3	2:40

Reading from the left, column one shows that 14 runs will be run in the first period, which is approximately 2min 10sec long. At the start of the stopwatch, the players run a three, which has to be completed in 25 seconds. They may finish in 15 seconds, so get ten seconds rest. At 25 seconds they then run a two, which has to be completed by 40 seconds etc. At the end of the first set, the players have one minute to recover, then the second set of runs commences, running the last two runs at 2min 15sec. A total of 18 runs are completed in this period, meaning the players have run 32 so far. Players always have one minute to recover at the end of each set. They ultimately aim to complete the 100 runs.

Nutrition

The following text provides a general outline on the subject of nutrition. For more expansive knowledge the reader should consult literature beyond the scope of this book.

Cricket is a sport that involves regular bursts of intense energy over a long duration. This principle definitely applies to bowling. Seam bowlers generally bowl in shorter, more intense spells, compared with the spinners, who generally bowl longer, less intense spells. To ensure a bowler has sufficient energy stores available to meet the demands of their role, it is essential that they have a basic knowledge of the importance of eating food that will deliver energy throughout the day's play.

The food sources needed can be divided in to the following categories:
- Carbohydrates
- Proteins
- Fats
- Vitamins
- Fibre

Carbohydrates

Carbohydrates can be divided into two forms: starches (complex carbohydrates) and sugars (simple carbohydrates).

During bursts of intense activity, it is the carbohydrates that provide the essential energy source. They should form the major part of a bowler's diet, approximately 50–60 per cent. They are stored in the muscles as glycogen. Glycogen is depleted rapidly during exercise, so it is essential that stores are kept topped up. Lack of glycogen in the muscles results in fatigue.

Good sources of complex carbohydrates are potatoes, pasta, rice, bread, porridge, cereals, baked beans, nuts, fresh fruit, dried fruit, etc. These carbohydrates are great at releasing glycogen to the muscles over a long period of time.

Good sources of simple carbohydrates are sugars, confectionery, jams, ice cream, etc. These carbohydrates are great at releasing glycogen to the muscles via a quick energy burst.

It is important to remember how long it takes glycogen to be produced for each type of carbohydrate.

The duration of exercise will determine how much carbohydrate is needed. A list indicating duration of exercise, amount of carbohydrate needed and recommended type of carbohydrate is shown below:

- 30–75mins – small amounts – single or multiple transportable carbohydrates
- 1–2hrs – 30g/hr – single or multiple transportable carbohydrates
- 2–3hrs – 60g/hr – single or multiple transportable carbohydrates

Proteins

Protein should only form approximately 10–15 per cent of a bowler's energy intake, and is found in meats, fish, eggs, yoghurts, milk, cheese, dairy products, nuts, beans, protein shakes, gels, etc.

Fats

A bowler should try to regulate their dietary fat content to no more than 35 per cent of their total energy intake. Fat is extremely high in energy but is not very suitable for the time durations encountered in a cricket match. Foods that are high in fat are: biscuits, chocolate, butter, mayonnaise, eggs, cheese, fried foods, etc.

Vitamins

Most vitamins are found in a balanced diet, but many can be found in vitamin supplements and drinks. Vitamin D can also be found in natural sunlight, in addition to natural food sources.

Fibre

While fibre is not an energy source, it is essential for digestive health and regular bowel movements, and it controls blood sugar levels.

Foods high in fibre are: wholegrain breakfast cereals, whole wheat pasta, wholegrain bread, fruit, vegetables, peas, beans, nuts, potatoes with skin.

The best way to sustain the relevant energy levels is to eat small regular meals, ensuring that their glycogen levels are replenished fully. Digestion of food takes approximately two to three hours, so timing this intake is very important. There is a good reason why it is said that breakfast is the most important meal of the day.

After a match or practice session it is important to replenish your energy stores. This not only replaces the energy sources used up, but helps in the body's recovery. Eating a high-carbohydrate meal within two hours of exercise is essential, as this is the most receptive time for storing glycogen.

Hydration

The following text provides a general outline on the subject of hydration. For more expansive knowledge the reader should consult literature beyond the scope of this book.

It is critically important that a bowler guards against the effects of dehydration. Seam bowlers generally bowl in shorter, more intense spells, and spinners generally bowl longer, less intense spells. Both types of bowler are susceptible, but the seam bowler will definitely need rehydrating sooner than the spinner due to the more intense nature of the bowling.

We have previously discussed the frequencies of intensities inherent in the various match formats, so it is essential that a player remains fully hydrated, as water plays a critical role in regulating body temperature.

Water and minerals are lost through sweating, so it is essential these are replaced. Crucially, for every kilogram loss in body weight through sweating, this equates to a litre loss in body fluid. Performance is impaired if dehydration is 2 per cent of body weight, and if it reaches 5 per cent this means that the body's capacity for work reduces by 30 per cent. Players can easily lose between two and five litres of fluid during a game. Dehydration will produce deterioration in coordination and decision-making, and an increase in fatigue.

It is recommended that bowlers only commence warm-ups and match play when sufficiently hydrated. This can usually be achieved by drinking between 400ml and 600ml of water approximately two hours prior to exercise starting. Sufficient water should be drunk during training or match bowling to prevent dehydration from exceeding 2 per cent of body weight.

To ensure hydration, the bowler should drink 5ml to 10ml per kilogram of body weight, two to four hours before a match. So, for a 75kg bowler, this would equate to approximately 750ml of water. A typical consumption rate during training or in a match is approximately 150ml to 300ml every 15 minutes. This may vary depending on the temperature and subsequent rate of sweating.

For activity of less than 90 minutes, water alone is sufficient to hydrate the body. For exercise in excess of 90 minutes, or when it is hot, it is recommended that carbohydrate electrolyte drinks are taken to sustain performance.

Dehydration can cause decreased sweat rates, decreased heat dissipation, increased core temperatures, increased blood pressure and the increased rate of depleting glycogen stores. To avoid this it is essential that players drink on a regular basis throughout training and matchdays. A good rule of thumb is to endeavour to drink every 20–40 minutes.

Coaches and players should ensure plenty of fluids are available before, during and after activity. If you become thirsty you are already dehydrated, so the key is to avoid this by taking regular fluid intakes. A great way of checking for dehydration is to check the colour of your urine. If it is yellow, you are already dehydrated. If it is clear, looking like water, you are rehydrated. Bowlers should avoid alcohol and caffeinated drinks at least 24 hours before a match, as these fluids both act as diuretics, thus promoting dehydration. Excessive alcohol consumption after a match is detrimental to the body's recovery system and can impair the following day's performance.

Symptoms of heat stress can be identified as follows: loss of coordination, feeling cold, dizziness, confusion and pale complexion. If a player ever displays these symptoms they should be removed from the field of play immediately, and appropriate medical attention sort.

Bowling in Hot Temperatures

Because cricket is a summer sport, a bowler will regularly be playing and training in hot temperatures and on sunny days. We have previously mentioned the importance of avoiding dehydration, so this has even greater importance on these occasions. In addition to this, bowlers can take certain measures to avoid the negative effects of these intense conditions.

The wearing of sun hats, caps, sunglasses, sun cream, lip balms and wrist sweatbands are all critical in ensuring bowlers play safely in hot and sunny conditions. It is essential that dehydration is avoided, so in addition to the allocated drinks breaks, full drinks bottles should be left around the full circumference of the boundary in the following six fielding positions (shaded if possible) to hydrate bowlers intermittently: third man and fine leg at both bowling ends, deep mid-wicket and deep extra-cover.

Bowlers may also wish to change into fresh clothing during sessions in multi-day cricket, with many bowlers understanding the benefits of changing into a fresh pair of woollen socks regularly. It is now very common in modern cricket for a bowler to leave the field after a long bowling spell, particularly beneficial in hot sunny conditions, as the cool shade provides a much-needed respite. This applies to both adult and junior cricket where a 12th man is available.

While wearing a long-sleeve shirt would be beneficial in terms of sun protection, it is very rare to see a seam bowler bowling in one, as the short-sleeve shirt offers more mobility to the bowler.

The application of a high-protection sunscreen or barrier screen is essential. Taking a cold shower between sessions of play is a great way to cool down after a long period in the sun. When waiting to bat, batters should endeavour to stay in the shade and keep cool as much as possible.

Bowling in Cold Temperatures

There will be days, particularly if playing in the UK, where both training and playing will be undertaken in cold conditions, particularly at the start of the season. Attempting to keep warm, particularly when waiting to bowl for the first time or in between bowling spells, presents different challenges to the bowler.

The two opening bowlers may still be warm after the initial warm-up, so their first overs may not be too much of an issue, as opposed to the first change and remaining bowlers who may have a prolonged period to wait to bowl. The opening bowlers will need to keep that initial warm-up heat, so they must ensure they wear appropriate layers of clothing to achieve this.

Body skins, both top and bottom halves of the body, are essential items of clothing worn under the cricket kit. These retain heat well, although the bowler must ensure they do not restrict body movements in any way. Long-sleeve and sleeveless cricket sweaters are another essential item of clothing, the long-sleeve ones only used for keeping warm in, as these are very restrictive for bowling. While it is uncommon to see a bowler bowling in a long-sleeve sweater, it is common to see sleeveless sweaters in use, as they do not restrict the bowler from bowling.

Long-sleeve shirts are generally worn by non-bowlers. Bowlers are rarely seen in these shirts as they may restrict the bowling action, so most seam bowlers generally bowl in short-sleeve shirts. However, it is more common to see spinners bowling in long-sleeve shirts.

On cold days it is a well-known fact that body heat is lost through the extremities of the body – head, fingers and toes. With this in mind, it is worth wearing a cap or sun hat, and in pre-season friendly matches, woolly hats are often seen.

Because gloves are not allowed in the outfield except for wicketkeepers, pocket-held hand warmers are a very popular way of keeping the hands warm on a cold day. They are widely available and come as both disposable air-activated warmers and rechargeable electronic versions. Bowlers should only use the soft, flexible air-activated disposable types, as these do not inhibit or cause injury when diving in the field. They are particularly desired by spin bowlers, who need warm fingers to help impart spin on the ball, as they may have been waiting a long time to come on to bowl in the cold conditions.

It is essential that the bowler attempts to stay warm by incorporating some form of movement and stretching while waiting to bowl. Obviously, the bowler will almost certainly be warming their hands with hand warmers, or by blowing on them while vigorously rubbing them together. They may also warm their body by doing some form of dynamic body movements such as jumping up and down on the spot, shoulder rotations, throwing their arms across their body, side-steps, jogging on the spot, running or even replicating their bowling action. Any associated stretching must only be carried out after the body has warmed up.

In the first-class game it is possible to come off the field to warm up again indoors, the bowler being replaced by the 12th fielder. However, in amateur and junior cricket this is not always possible, so it is essential the bowler is prepared with a plan for keeping warm in cold conditions. If it is possible to take on a hot drink at some stage, this is advisable, but on most occasions, apart from when training, this is difficult to achieve.

Sleep

The following text provides a general outline on the subject of sleep. For more expansive knowledge the reader should consult literature beyond the scope of this book.

In addition to nutrition and hydration, another important element of a bowler's preparation is having enough sleep. Sleep is the body's natural way of recovering from the day's exertions. It is essential for our health and wellbeing, particularly in the sporting environment, and it is recommended that a minimum of eight hours of sleep is required. If this can be achieved, a bowler enhances their chances of performing well.

There are numerous ways this can be achieved. Have a warm bath or shower directly before getting into bed, refrain from using mobile phones at least 30 minutes before getting into bed, refrain from watching TV in bed, keep your bedroom cool and well ventilated, sleep in fresh bed linen as often as is practically possible, take a milk or vitamin-fortified drink before going to sleep, avoid chocolate or cheese directly before bed, and avoid a big meal late at night.

The use of scented candles in a bedroom prior to turning in can promote a more peaceful sleep, as can relaxing music or listening to natural sound mood recordings, such as birds singing or waves washing on a beach. Research also suggests that performing some stretching or undertaking yoga before bed can aid restful sleep, as can reading a book prior to turning the light off.

More recently, tinted night-time blue light blocking glasses are gaining popularity as an aid in promoting better sleep. Wearing an eye mask can also be beneficial, as they darken the room and stop early morning light waking you up.

Taking herbal sleeping tablets can also help in attaining a good night's sleep, but the potential side-effects should be ascertained prior to taking.

It is not just the duration of sleep that is important; there are different cycles of sleep that ensure you wake fully refreshed and ready for the day ahead.

Bowling Equipment

Buying the right equipment and looking after it is important, and below is a list of the essentials that you will need:

- Bespoke studded fast-bowling boots (ankle protection)
- Studded spin-bowling boots (traditional batting/fielding boots)
- Socks
- Cap/sun hat
- Sunglasses
- Hand warmer
- Wrist sweatbands
- Medical bag

What you can afford will obviously influence your decision on the quality of these items unless you are fortunate enough to be a sponsored player.

Spiked Bowling Boots (Bespoke Fast Bowlers Boots and Spin Bowlers Boots)

It is essential that the bowler has comfortable footwear when bowling. Fast and seam bowlers generally wear bespoke studded bowling boots, which have added ankle protection inherent in their design. This is an essential feature that adds greater protection against twisting an ankle, an injury that is much more likely considering the additional speed, higher forces and balance and stability issues associated with this intense form of bowling.

Spin bowlers generally wear the more traditional spiked batting/fielding boot, which does not have the additional ankle protection. Spiked boots are always recommended, but on hard, dry surfaces some spin bowlers do prefer to wear pimple-soled cricket boots. Tactically, this does not happen much in 50-over or multi-day cricket, as bowlers wearing this type of footwear do not leave any footmarks in their follow-throughs for their bowling partners to aim at.

If the footwear is the wrong size, or inappropriately fitted, this will create additional physical problems, while also producing mental distractions. Additionally, if laces are not done up securely, this could also contribute to the physical and mental challenges highlighted, as well as potentially contributing to the bowler bowling in a detrimental manner.

Many fast bowlers like to cut a hole in one of their bowling boots, around the big toe area. This is to stop the big toe persistently rubbing against the inside of the boot, which can lead to severe blisters and swelling under the big toenail, which can be very painful and debilitating. It is always on the bowler's front foot – left foot for a right-arm bowler, and right foot for a left-arm bowler. This situation usually only happens once a bowler reaches their late teens and beyond due to the fact that they are now physically adults, capable of producing immense forces through their heavier and stronger bodies into the ground.

Generally, this outcome is more prevalent with 'toe-strike' bowlers than 'heel-strike' bowlers. A 'toe-strike' bowler is one whose front-foot toes hit the ground first on front-foot contact, after the transition from back-foot contact to front-foot contact has taken place. This type of foot placement places severe stress on the booted big toe, hence why the bowler removes the restraining piece of leather. A 'heel-strike' bowler's front-foot heel hits the ground slightly before the full profile of the foot, including toes, hits the ground on front-foot contact. Once again this happens after the transition from back-foot contact to front-foot contact has taken place. This second type of landing produces more stress on the heel, but less stress on the toes, as the impact forces are spread out more evenly over the full profile of the landing foot. We would never suggest young players start cutting holes in their brand-new bowling boots!

Many seam bowlers insert pairs of impact protection insoles into their bowling boots, which help hugely with dissipating the severe forces generated by the bowling action. These can be purchased from all pharmacies, and usually come in one large size. The individual can then cut the insole down to their specific boot size and shape, using the marked template printed on the insole. Cutting should be carried out in a staged regression, ensuring that the insole fits tightly into the boot. If it is reduced too much, the insole and foot will slide in the boot, eventually causing discomfort to the bowler.

It is advised that you carry some spare spikes in your kit bag to replace any that wear down or come out. A full set of spikes on your footwear is essential, particularly if you are a fast or seam bowler. These ensure you do not slip at any point in the bowling action, thus holding solid bases, from run-up through the bound, during back-foot and front-foot contact, ball release and follow-through.

Additionally, a full set of studs guarantees that your weight is evenly distributed into the ground, reducing the chance of sore feet caused when a stud or two are missing. Regular tightening of the studs with the spanner supplied ensures they will not fall out while you are bowling.

Some boot manufacturers supply a compromise alternative known as a 'half-spiked' or '50/50' boot. This option has spikes around the toes/balls of the feet, with a pimpled surface to the rear half of the feet around the heel area.

It is not unknown for a player to have studs inserted into a normal pair of trainers, preferring to have the comfort of the generally lighter feel these trainers give. The studs need to be fixed in professionally, as there is the potential for this type of modification to have adverse effects on the soles of the bowler's feet. Additionally, this type of trainer offers minimal protection to an accurate yorker homing in on the feet if used for batting! Purpose-built leather cricket boots, whether studded or pimpled and rubber-soled, offer more protection to the feet due to their more robust and stronger construction.

It is also a good idea to clean your boots regularly with soap and water. Boots should not be left near radiators to dry, as the intense heat can crack the leather, thus damaging their integrity.

Socks

A good pair of lamb's wool socks will provide great comfort and cushioning when bowling and they also have better breathing/sweating qualities than man-made synthetic socks. If possible, it is advantageous to have multiple pairs of socks, so the bowler can change into a fresh pair when needed. Socks should not be dried on radiators, as the intense heat can damage their integrity.

Cap and Sun-hat

Both caps and sun hats should be of an appropriate size, suitable to the age/size of the player. They should be correctly adjusted so that they fit snugly on the head, ensuring they are neither too tight, which can cause discomforting headaches, nor too loose that they could fall off and blow over your eyes when you are fielding the ball or taking a catch!

It is essential that all the bowler's clothing is in good order and fits correctly, as any discomfort or distraction can adversely affect concentration and subsequent performance.

Sunglasses

Sunglasses should provide 100 per cent protection from both UVB and UVA rays, therefore the lenses must give 400UV protection. The glasses should fit snugly to the head, and the lenses be kept diligently clean and scratch free. They should be comfortable, light, strong and robust, as there is a high probability they will be dislodged when diving if they are stored on top of headwear while not in use.

Sunglasses lenses come in a variety of colours, and each one provides slightly different vision enhancements and characteristics. The bowler is encouraged to research this further, as this is beyond the scope of this book.

Hand Warmer

Pocket-held hand warmers are a very popular way of keeping the hands warm on a cold day. They are widely available and come as both disposable air-activated warmers and rechargeable electronic versions. Bowlers should only use the soft, flexible air-activated disposable types, as these do not inhibit or cause injury when diving in the field. They are particularly desired by spin bowlers, who need warm fingers to help impart spin on the ball, as they may have been waiting a long time to come on to bowl in the cold conditions.

Wrist Sweatbands

These can be widely purchased, and many bowlers find these essential in removing sweat from their foreheads and arms during their bowling spells. Wash and dry between uses.

Medical Bag

While most cricket teams will have a team medical bag, it is beneficial for the bowler to have a small one of their own containing essential items for general bowler maintenance. The items listed below are for guidance purposes, and the individual may wish to add to these:

- Plasters
- Plaster rolls
- Scissors (small)
- Sun cream
- Sun-protection lip balm

- Lubrication gel
- Ice packs
- Portable electronic massager

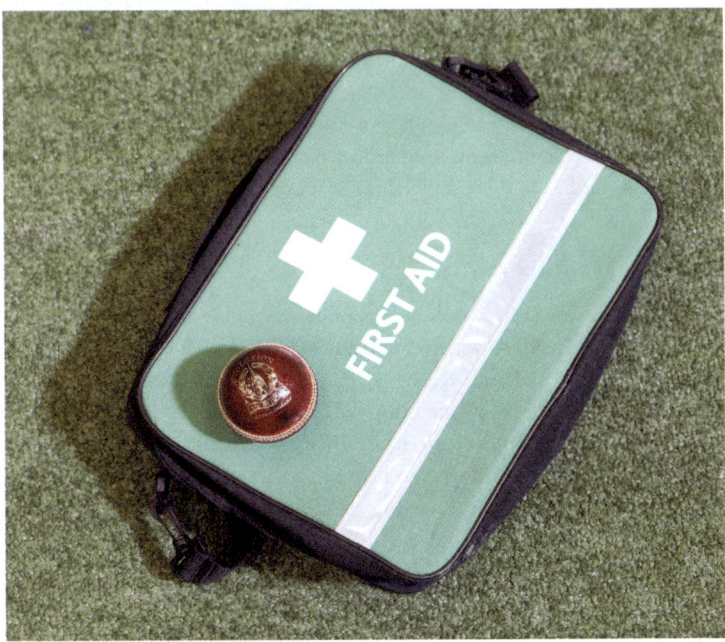

The items are self-explanatory, though the bowler should ensure a healthy supply of plasters and plaster rolls are ever present, as these can be used frequently, particularly when breaking in new bowling boots.

NINE
BOWLING DRILLS

'The bowling drill has to be specific to the bowler on what they want to improve or get stronger in, and then that drill needs to be built into their bowling to help improve the outcome or consistency.'
CHRIS LIDDLE
Northants & England Women's Seam Bowling Coach

Coaching Styles

There are three main coaching styles: fixed, variable and games-based learning. This chapter provides a comprehensive list of drills and practices broken down into the following categories:
- Technical development
- Tactical development
- Bowling games
- Hand-eye-foot coordination
- Training on your own
- Pre-match
- Introduction to video analysis
- Safety when practising
- Useful coaching quotes to remember

Where appropriate, we list the equipment needed and describe how the drill works, with text and photos, additionally offering ideas for progression. We also hope that you will be inspired to adapt the drills specifically for your target audience, and even start producing your own.

Cricket training in the UK is unusual, as there is a distinct difference between the surface a bowler will train on during the indoor winter training programme and the playing surface a bowler will play on during the outdoor summer playing season.

During the indoor winter period, October–March, the indoor surface is hard, fast and bouncy, due to the construction of indoor sports hall floors. Because of this, there can be a tendency for bowlers to bowl too short, as they now have the possibility to dig the ball in to the batters more than they would outside.

The ball comes on to the bat well, so there is the potential for batters to reduce their amount of footwork, play through the line of the ball when the ball is pitched further up, and generally be quite free-scoring. To counter this, the bowlers may then bowl a bit shorter to stop being driven regularly. While tactically this is a good decision, over the winter period the bowler may develop muscle memory for bowling on the indoor surface, which is totally different to the outdoor wickets they will encounter at the start of the playing season in April in the UK, where the surface of the natural grass is softer, slower and has less bounce and carry.

Another trap bowlers can fall into over the indoor winter period is the bowling of front-foot no-balls. This is a very common occurrence, and can once again lead to issues of no-balling at the start of the outdoor season. Once again, muscle memory has developed for bowling over a shorter pitch distance, therefore front-foot no-balls and bowling too short are exacerbated.

Seam bowlers will argue that the reason they bowl no-balls is because they are unable to fit in their full run-up indoors. This is obviously true, but they need to accept responsibility that they are actually bowling no-balls all the time. The coach can make a point by calling 'no-ball' every time they bowl one. It is best for the bowler to have an accurate shorter indoor run-up, thus ensuring they do not bowl no-balls for the reasons previously explained.

Bowlers Coaching Development Methods

The ECB (England & Wales Cricket Board) differentiates a player's coaching development methods into three distinct areas: fixed, variable and games-based learning. Each type of coaching method has its own separate characteristics and is appropriate to the age, ability and experience of the individual player. There are certain elements that are cross-referenced in all three methods, but ultimately there is a clear progression through the three-practice type continuum. The continuum is:

FIXED – VARIABLE – GAMES BASED LEARNING

Descriptions and characteristics of the practice methods are listed below.

Fixed Practice

This is a bowling practice activity that requires the bowler to repeatedly perform a certain task, such as hitting a predetermined line and length, target bowling at cones or hitting a 'top of off' foam bullseye target. It could also involve repeatedly producing swing, seam or spin on the ball for a series of deliveries. Fixed practices are generally carried out alone or with the coach, as no batters are needed.

Working on technical points such as stationary set-ups, walk-throughs, run-ups, wrist flicks and alignment corridors are further examples. Bowlers can immediately improve their technique and confidence. This form of practice can otherwise be described as 'grooving' or 'gaining muscle memory'.

Variable Practice

This is a bowling practice activity that requires the bowler to bowl different balls from one ball to the next. It could be a form of target bowling practice, where the bowler has multiple coloured cone lengths to aim at, with the coach calling out a colour just before the bowler bowls the ball. The bowler could also bowl at a combination of right- and left-handed batters, who rotate the strike after each ball. The bowler could also be encouraged to bowl over and around the wicket after each delivery, and even have sessions where they bowl with new or old cricket balls, so they have the opportunity to practise with a hard and soft ball.

Variable practice attempts to replicate the random decision-making and execution of bowling skills required from the bowler. It is a good form of practice for developing game-specific technical skills, but can be challenging initially, leading to a potential temporary drop in accuracy for a while.

A good example of variable practice is a bowler bowling at batters in the nets, with or without any scenario or conditioned games being incorporated. Every batter bats differently to the ball delivered to them, so the bowler has to adapt their bowling for each batter. It is also a great opportunity to practise variations such as slower balls, yorkers and cutters.

Games-Based Learning

This final form of practice is usually carried out setting up conditioned scenario games, aimed at replicating various random situations that regularly occur when bowling in a real match. For example, this could be bowling to real batters, attempting to stop them chasing down 25 runs to win off four overs with five wickets remaining, or opening the bowling in a T20, bowling in the powerplay. Another could be trying to take the final wicket to win a multi-day match, with only four overs remaining. The options are endless. It could be carried out with right-handed or left-handed batters, or a combination of both.

The bowlers should set their own fields and outline their bowling plans to the coach. These plans and subsequent outcomes can then be discussed in the post-practice scenario debrief, with a particular note made of how the bowler performed against both right- and left-handed batters.

These scenarios could be set up on a full outdoor ground with a full team of fielders, indoors in a sports hall, or even in nets with cone fielders and the coach umpiring and adjudicating the course of play. This form of practice is as close as you can achieve to match play when training.

Games-based learning sessions give the coach a great opportunity to assess the individual bowler's skills development. When challenging scenarios are set, the bowler's decision-making skills and self-awareness under pressure are revealed, thus enabling further development plans to be made accordingly. It is a great way to stretch good players and improve the player's performance under pressure.

Any form of practice should have a purpose at its heart, so whether a bowler is practising in a fixed, variable or games-based learning session, the coach should consider the bowler (person) themselves, their specific bowling needs and the form of practice most suitable to achieve those needs.

Bowlers Coaching Development Methods
(sizes appropriate to age and ability of bowler where applicable)

- New cricket balls (white/pink)
- Old cricket balls (white/pink)
- Red/white coaching cricket balls
- Incrediballs (plastic)
- Swingballs
- Taped tennis balls
- Aggot balls
- Flexi-stumps (outdoor)
- Flexi-stumps (indoor)

- Mini yorker flexi-stumps
- Wobble stumps
- Foam top of off bullseye targets
- Fielding net
- Intervention poles
- Cones
- Wobble cushion
- Crash/gym mats (horizontal and vertical)
- Agility ladders
- Agility hoops
- Hurdles
- Skipping rope
- Bungee restraint band
- Theraband
- Weighted cricket ball
- Weighted medicine ball
- Target mats
- Katchet board (target)
- Stick-on fluorescent stickers
- Additional gateway stumps (spinners)

General Technical/Tactical Net Drills

The following suggestions for progression should be incorporated into all the bowling drills described in this book where appropriate.

Record the results on data performance sheets. The bowler should include practice from over and around the wicket, bowling to right- and left-handed batters, switching to alternate ball combinations and bowling different variations. They should use different ball types where possible, and bowl with red and white balls regularly. Introduce point-scoring games whenever possible. Introduce balls that swing excessively. Video record the session and give each delivery a reference number, so that the coach and bowler can correlate a poor or good delivery with a certain 'feel' or visual technical breakdown in the bowling action.

> *'Ensure you practise and can bowl all types of deliveries with confidence and under pressure, and according to different match situations. Any drills that improve control and accuracy of line and length are essential. Place targets*

on different parts of the wicket, and see how many times you can hit them or get close to them. Keeping the head and body moving towards the target area, wicketkeeper, stumps or batter will greatly assist in improving accuracy.'
BRENDEN FOURIE

Bowling in Nets Training Sessions

Equipment

Cricket ball, stumps, cones.

Description

Virtually all bowling practice is undertaken in cricket nets, the bowler bowling at batters, or honing their skills alone, working on line and length, variations, over and around the wicket, right-handed/left-handed batters, wide of the crease, etc. Whenever possible, a match scenario or jeopardy should be applied to the session, so that both bowlers and batters are being tested in the technical, tactical and mental elements of the game. Additionally, by thoughtful planning, an increased physical session can be incorporated. These give the coach the opportunity to observe the players' responses to orchestrated match scenarios.

Nets where players just go in and 'have a bowl' or 'have a bat' should be kept to a minimum. A fun, positive learning environment should be present at all times.

Progression

Imaginary fielders can be incorporated into the session by the use of cones. Fielders in the ring can be shown using the same colour cones, and fielders outside the ring can be indicated by using a different colour cone.

Bowlers should then be encouraged to bowl to a predetermined scenario bowling plan and field placement layout, and on assessment of their level of success adapt their plans and field placing accordingly. Bowlers should be encouraged to assess the batters' strengths and weaknesses, and adapt field placing and bowling strategies, including bowling over or around the wicket accordingly. Having a pair of batters in a net, particularly a right- and left-handed pair, is great practice. Batters could be encouraged to rotate the strike to attempt to disrupt the bowler's rhythm.

The number of scenarios is endless, but ones such as 'opening the bowling in a T20 powerplay', 'bowling in the middle overs of a 50-over game', 'bowling at the death' are all firm favourites. Coaches are encouraged to be inventive with their scenarios. 'Needing to take the last wicket with only 12 balls remaining, fielders around the bat' is a particular favourite with bowlers!

Bowling with brand-new balls and very old ones is an extremely useful exercise for bowlers, as is bowling with the different-coloured balls used in the various formats of the game. A bowler could occasionally use a ball they have artificially shined themselves, one that swings excessively, as this is great practice for bowling with a ball that could swing around corners in a game. It is good practice for the batters too!

To increase the physical demands on the bowler, they could be asked to run back to the start of their run-up after every delivery or, if they have other bowlers in the net, they could bowl six balls in a row, running back between each ball.

The bowlers could be asked to record the line, length and subsequent outcome of their spell, or even introduce a scoring game where the bowler scores points for taking wickets, bowling for the 'three in play' line and length, bowling dot balls, play and misses, hitting the batter's pads, successful variations, etc. Points are removed if they bowl no-balls, wides, down the leg side or get hit for two consecutive boundaries. You could even remove points if they do not bowl any variations!

Coaches should endeavour to create a fun, competitive, positive learning environment at all times.

Bowling in Outdoor Middle Practice Sessions

Equipment

Cricket Ball, Stumps.

Description

Exactly the same as indoor/outdoor nets, but the session takes place outdoors on the square, on a wicket, out in the 'middle'.

The bowler will be bowling to two batters, with a full field of live fielders. The bowlers will have the opportunity to bowl from both ends, off their full run-ups and will encounter different weather and wicket conditions, variations in boundary distances, lengths of grass and slopes. Bowlers should also be encouraged to assess their own fielders' ability, ensuring they have the most suitable fielder in the most suitable fielding position. It also gives the bowler the opportunity to practise adapting the field quickly.

This is the most realistic of practice environments as it now involves every cricket discipline being utilised. It is particularly useful if used early in the season, as bowlers are reminded of the lengths to bowl on real outdoor grass wickets.

All the scenarios, bowling plans, performance data recording, scoring games listed in the indoor/outdoor net sessions can be incorporated into this form of practice. Coaches should again endeavour to create a fun, competitive, positive learning environment at all times.

Progression

In addition to the points-scoring games already suggested, bowlers could score additional points for bowling a dot ball on the first ball of the over, not being hit for two consecutive boundaries or finishing the over with a dot ball. Negative points can be applied to bowlers if they do not bowl a variation in the over. To create pressure on the batters, an 'out when you're out' rule is applied, or even apply a rule that both batters are out if one of the pair is dismissed!

Combat Nets

Equipment

Cricket Ball, Stumps. Cones.

Description

Identical to the Bowling in Nets Training Sessions, but only 2v2, or 3v3 batters and bowlers. The first pair bat for a period of time under a set of rules while the other pair bowl at them. The pairs swap over and repeat. The pair with the highest score wins.

Progression

In addition to the points-scoring games already suggested, bowlers could score additional points for bowling a dot ball on the first ball of the over, not being hit for two consecutive boundaries or finishing the over with a dot ball. Negative points applied to bowlers if they do not bowl a variation in the over. To create pressure on the batters, an 'out when you're out' rule is applied, or even apply a rule that both batters are out if one of the pair is dismissed! Points-scoring game for a wicket, play and miss, hit on the pads, leave, or wicket from a variation ball.

Target Bowling (Line and Length)

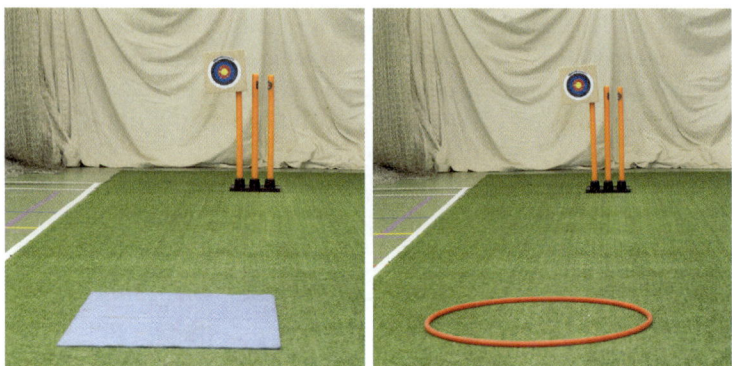

Equipment

Cricket ball, stumps, cones, target mats, hoops, sponge 'top of off' bulls eye target.

Description

Target bowling is the mainstay of practice for any bowler, irrespective of age or ability.

A cone or group of cones laid on the ground are the usual items used for marking the approximate lines and lengths that bowlers are consistently trying to hit. For seam bowlers the lengths are good length, back of a length, bouncer and yorker. For spinners the lengths are good length and yorker. Target mats can also be used on the ground, as can a foam 'top of off' bullseye target, placed on top of off stump. This item is very useful for a bowler looking to find the top of stumps length.

Bowlers try to hit their required target as often as possible using their normal run-up. Seam bowlers may not be able to use their full run-up when training indoors in the winter period.

Progression

Introduce a point-scoring game. Spinners could also have cones wide of off stump on both good and yorker lengths. This would replicate an area they might try to target for a stumping dismissal, if a batter was coming down the pitch to hit the ball. Video record the session and give each delivery a reference number, so that the coach and bowler can correlate a poor or good delivery with a certain 'feel' or visual technical breakdown in the bowling action.

Target Bowling Length Reaction

Equipment

Cricket ball, stumps, cones, target mats, hoops, sponge 'top of off' bullseye target.

Description

Equipment and procedures set up as listed in the Target Bowling (Line and Length) drill description. Three different-coloured cones are laid on the ground at good length, bouncer and yorker lengths. The bowler is told which cone to aim at just before they start their run-up. They then proceed and bowl at the target.

Progression

The bowler commences their run-up, and halfway down the coach calls out the length to hit or cone colour. The bowler commences their run-up, and three-quarters of the way down the coach calls out the length to hit or cone colour. Repeat again, but this time the length or colour is called as the bowler prepares to initiate the bound. (There is less reaction time to prepare for release of ball to match the coach's call.) Introduce a back-of-a-length target for the seamers. Spinners could also have cones wide of off stump on both good and yorker lengths. This would replicate an area they might try to target for a stumping dismissal if a batter was coming down the pitch to hit the ball. Introduce a points-scoring game.

Target Bowling Score Recording (Length and Line Sheets)

Bowlers Pitch Maps

Name: ....
Bowler Type: ....

Right Handed Bat	Left Handed Bat
Yorker / Half Volley / Good Length / Short Off-side width — Good line — Legside	Yorker / Half Volley / Good Length / Short Legside — Good line — Off-side width

Description

The coach indicates where the ball landed with an X, and indicates the ball number next to it, and subsequently reviews with the bowler. Record results for a period of two to five overs. Coach to inspect data to see if the bowler's stats indicate they bowl more accurately when warmed up, and less accurately when tired.

Progression

The bowler also records the results on their own sheet. The two sheets are compared to see if the bowler visually misjudges the length they are actually recording.

Can be used with multiple bowlers to add a competition element to score points for hitting targets in a certain number of balls/overs. Winner is the one with the most points.

Target Bowling (Height)   7

Equipment
Cricket ball, stumps, foam 'top of off' bullseye target.

Description
A foam 'top of off' bullseye target, placed on top of off stump is a very useful piece of equipment for a bowler looking to find the 'top of stumps' length. The bowler simply bowls the ball on a line and length, which after bouncing hits the target.

Progression
Reposition the target on top of a left-handed batter's off stump.

Target Bowling Score Recording (Height Sheets)   8

Target Bowling Score Recording (Height Sheets) 8

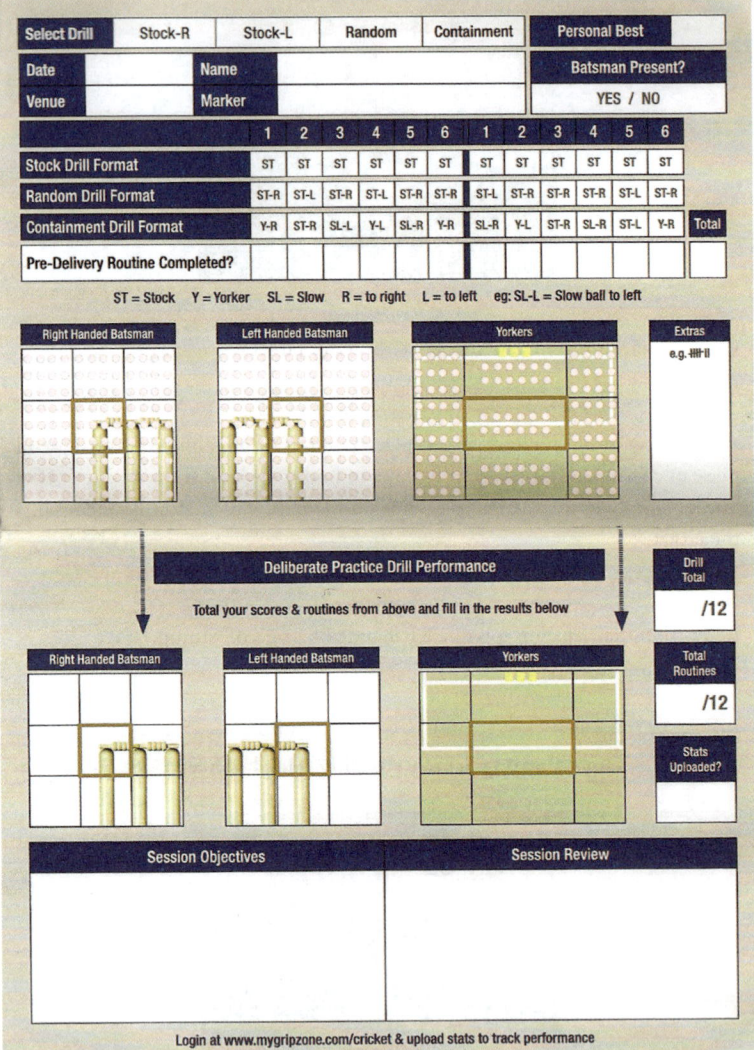

Description

The coach indicates the height and line where the ball missed or hit the stumps with an X, indicates the ball number next to it, and subsequently reviews with the bowler. Record results for a period of two to five overs. Coach to inspect data to see if the bowler's stats indicate they bowl more accurately when warmed up, and less accurately when tired. The X should ideally be around the top of stump height, or a height requested by the coach. The results recorded look similar to the 'beehive' graphics used on cricket television coverage.

Progression

The bowler also records the results on their own sheet. The two sheets are compared to see if the bowler visually misjudges the length they are actually recording.

Can be used with multiple bowlers to add a competition element to score points for hitting targets in a certain number of balls/overs. Winner is the one with the most points.

Katchet Board Target Bowling (Outside with Wicketkeeper)

Equipment

Cricket ball, stumps, (Flexi-stumps), Katchet deflection board.

Description

Full-length pitch set-up. Bowler runs in off full run, bowls the ball, attempting to hit the Katchet deflection board positioned on a good length, therefore giving the wicketkeeper a straight or diving catch. Board to be positioned for both right- and left-handed batters. Wicketkeeper also gets invaluable catching/reaction practice.

This drill could also be used for spin bowlers with an experienced keeper standing up.

Spin Bowling Stump Gate

Equipment

Cricket ball, sets of plastic stumps in bases, stumps, foam 'top of off' bullseye target.

Description

Pitch set up as normal. Two sets of plastic stumps/bases are positioned on a good length, coinciding with the anticipated ball landing point for an off spin or leg spin bowler, etc.

The plastic stumps are to run at 90 degrees to the playing stumps, set approximately 450mm apart, facing each other to form an entrance gate. The bowler should only see one stump out of each set.

The bowler bowls, attempting to land the ball through the gate, spinning the ball back appropriately to hit the off stump of the playing set of stumps. A foam 'top of off' bullseye target could be placed on off stump. The bowling surface will dictate how much the ball will turn. This drill can also be used for seam bowlers swinging the ball.

Progression

Pair of plastic stumps set wider from off stump to encourage the bowler to extract more spin. Gap between stumps reduced.

New Ball, Old Ball, Swing Ball Practice (incl. Multicoloured Balls)

Equipment

Stumps, foam 'top of off' bullseye target, new/old/swinging/multi coloured balls.

Description

Bowlers bowl using either brand-new, old or balls shined up to swing excessively, as these types of ball have different movement characteristics. This drill is also used for the different-coloured balls used in multi-format cricket – red, white and pink.

A foam 'top of off' bullseye target is placed on off stump.

Classroom Tactical Session

Equipment

Cricket balls if appropriate.

Description

This is an invaluable part of cricket coaching, no matter what the age or ability of the players, and should never be underestimated. Sessions can take the form of PowerPoint presentations, whiteboard brainstorming, videos, Q&As, field placing sessions, tactical scenarios, pitch and ground assessments, quizzes and games, etc. The length of the session is to be age appropriate.

Coaches should again endeavour to create a fun, competitive, positive learning environment at all times.

Google Map of Ground

Description

This can be done as a group classroom session or by the individual bowler. It is a great method of obtaining advance information about a cricket ground, especially if you have never played there before, particularly regarding areas such as wicket orientation, boundary shape and dimensions. A major factor to consider in any cricket match is the wind direction. As the prevailing wind in the UK generally comes from a south-westerly direction, by looking at a plan view of the ground, knowing that north and south are at the top and bottom of the screen, a bowler can assess which may be the best end for them to bowl from, bearing in mind whether they are a seam or spin bowler. It is always worth rechecking the weather forecast on matchdays as a final check, because the wind may be coming from a different direction. It may of course change during the match!

Width and Depth of Crease Variation Drills

Equipment

Cricket ball, stumps

Description

This is a general variation target bowling drill, with the bowler experimenting with their bowling release position in relation to the crease line. The bowler practises delivering the ball from much closer to the stumps, or alternatively much wider on the crease. Additionally, they can practise releasing the ball from level with the stumps or further back.

These changes of angles and distance can be just enough to cause a batter to lose their timing, contributing to the bowler taking a wicket.

Manual Cone Pitch Map

Equipment

Cricket ball, stumps, foam 'top of off' target, 24 cones (6x4 of different colours).

Description

This exercise is best suited for a 1-2-1 coaching session. The bowler bowls their stock length or a length requested or marked by the coach. After each delivery the coach places a cone on the ground at the exact ball pitch mark. This is repeated for six balls until the first over is complete. Identical colour cones are used for the first over and are left in place. The second, third and fourth overs are bowled, using different-coloured cones for each over. All cones are left in place.

A pitch map has now been made. Coach and bowler assess the evidence. An assessment on the cone grouping can be made for each over by determining the floor area covered for each over bowled, by pacing out or accurately measuring the width and length surrounding the six blue cones, for example. This is carried out for the four different-coloured overs. The best over can be determined in relation to the target agreed between coach and bowler. This drill indicates whether the bowler is generally too short or too full, and at what line they generally bowled.

Finally, the coach can ask the bowler to remove any cones they thought were bad balls. This leaves a pitch map of good deliveries. So, if only six cones remain, that is 6/24, hence a good ball ratio of 25 per cent. The most frequent colour cone remaining may indicate that that was the best over. Coach and player can then discuss why that might have been.

Leaving the Ball Practice

Equipment

Cricket ball, stumps.

Description

The bowler bowls at a batter, trying to make them play at every ball they bowl. The objective of the drill is to not let the batter leave a single delivery.

Yorker Training

Equipment

Cricket ball, stumps, cones, bucket etc.

Description

The bowler attempts to bowl a yorker. Cones or a bucket, for example, are used for a visual guide and target. A chair can be used instead of a bucket to bowl through the legs of the chair.

Slower Ball Training

Equipment

Cricket ball, stumps.

Description

The bowler attempts to bowl disguised slower balls. They should be encouraged to experiment with as many methods and grips as possible. Coaches should again endeavour to create a fun, competitive, positive learning environment at all times.

Speed Gun

Description

The bowlers bowl at their normal pace for their specific type of bowling. The coach records the speed of delivery. Bowlers should also be encouraged to bowl as fast as they can, and to also record the speed of their disguised slower balls. There are apps now available to allow speed recording on mobile phones.

Progression

The fast seam bowler is asked to bowl a number of overs at full pace, recording the moment when their pace starts to drop through tiredness.

Pole Channel Outside Off

Equipment
Cricket ball, stumps, two training agility poles.

Description
The bowler bowls, aiming to place the ball between the two agility poles, stationed outside the back of the net, approximately 300mm apart. If they are bowling to an imaginary right-handed batter, the pole on the right should be positioned on the line of middle and off guard, and the one on the left 300mm to the left. The reverse is applied to a left-handed batter. This is great training for putting the ball down the 'corridor of uncertainty'.

Catching and Fielding Off the Bowler's Own Bowling

Equipment

Cricket ball, stumps, fielding bat.

Description

The bowler runs into bowl, but without a ball. They go through their complete action including follow-through. Upon completion of the follow-through, the coach, situated where the batter would be, hits the ball back at them, replicating a caught-and-bowled opportunity or a fielding stop. The timing of the hit should replicate a match situation, suitable for the speed of the bowler.

Progression

Hit to the bowler's weaker side. Progress from two-handed catches and stops to one-handed. Coach stands closer to the bowler, or hits the ball harder. Upon a successful stop, the bowler throws at either set of stumps, attempting to hit them.

Backing-Up Bowler's Stumps

Equipment

Cricket ball, stumps.

Description

The bowler runs in to bowl, but without a ball. They go through their complete action including follow-through. Upon completion of the follow-through, the bowler quickly returns to the stumps at the bowler's end, and receives the ball thrown in on the full by the coach, who is situated anywhere in the outfield. The bowler attempts to replicate a body position similar to that of a wicketkeeper receiving a throw – near to the stumps, bent knees, staying low, with hands together. Upon catching the ball, the bowler completes the run-out attempt.

Progression

Coach throws bounce throws and half-volley takes. Throw the ball in slightly wider of the stumps. Throw ball in earlier before bowler gets completely to the stumps. Bowler throws at batter's stumps. Rapid-fire feed, where the coach throws ten balls, one immediately after another, calling 'bowler's' or 'batter's', indicating which set of stumps the bowler should effect a run out at. Use three fielders throwing in from different positions – rapid-fire.

Bowler Run Out at Each End

Equipment

Cricket ball, stumps, fielding bat.

Description

The bowler runs in to bowl, but without a ball. They go through their complete action including follow-through. Upon completion of the follow-through, the coach, situated where the batter would be, hits the ball back at them, replicating a hit from the batter, culminating in a fielding stop leading to a run-out attempt. The timing of the hit should replicate a match situation, suitable for the speed of the bowler. The bowler throws at either end, called by the coach. The bowler is encouraged to align their feet, hips and shoulders towards the target stumps as quickly as possible in the short time available.

Progression

Coach throws bounce throws and half-volley takes. Rapid-fire feed, where the coach throws ten balls, one immediately after another, calling 'bowler's' or 'batter's', indicating which set of stumps the bowler should effect a run out at. Bowlers practise spin throws when stopping balls on their reverse throw side. Throw the ball underarm. Throw from a kneeling or sitting position.

Stump Number Movement Game (Two Sets of Stumps)

Equipment

Cricket ball, plastic stumps, empty stump base.

Description

Stumps and empty stump base are set up next to each other at the batter's end, giving stump reference numbers one to six. (Set up for a right-handed batter.)

For away-swing and leg-spin bowlers the stump arrangement is as follows: 1 – imaginary leg stump base; 2 – imaginary middle stump base; 3 – imaginary off stump base; 4 – leg stump; 5 – middle stump; 6 - off stump.

For inswing and off-spin bowlers, stump arrangement is as follows: 1 – leg stump; 2 – middle stump; 3 – off stump; 4 – imaginary base; 5 – imaginary base; 6 – imaginary base.

Bowlers attempt to swing, seam or spin the ball. They should be looking to pitch the ball on one of the imaginary stump numbers, with a view to hitting one of the real stump numbers (ideally off stump). They should record which imaginary stump number the ball pitched on, and which real stump number the ball hit. The difference between the stump numbers gives a score number for the amount of ball movement.

Target Bowling Cones Game

Equipment

Plastic stumps in bases, tennis balls, 15 cones.

Description

This group bowling game is ideal for beginners and young players, but could also be used for group or individual adult players. It is a very active and fun game. Bowlers are split into teams. The 15 cones (five rows of three) are placed in front of the stumps, on a good-length distance, positioned on a middle stump to imaginary stump No.4 line.

At the shout of 'go' the bowlers have three minutes to bowl, with a view to hitting either the cones or the stumps. Bowlers take it in turns to bowl. If they hit the cones they score one point, if they hit the stumps one point, and if a cone and the stumps two points. The score is kept by sliding a cone or cones, taken from the 15 on the ground, down the stumps each time a point is scored. Cones taken from the ground are not replaced. The team with the most cones on the stumps in three minutes wins.

Progression

Bowler to include practice from over and around the wicket, bowling to right- and left-handed batters. Introduce balls that swing excessively. Bowlers could compete in a combat game against each other. Reduce the number of cones, i.e. length and width. Change the length at which the coned target area is positioned. Bowlers run back to the top of their run-up. Replace a time duration with a number of balls bowled.

Length and Line Cones Game

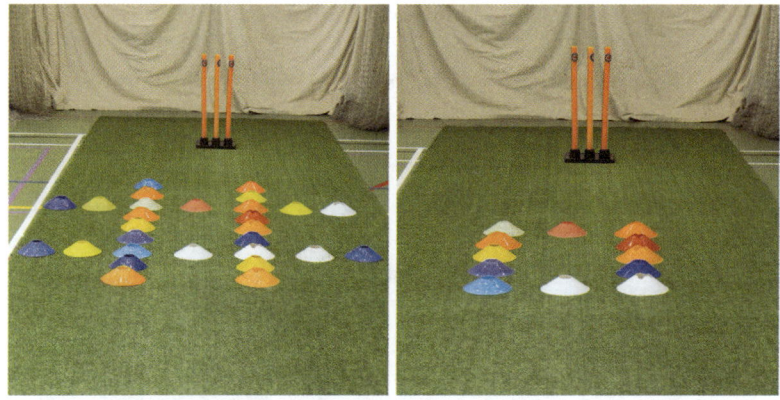

Equipment

Cricket ball, stumps, cones.

Description

This length bowling game is suitable for beginners and young players in both groups or as individuals. A line of cones is placed across the full width of a cricket wicket at a position deemed by the coach as the shortest acceptable length to bowl. Bowlers then bowl, looking to regularly land the ball beyond the cones. Another line of cones is placed at another position deemed by the coach as the fullest acceptable length to bowl. Bowlers continue to bowl, looking to regularly land the ball between the two lines of cones.

Another two lines of cones are introduced to form a wide target area to control the line of the ball, the width as deemed appropriate by the coach. The bowlers now have a line and length target rectangle to aim at.

Progression

Reduce the length and width of the target area. Remove all cones outside the target rectangle. Reposition the target bowling length.

Technical Remedial Work Drills

Stumps Showing Side-On, Front-On and Midway Actions

Equipment

Three plastic stumps.

Description

Three stumps are very useful for visually helping to identify the three types of bowling action: side-on, front-on and midway. One is placed across the bowler's shoulders, one across their hips, and the final one across their feet. The differences are already explained in greater detail earlier in this book. Please remember: 'Hips and shoulders in line and you'll be fine.' 'Twist the back and it will crack!'

Three Stump V Showing Counter-Balance Issues

Equipment

Three plastic stumps.

Description

Using three stumps on the ground is a simple yet powerful way of visually indicating how issues can develop in an inappropriate misaligned bowling action. If the bowler's momentum is heading in a direction down the leg side, their brain will tell them that they need to go straight to bowl at the stumps, therefore the body will then somehow compensate in the opposite direction to enable the ball to be delivered. The compensation angle is normally the same amount but opposite of the initial momentum angle. This invariably produces an unbalanced and potentially unsafe action. There is a high chance of back injuries inherent in this situation, along with less control of bowling accuracy.

By using three stumps (three different colours is preferable), the initial momentum direction, desired delivery direction and compensation angle can all be demonstrated. (Photo 1)

If the initial momentum direction can be straightened to match the desired delivery direction, the compensation angle can be eliminated, and a much-improved bowling action and balanced delivery are achieved. The risk of back injury is therefore greatly reduced, and an improvement in bowling accuracy will follow. (Photo 2)

Cone Run-Up Corridor

Equipment

Cricket ball, stumps, cones.

Description

A corridor of cones along the full extent of a bowler's run-up and follow-through is an invaluable way of realigning the run-up of a bowler who may be snaking along its length, or cutting/jumping in as they execute their bound. This can cause balance and stability issues, leading to injuries, inaccuracy and inconsistency.

The cone corridor forces the bowler to run in a more stable way, momentum heading towards the stumps, reducing the possibility of any oscillation occurring within the body that could be detrimental when executing the bound. The width of the corridor should be wide enough to accommodate the width of the bowler's natural running gait, with a tolerance added in. The use of video footage is very powerful, especially if taken before, during and after intervention.

Intervention Pole Corridor

Equipment

Cricket ball, stumps, agility poles.

Description

A corridor of agility poles along the final part of a bowler's run-up and follow-through is another invaluable way of realigning the action of a bowler who may be snaking or cutting/jumping in as they execute their bound. This can cause balance and stability issues, leading to injuries, inaccuracy and inconsistency.

Additionally, this drill controls both the top and bottom halves of the body. Because the poles are high, there is more awareness from the bowler for the need to keep the body upright and the arms tucked in as they make the transition from run-up through the bound, back-foot contact, front-foot contact, delivery and follow-through. Forward momentum is in a more stable condition, heading towards the target.

The width of the corridor should be wide enough to accommodate the width of the bowler's natural running gait, with a tolerance added in. When used with the bowler running in at normal speed, the width can be increased slightly, but when used in a 'standing' or a 'walk-through' situation the poles should be closer, to squeeze stability into the bowler.

The use of video footage is very powerful, especially if taken before, during and after intervention.

A good description for the purpose of this drill is to ask the bowler to imagine bowling through a doorway. If the body falls to one side or either of the arms stick out during the bowling action, they will hit the door frame!

This drill works very well when accompanied with the Cone Run-Up Corridor and String Line alignment drills.

String Line on Ground

Equipment
Cricket ball, stumps, long ball of gardener's string line.

Description
This drill is similar to the Cone Run-up Corridor, as it guides the bowler to run in a straighter, more stable attitude, momentum heading towards the stumps, reducing the possibility of any oscillation occurring within the body that could be detrimental when executing the bound. The string starts at the very start of the run-up and finishes tied around middle stump. The bowler simply runs down the string line as they make the transition from run-up through the bound, back-foot contact, front-foot contact, delivery and follow-through. Forward momentum is in a more stable condition, heading towards the target.

For more experienced bowlers, the string line can pass over the point where they are trying to land the ball, with the string anchored around a single stump behind the batting crease line. The line approach angle may need to be reorientated slightly when bowling around the wicket.

Bowler to include practice from over and around the wicket, bowling to right- and left-handed batters. The use of video footage is very powerful, especially if taken before, during and after intervention.

Stationary (Standing) and Walk-Through Sequence

Equipment

Cricket ball.

Description

Stationary and walk-through bowling technique grooving can be done anywhere, especially if it is done without bowling a ball. (A soft foam ball could be used in a sensitive indoor environment.) Ideally it should be carried out in a net using a real cricket ball. This is a great opportunity to use red and white balls, as seam position and spin direction can easily be seen.

These drills are generally used when refining a bowler's action, to remove safety, balance, stability, momentum and general bowling consistency issues. It is wise for the bowler and coach to invest a lot of time in these procedures, as the body and mind need to establish great levels of proprioception or kinaesthesia, otherwise known as 'muscle memory' or 'feel'.

Stationary or Standing Bowling

The bowler sets up with the front and back foot a comfortable distance apart. They then arrange their upper body into a coil position at the point where they would commence the rotation and delivery of the ball. They then shift all their body weight by gently rocking on to the back foot, lifting the front foot off the ground, keeping the back leg straight, and being perfectly balanced with no wobbling. When this is achieved, they push firmly forward on to the front foot and bowl the ball, this time bowling off a braced front leg. A one- or two-step follow-through is acceptable at this point, as there is a minimal amount of forward momentum available.

During this movement the coach continually observes or films the specific bowling action component being worked upon. Because there is no run-up or bound, it is quite easy for the bowler to control their balance, stability, momentum and direction; therefore, they experience and feel the perfect condition they are searching for.

Walk Through Bowling

This drill is a natural progression from the Stationary or Standing Bowling drill. The bowler initially takes two steps forward before walking on to the back-foot contact and subsequent delivery of the ball. A natural follow-through is acceptable at this point, as there is a little more forward momentum available.

During this movement the coach continually observes or videos the specific bowling action component being worked upon. Because there is no run-up or bound, it is relatively easy for the bowler to control their balance, stability, momentum and direction; therefore, they experience and feel a perfect condition they are searching for.

A further progression is to walk through faster with a bound, landing on the back foot with more force. This is the critical moment of the bowling action, as prior to landing (back-foot contact), the body is off the ground, turning into its delivery shape and orientation. The moment the foot hits the ground the body is totally susceptible to balance, stability, momentum, direction and safety issues, due to the increased forces generated through the body.

Walk-Through Using Vertical Barrier

Equipment
Cricket ball, intervention poles, mats, wall, nets.

Description
Following on from the Stationary (Standing) and Walk-Through drills, if a bowler is experiencing serious balance, stability, momentum or direction issues, a great form of remedial action is to create a high vertical restraint corridor. This will be both a visual and physical help in stabilising the complete body height of the bowler, and can be invaluable in removing incidents of back-foot or front-foot collapses, which invariably lead to lateral deflection spine issues, such as trunk rotation and trunk flexion.

The use of intervention poles has already been explained in the book, but using crash mats, walls and bowling nets are equally good options for this exercise.

Removing a Hop from Bowling Action

Equipment

Cones.

Description

Some bowlers have a hop in their run-ups, which always occurs just before they into the take-off, or bound. If possible, this is to be eliminated, as a hop contributes to a loss of momentum and causes stability/balance issues. Basically, instead of initiating the bound by pushing off the front foot, a hop is produced by pushing off the back foot. The bowler then immediately lands on the back foot. Removing a hop is not easy, as this is a natural movement that may have been present for many years. It may need a big investment of time from both player and coach.

A good method for removing the hop is to ask the bowler to imagine they are jumping across a stream. Two rows of cones are set up in parallel, approximately 500mm apart. The bowler places their front foot behind the first row of cones and is asked to jump across the 'stream', clearing the second set of cones and landing on their back foot. When successful, the bowler is then asked to immediately commence the bowling action upon landing.

This will need to be practised many times to remodel the take-off and landing, thus training the muscle memory. The cones can be kept in place when the bowler initially goes back to bowling off their full run-up.

The big test of success is always when the bowler goes back to bowling off their full run-up with the cones removed.

Wrist Flick (Seam Bowlers) 35

Equipment

Cricket ball (preferably red and white).

Description

Seam bowlers can add pace and put backspin on the ball if they flick their wrists in a downwards motion upon ball release. By imparting backspin on the ball (the fingertips running down the back of the seam), the seam presentation will be held in a favourable plane for swinging the ball in the air, or hitting the seam for movement off the pitch.

The bowler sits on the ground, legs crossed, the bowling arm elbow resting on the knee of the back leg. The non-bowling hand grips just below the wrist of the bowling hand, thus isolating any movement of the lower arm. The bowler then flicks the ball out of the hand towards a target a short distance away, ensuring the wrist flicks downwards. The bowler should be encouraged to get the maximum wrist power for maximum speed.

Red-and-White Ball Release

Equipment

Red and White Cricket ball.

Description

Using the red-and-white ball gives the bowler and coach the perfect opportunity to assess how the ball is being released from the fingers. The correct seam position and rotation of the ball upon release is essential for the desired bowling outcome to be attained, whether it be a seam or spin bowler.

The coloured ball seam position is clear to see in flight when compared to a red ball, as the two colours are separated by the seam. The seam positions on the white and pink balls are slightly easier to see in flight when compared with the red ball.

This allows an instant assessment of the seam position through the air and upon contact with the ground. Remedial action, if necessary, can then take place regarding release position, grip, finger orientation, wrist position or bowling action. The use of video confirmation is a powerful tool in this situation.

Every bowler must have a red-and-white ball, which should be used regularly when practising stock balls and all variations.

Off-Spinner Undercutting the Ball

Equipment
Red and White ball, surgical tape, highlight pen etc.

Description
The coach may have discovered that an off-spinner is undercutting the ball upon release, meaning that the ball pitches on the side of the ball, rather than landing on the spinning seam. Invariably this means the ball will not spin. In this situation, instead of the wrist staying stiff and not bending at release, the wrist is in front of the ball and not behind it, caused by the bowler pulling the hand back slightly, bending the wrist backwards. This alters the seam release angle, taking it away from the desired position. This is a common occurrence when an ex-seam bowler takes up bowling off spin.

 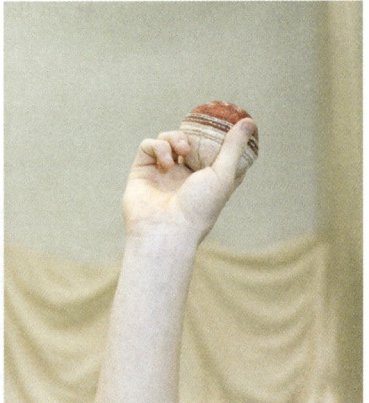

If attempts to remove the undercut wrist action naturally have failed, a great training drill to counteract this is for the bowler to create a method of making the movement physically impossible. This can be done by taping a physical restraint to the back of the wrist. A highlighter pen or wooden rule is ideal for this, as it does not impede the bowling action in any way. If the bowler has hairy arms, it may be advantageous to use a bandage tie rather than surgical tape!

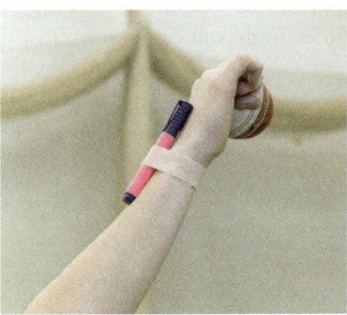

It may feel uncomfortable for a while, but if the bowler perseveres they will start to spin the ball much more. Once the bowler has visual proof of the benefit of the correct wrist position and has obtained the 'feel', the restraint can be removed.

It is worth remembering that the occasional ball undercut and not turning will be a great variation ball.

Aggot Ball Bowling

Equipment

Aggot ball.

Description

Bowling with this disc-shaped ball is another way of confirming seam position upon release. It can be used for both seam and spin bowlers. If there is any fault in the release position, the ball will fall end over end on pitching, but a ball hitting the seam correctly will continue on its path, even spinning as anticipated.

Spinner's 180-Degree Rotation (Two Sets of Stumps)

Equipment

Two sets of stumps, one cone.

Description

This is a great drill for a spin bowler, reinforcing the importance of rotating the whole body 180 degrees during the bowling action. It is done without a ball. A cone is placed on the ground, and two sets of stumps are placed a pitch length behind and in front of the intended bowling direction, 180 degrees apart.

The bowler stands directly over the cone, in a standing coil position, side-on, left side facing one of the sets of stumps.

They then bowl an imaginary ball, spinning around on their front foot until their back foot lands following 180-degree rotation, now facing the other set of stumps. Full follow-through of shoulders and arms 180 degrees into a new bowling coil position.

The bowler now just turns their head and slightly readjusts their feet to execute another imaginary delivery.

It is worth reminding players that at the start of delivery the left side faces the stumps, then after completion the right side faces the stumps (right-arm spinner) – 180-degree rotation.

This drill could be reinforced by placing a string line on the ground or, if in a sports hall, aligned with floor markings. Progression of the drill could be through bowling real balls. In a match or net situation the bowler would return to the catching position after delivery.

Off-Spinners Knee Drive 40

Equipment
Cricket ball, baseball glove or suitable debris.

Description
Lots of off-spinners bowl with a weak follow-through. To help an off-spinner obtain more zip, power, dip and turn it is vital to have a dynamic knee drive towards the target.

To promote this the bowler stands in their coil position ready to bowl. An object such as a baseball glove is placed on the floor to the leg side of and slightly in front of the front foot. The bowler then bowls the ball, looking to rotate, while driving the back-leg knee up and over the glove. This can be carried out over a full pitch length, into a side net five metres away, or a full toss bowled to the coach standing halfway down the pitch.

Progression

To promote more drive height, the glove could be replaced with a small hurdle. The hurdle could even be pushed slightly further down the pitch if required. Finally, the bowler can come in off their normal run-up. Remember, 'off-spinners' knee, leg-spinners hip'.

Leg-Spinner's Hip Drive

Equipment

Cricket ball, baseball glove or suitable debris, foam bowling target on top of stump.

Description

Lots of leg-spinners bowl with a weak follow-through. To help a bowler obtain more zip, power, dip and turn, it is vital to have a dynamic hip drive towards the target.

To promote this the bowler stands in their coil position ready to bowl. An object such as a baseball glove is placed on the floor to the leg side of and slightly in front of the front foot. Next to it, but further away is plastic stump with a foam bowling target on top. The bowler then bowls the ball, looking to rotate, while driving the back leg up and over the glove. They simultaneously try to hit the foam target with the ankle side of their foot. This can be carried out over a full pitch length, into a side net five metres away, or a full toss bowled to the coach standing halfway down the pitch.

Correct positioning of the stump and foam target is essential, so that the actual follow-through technique is not compromised.

Progression

The bowler can come in off their normal run-up. Remember, 'off-spinner's knee, leg-spinner's hip'.

Off-Spin Overarm Throw

Equipment

Cricket ball or incredi-ball.

Description

This is a great way of introducing young bowlers or beginners to the finger and wrist action needed to bowl off spin. It can be used as an introductory to off spin or as a remedial drill. Once it is mastered it can be introduced into the full, straight-arm bowling action.

The player holds the ball using the off-spinner's grip. They then simply throw the ball overarm with a clockwise finger-spin direction, bouncing the ball up against a wall or to the coach (note – the elbow should be bent here). If the correct spin is put on the ball, it should turn. Once it is mastered it can be introduced into the full, straight-arm bowling action.

Leg-Spin Underarm Throw

Equipment

Cricket ball or incredi-ball.

Description

This is a great way of introducing young bowlers or beginners to the finger and wrist action needed to bowl leg spin. It can be used as an introductory to leg spin or as a remedial drill. Once it is mastered it can be introduced into the full, straight-arm bowling action.

The player holds the ball using the leg-spinner's grip. They then simply throw the ball underarm with an anti-clockwise finger-spin direction, bouncing the ball up against a wall or to the coach. If the correct spin is put on the ball, it should turn. Once is it mastered it can be introduced into the full, straight-arm bowling action.

Front-Arm Hand Trace

Equipment

Mirror, window etc.

Description

This is a simple drill used for showing the general path of the front-arm, non-bowling-arm hand, from the coil position through to the completion of the bowling action. The bowler simply stands in front of a mirror, window or picture reflection, and slowly goes through the full bowling action using both arms. They then isolate the front-arm movement and observe it in their reflection. The bowler and coach can then assess, incorporate any technical changes and see the results instantly.

The bowler instantly gets a feel for the complete movement. The use of video footage is also a powerful learning method.

Progression

The bowler could pull a resistance band to add a physical resistance to the arm action.

Bowling-Arm Hand Trace

Equipment

Mirror, window etc.

Description

This is a simple drill used for showing the general path of the bowling-arm hand, from the coil position through to the completion of the bowling action. A ball is not required for this drill. The bowler simply stands in front of a mirror, window or picture reflection, and slowly goes through the full bowling action using both arms. They then isolate the bowling-arm movement and observe it in their reflection. The bowler and coach can then assess, incorporate any technical changes and see the results instantly.

The bowler instantly gets a feel for the complete movement. The use of video footage is also a powerful learning method.

Progression

The bowler could pull a resistance band to add a physical resistance to the arm action.

Fluorescent Stickers

Equipment

Fluorescent stickers.

Description

This drill forms a simple visual method of assessing the alignment of different body parts and joints, if remodelling a bowler's action. The component being observed has a sticker placed on it, and a video is taken of the element within the part of the bowling action being analysed. It is a very simple and rudimentary version of a skeletal motion examination used by sports scientists.

It is important that the coach knows exactly where the sticker should be facing at a particular moment in the full bowling action, proceeding from start of run-up, through the bound, back-foot contact, front-foot contact, delivery, release, to the completed follow-through. This will also determine whether the bowler is recorded from behind, to the side or in front during the delivery of the ball.

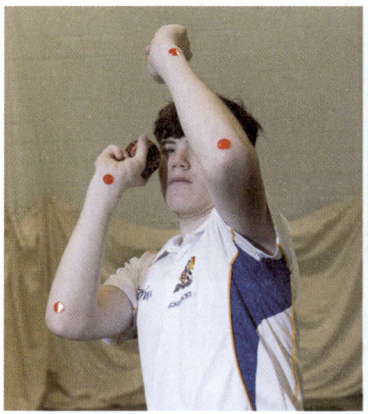 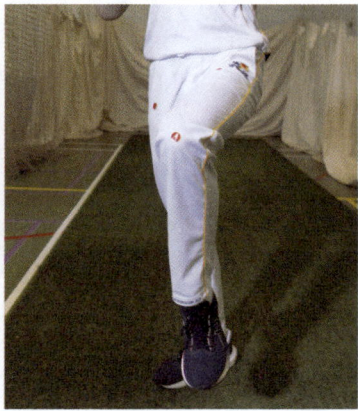

Useful components to look at include feet, knees, hips, elbows, wrists and hands. For the best results, the bowler should be wearing shorts and a short-sleeve shirt if possible.

Fitness and Stability Drills

Weighted Ball Training

Equipment

Weighted cricket ball.

Description

This fitness drill is great for strengthening all the body parts specifically used in the upper-body bowling cycle.

The bowler adopts a kneeling position, left knee on the ground if a right-arm bowler, right knee on the ground if a left-arm bowler. The bowler then gently bowls the ball into a nearby net, executing a full toss. The bowler tries to ensure complete shoulder rotation and full follow-through of both arms.

The body parts become used to bowling the heavier ball, so that when the bowler returns to using the normal cricket ball the body is under less stress. It will also help a fast bowler increase their pace.

Progression

The bowler could stand and deliver from a stationary position, proceeding to a gentle walk-through.

Bowling Over Crash Mats

Equipment

Crash mat cricket balls, stumps.

Description

An excellent method for improving a bowler's stability during the various elements of their bowling action can be produced by using crash mats. By walking and running on one, or jumping on to or off a crash mat, the bowler has to engage their whole body system to obtain the necessary balance and stability to deliver the ball.

The bowler can progress from a standing position at back-foot contact, through front-foot contact, and delivery. Then further progression can be made by walking through, finally finishing with running through. The bowler could deliver the ball from the mat, or jump off it on to normal ground to deliver.

Any number of mats could be pushed together. This is also a very tiring drill, so pushes the bowler physically too. Wobble cushions can also be used under each foot, either together or individually, for stationary deliveries.

Stamina Drills
(Bungee Rope, Running Back to Start of Run-Up, Fartleks, etc.)

Equipment

Bungee restraint rope, cricket balls, five cones.

Description

In addition to spending lots of time in the gym, there are some simple bowling-specific fitness drills that can increase power, speed and endurance of the bowler.

A bowler can increase their power by using the resistance of a bungee restraint rope in their run-up. The rope is attached around the bowler's waist and, as the bowler proceeds down their run-up, resistance is provided by the coach running behind them, pulling on the rope. This normally terminates when the bowler reaches the crease, but could be continued as they deliver the ball.

In the training environment, another simple yet effective way of building a bowler's stamina and endurance is to ask them to jog or run back to the start of their run-up after each delivery. They should immediately then run in and bowl the next ball. This should be repeated for a six-ball over. The bowler could then progress to ten balls, etc. (The coach should strictly monitor the number of balls bowled, as the bowler will have strict weekly workloads to adhere to.)

A final speed, power, stamina and endurance drill is called Fartleks. These are best done outdoors, as they involve 40m sprints. The exercise is a series of random variations in speed and intensity, alternating between bursts of sprinting over varying distances and recovery jogging and walking over shorter distances. Fartleks were invented by a Swedish athlete in the 1930s, and the Swedish term Fartlek means 'speed play'.

A line of cones is set out at 10m intervals covering a total distance of 40m. A typical start could be:

- Walk the first 10m, jog the second 10m, sprint the third 10m, jog the last 10m; then
- Walk the first 10m, sprint the second 10m, jog the third 10m, jog the last 10m; then
- Sprint the first 10m, sprint the second 10m, jog the third 10m, walk the last 10m; then
- Sprint the first 10m, sprint the second 10m, sprint the third 10m, walk the last 10m;
- etc., etc.

The bowler increases the intensity and duration as their fitness improves.

Athletic Run-Up, Lifting Feet (Seam and Pace Bowlers)

Equipment

Mini-hurdles.

Description

A good seam or fast bowler will normally have a fluent, light-footed, relatively fast-running action, with both lower and upper body contributing to the run-up. Very often a bowler will possess a flat-footed run-up, or one that contains very little knee lift. This style of run-up does not look very athletic, as it lacks approach speed, rhythm and balance, and has variable stride patterns and lengths. When executed in an indoor sports hall, these run-ups are often very noisy due to the heavy impact sound generated.

Bowlers with this type of run-up can be susceptible to shin splints and other joint impact injuries, as they are running flat-footed rather than running on the balls of their feet and toes. Additionally, a lack of arm pump (both bowling and non-bowling arms) and upper-body rhythm is generally associated within this run-up. Some bowlers even pump their non-bowling arm, while holding the ball out straight in their bowling-arm hand.

From a technical standpoint, these bowlers are losing speed from their delivery, and potentially accuracy from their bowling.

To encourage a bowler to raise their knees when running in, subsequently putting more emphasis on landing on the balls of the feet and toes, running over mini-hurdles is a great drill for promoting an athletic run-up. A long line of hurdles is placed a suitable distance apart. The bowler is then asked to run over the hurdles at approximately 75 per cent full sprint speed. The length of hurdles does not have to match run-up length at this stage, as the bowler is just being encouraged to run in a more athletic manner. (For a good running action, the bowler is encouraged to look at footage of middle-distance runners.) Both arms should be pumping equally in a rhythmical manner.

The run-up should now sound quieter if performed in an indoor sports hall.

Progression

Hurdles positioned accurately in the bowlers run-up, so that after running in over the hurdles they bowl the ball and complete their follow-though. Progress finally to removing the hurdles completely, with the bowler looking to run in smoothly and athletically.

The bowler should remember this phrase: a seam bowler is made up of two people, the first 'runs in like an athlete' and the second 'turns into a bowler', the turn being executed in the air as they perform their bound prior to back-foot contact.

There are many more training drills beyond the scope of this book, so the reader is encouraged to investigate further resources.

Useful Coaching Quotes to remember

Listed below is a collection of bowling coaching and motivational quotes to remember, which may strike a chord or be a good prompt for bowlers. They are in no particular order, but are relevant to the technical, tactical, physical, mental and lifestyle elements of a player profile. It may be worth remembering where they are located in the book. They are:

- Heart in the oven, head in the freezer.
- Train hard, play easy.
- Hard work beats talent when talent fails to work hard.
- Never give up, whether you're winning or losing.
- Failsafe, it's safe to fail.
- Fear of failure or fear of success?
- FEAR – False Evidence Appearing Real.
- FAIL – First Attempt In Learning.
- PRIDE – Personal Responsibility In Developing Excellence.
- Are you prepared to risk failing to achieve success?
- Someone who never made a mistake never made anything.
- Form is temporary, class is permanent.
- Believe and you will receive.
- Pressure makes diamonds.
- Uncertainty + Importance = Anxiety
- To use a springboard you have to go down first!
- 3 Ps – Preparation, Perseverance, Patience.
- PRIDE – Personal Responsibility In Developing Excellence.
- Plumbing teamwork, are you a drain or a radiator?
- A=1%, Z=26%, ATTITUDE = 100%
- Paralysis by analysis.
- Who's winning? Why?
- Feet are the servants of the body.
- Risk, reward.
- Cause and effect.
- To make things better you have to know what's wrong.
- Don't underrate your value, and never overrate it!
- Question your knowledge into your player.
- Do you 'push' or 'pull'?

- Find the pace of the pitch.
- Three in play.
- Be unpredictable.
- Its 'place' not 'pace'.
- Wicket-taking balls or wicket-taking overs?
- Prehab or rehab?
- Feet up – Head down.
- Look in the mirror.
- A seam bowler is an athlete who turns into a bowler.
- Leakage or wash-off.
- Tall, narrow and straight.
- Take a look at yourself in the mirror.
- Vision without action is a daydream. Action without vision is a nightmare.
- You cannot remain the same and improve.
- Was it fun? What did you learn?

TEN
INTRODUCTION TO VIDEO ANALYSIS

Mobile phones, tablets and iPads are commonplace today, so these offer a great opportunity for recording, assessing and making technical changes to bowlers, both young and old, and experienced or inexperienced. They also provide an accurate record of a player's level of play at a particular moment in time and, if the player has access to the footage, it encourages them to take ownership of their own analysis. This brief introduction to video analysis may give the parent, or inexperienced person, a basic introduction to some fundamental areas to look at, which may help with the development of their bowler.

In most cases a perceived flaw in technique will be compared with a proven successful method by the use of photos. Some apps enable a side-by-side comparison with a bowler demonstrating good solid technique, and these can be synced together so a player and coach can compare from start to finish the bowling element being worked on.

The art of good video analysis is to determine the catalyst causing the breakdown in a bowler's technique. They may have three things wrong with their action, but if the catalyst is found the other two may disappear immediately without any intervention needed by coach or player.

Advantages of Video Analysis
- Does not lie
- Provides a permanent record at a moment in time
- Can be viewed instantly, repeatedly and in great detail
- Provides freeze-frame and slow-motion analysis
- Progress evidence is produced
- Technical strengths and improvements are motivating for the player

Limitations of Video Analysis
- Requires bowling technical knowledge for correct feedback
- Potential to over-emphasise technical weaknesses
- Paralysis by analysis

Remember that video analysis can only highlight flaws in technique – it cannot correct them. This can only be done by adopting the appropriate remedial drills, reinforced with high repetition. It is essential that video analysis is also used for highlighting strengths in technique.

It is important to remember that we are all made differently, and no two body compositions are the same. If a bowler's action is proven to be biomechanically safe (i.e. does not have a 'mixed' action), is free from persistent stress and impact-related injuries, and they are bowling consistently well, their action may not need any intervention. Ultimately, will the coach's intervention improve the player?

Filming location

To obtain the best footage, filming should take place in the following three locations and for the Bowling durations indicated:

• In line with the stumps at the bowler's end, from start of run-up to completion of follow-through. (Camera located behind the start of the bowler's run-up.)

• Zoom in as bowler approaches their bound, ensuring that the view captures the bowler from feet to top of bowling action.

• Square of the stumps at the bowler's end (bowling arm nearest the camera), from start of run-up to end of follow-through.

By using the three different locations, the coach and player gain more detailed evidence of the movement of all the body parts.

When analysing bowlers, the coach should remember the phrase 'feet up', and for batters the phrase 'head down'. These refer to the order in which analysis of body parts is recommended, encapsulated by a term relevant to each cricket discipline.

Key Elements to Study in the Bowling Action

Run up

Bound

Back foot contact

Front foot contact (Delivery)

Ball release

Follow through

The following pages contain some examples of commonly found chronological elements within a weak bowling technique, easily identified using video analysis. In each example a cause, effect, solution and remedial drill will be provided.

The examples apply to both seam and spin bowlers unless specifically noted.

Snaking Run-Up

Some bowlers have what is commonly known as a snaking run-up. They do not approach the crease in a continuous straight line, but move from side to side. This is very often accompanied with a stuttering run, an inconsistent stride length and occurs without much natural rhythm. Momentum can also be lost in this situation. As the bowler approaches their bound, the body may be oscillating, thus making an unstable, unbalanced position, from which it is difficult to jump towards the target. This will then have a huge detrimental effect on the rest of the bowling action.

Some bowlers even run up with their bowling arm straight out in front of them, while their non-bowling arm can be seen pumping.

A straight, rhythmical run-up is crucial to a good bowling action. It keeps all the momentum going towards the target, and there is no 'leakage' or 'wash-off' of energy. A good run-up, particularly for a seam bowler should see the knees and arms pumping strongly as they approach the bound. It is so important to have a good running technique because a seam bowler is actually 'an athlete who turns into a bowler'. It is critical that the bound is executed with all the energy directed towards the target.

A good way to start the run-up is to slightly lean the upper torso forward to a point where the feet want to naturally start moving. By using gravity, the bowler can save some energy, as they do not have to push off their foot as hard to initiate forward momentum.

It is crucial for the run-up to be accurately paced out. Bowlers should count out the normal walking paces to the start of their run-up, measured from the bowling crease. When commencing the run-up, it is crucial that the correct foot is on the bowler's mark. This can be either foot, but it must always be the same one. If not, the bowler will repeatedly lose their run-up.

Methods for marking the starting point of a run-up include: rubbing the sole of the foot on the ground, using marker discs, and at the higher levels of the game by accurately measuring with a long tape measure and marking the position with spray paint. At professional levels the bowler will measure and spray their positions at all four corners of the pitch, covering over and around the wicket at both ends.

When young players are going through the growth spurt they may have to remeasure their run-ups two or three times if it takes place during the outdoor season.

Relevant remedial drill (see Technical Remedial Work Drill section):
- Cone Run-Up Corridor
-    Athletic Run-Up, Lifting Feet

'Cutting in' or 'Jumping in' during the Bound   2

Some bowlers can 'cut in' or 'jump in' during their bound, meaning that they change their approach and delivery alignments whilst in the air. They will have had a wider run-up position, when compared with where they bowl from after completing the bound. Some can even cut in just before they commence their bound. This re-alignment will have a huge detrimental effect on the rest of the bowling action, as the bowler's momentum is now heading down the leg side of the wicket, rather than straight towards the target. This will mean the body's preferred direction will fight against its momentum, so balance and stability issues will undermine the efficiency of the bowler's action, thus contributing to potentially unsafe biomechanical movements. This may also affect ball movement, accuracy, and consistency.

Cutting in or jumping in is the term used when a bowler is bowling over the wicket. When a bowler is bowling around the wicket the term is changed to cutting out or jumping out. Either way, the effect is the same.

Therefore, it is crucial for the run-up and bound to be continuously aligned towards the target, encouraging a more stable, balanced, efficient and biomechanically safe action. This will also improve ball movement, accuracy and consistency.

Relevant remedial drills (see Technical Remedial Work Drills section):
- Three Stump V Showing Counter-Balance Issues
- Cone Run-Up Corridor
- Athletic Run-Up, Lifting Feet

Excessive Bound Height with Backward Body Lean

This is a crucial moment in the bowling action, as prior to landing (back-foot contact), the body is off the ground, turning into its delivery shape and orientation. The moment the foot hits the ground the body is totally susceptible to balance, stability, momentum, direction and safety issues, due to the increased forces generated through the body.

If the bound is too high, the forces generated on contact with the ground are drastically increased. A scientific survey of professional fast bowlers discovered that as the ball is delivered the force generated into the ground is between six and ten times their body weight. Therefore, a strong body is required to sustain these impact loadings, and many fast bowlers do have long periods of injury due to this.

A high bound can be a particular problem for young, physically under-developed bowlers, as their bodies are not strong enough to deal with the demands asked of it, particularly on back-foot landing, where the back leg can collapse very easily. This breakdown then affects the rest of the bowling action. Additionally, there is a loss of forward momentum, leading to wash-off or leakage of potential energy, and the distinct possibility of back injury.

Leaning too far backwards in the bound is detrimental, as this also leads to a loss of forward momentum in the air and hinders stability upon back-foot contact.

Adult bowlers should be encouraged to lower the height of their bound to a maximum of approximately half the height of the stumps, and for juniors approximately one-third of the stump height. By doing this the bowler loses less forward momentum, increases the chance of a strong back-foot contact being made, thus increasing the possibility of delivering the ball from a stable, balanced and well-aligned, strong release position.

If the bowler also reduces the backward lean of the upper torso as they enter the bound, by keeping the head going forward they will sustain forward momentum, again ensuring they deliver the ball from a strong release position.

Relevant remedial drills (see Technical Remedial Work Drills section):
- Intervention Pole Corridor
- Stationary (Standing) and Walk-Through Sequence
- Athletic Run-Up, Lifting Feet

Excessive Back-Leg Collapse

This is the critical point in the bowling action. The moment the foot hits the ground the body is totally susceptible to balance, stability, momentum, direction and safety issues, due to the increased forces generated through the body. Because of the high forces generated at this point in the bowling action, particularly by fast bowlers, it is crucial that bowlers maintain a strong, stable, balanced and well-aligned attitude on back-foot contact. If this is absent, it can lead to many other difficulties with the bowling action and its outcome.

This can be a particular problem for young, physically under-developed bowlers, as their bodies are not strong enough to deal with the demands asked of them, particularly on back-foot landing, where the back leg can collapse very easily. The body will invariably fall to the off side as the back leg bends excessively at the knee, producing a conflict between the actual body momentum and the desired one towards the target. Lateral deflection will inevitably take place at the point of ball release. Additionally, there is a loss of forward momentum, leading to wash-off or leakage of potential energy, leading to the distinct possibility of back injury when delivering the ball.

Back-foot collapse in young players will greatly reduce over time as the bowler becomes physically stronger. A small amount of collapse will naturally always be present in a bowling action. As the bowler makes the transition from jumping into the air to landing back on the ground, the knees will always act as shock absorbers. The stronger the back leg can be on contact, the less chance there is of the upper body falling away from its desired attitude and direction of travel. Physical training for the development of all the leg muscles, glutes and core are essential for this to happen.

Lots of hopping on both legs, star jumps and squats are a simple but effective way of strengthening these areas. With this in mind, lots of walk-throughs and jog-throughs will help a bowler get a feel of controlling their back-leg balance, which can then be taken into their full-speed action.

Relevant remedial drills (see Technical Remedial Work Drills section):
- Three Stump V Showing Counter-Balance Issues
- Intervention Pole Corridor
- String Line on Ground
- Stationary (Standing) and Walk-Through Sequence
- Walk-Through Using Vertical Barrier
- Fluorescent Stickers
- Athletic Run-Up, Lifting Feet

Falling to Off Side

Falling to the off side is mostly a symptom of excessive back-leg collapse at back-foot contact. Because the body starts to lean to the off side as the bowling action progresses through to front-foot contact, the body has naturally aligned itself to head in the off-side direction, as it is now out of balance. Another case of leakage or wash-off.

A misaligned run-up angle can also lead to falling to the off side. Additionally, this breakdown in bowling alignment can be caused by the front arm (non-bowling arm) being redundant in the bowling action. This is quite common, particularly with young bowlers.

The front arm should be up and active, with the elbow at eye level, pointing towards the target. This acts like a rudder, directing the bowler forward. It is vital that both the front foot and the front arm head towards the target.

The contribution of the front arm (non-bowling arm) into the bowling action, combined with a strong, stable back-leg contact will remove the possibility of prematurely falling to the off side.

Relevant remedial drills (see Technical Remedial Work Drills section):
- Three Stump V Showing Counter-Balance Issues
- Intervention Pole Corridor
- String Line on Ground
- Stationary (Standing) and Walk-Through Sequence
- Walk-Through Using Vertical Barrier
- Front-Arm Hand Trace
- Bowling-Arm Hand Trace
- Fluorescent Stickers

Front Leg Not Braced

There are two main reasons why a bowler's front leg may not be braced upon release of the ball: collapsing of the back leg, and running in too fast.

If the back leg collapses excessively, it is difficult to push back up to take the body into a position where the front leg has a chance to brace itself on or a fraction after front-foot contact and subsequent delivery of the ball. This is exacerbated if the bowler runs in too fast, as they do not have time to create the braced front-leg component. The ball is also delivered from a lower release position.

A technical improvement would be to have the bowler releasing the ball from a fully braced front leg position. Not only will the ball be released from a much higher position, giving more bounce, but a powerful stable base position is created to activate the correct timing of shoulder and hip, thus acting like a slingshot catapult. Notwithstanding this, it is still possible to bowl very fast without a braced front leg, and many bowlers do so!

Once again, a stable back leg and a slightly reduced run-up speed will help create the perfect bowling release condition, particularly for fast bowlers.

Generally, seam bowlers whose front foot contact is of the 'toe strike' variety, have a slim chance of bowling with a braced leg, where as a 'toe strike' spinner probably can.

Relevant remedial drills (see Technical Remedial Work Drills section):
- Stationary (Standing) and Walk-Through Sequence
- Spinner's 180-Degree Rotation (Two Sets of Stumps)
- Off-Spinner's Knee Drive
- Leg-Spinner's Hip Drive
- Fluorescent Stickers

Front Foot Cutting Off

This misalignment is very often accidental, but the main reason for it is when a run-up or a bowler's bound are misaligned. This could be by design or by accidently jumping in just before or during the bound. The back foot lands, and as the bowling action proceeds to front-foot contact, rather than aiming towards the target, an imaginary line drawn between both feet points down the leg side. Once again there is a mismatch between where the momentum is going and where it needs to go. This type of misalignment can restrict the back leg in its attempts to drive through to the target.

There is potential for the body to start to lean to the off side to compensate for this, which can then lead to potential back problems associated with misalignment of shoulders and hips, caused by the twisting required to realign to the target for the ball release and subsequent follow-through. Very often a seam bowler's momentum can be reduced because the front foot can end up spinning round like a spin bowler's as the body compensates for the misalignment. There is also a good chance that the bowler will run on the 'danger area' part of the wicket, leading to the umpire withdrawing the bowler from the attack.

The bowler's foot realignment and momentum should always head towards the target, and should be correctly arranged to be conversant with a side-on, front-on or midway bowling action. Some spinners do like to cut the front foot off slightly, as they suggest they can spin and drift the ball more. This has never been scientifically proven to be true. Bowling with the corrected foot alignment will now provide a more balanced and stable environment to bowl from, allowing the back knee to drive through without restriction.

Relevant remedial drills (see Technical Remedial Work Drills section):
- Three Stump V Showing Counter-Balance Issues
- Intervention Pole Corridor
- String Line on Ground
- Stationary (Standing) and Walk-Through Sequence
- Walk-Through Using Vertical Barrier
- Spinner's 180-Degree Rotation (Two Sets of Stumps)
- Fluorescent Stickers

Redundant Front Arm or Non-Bowling Arm

Bowling with a redundant front arm (non-bowling arm) gives a bowler stability and balance issues, and can contribute to a loss of power and swing if a seam bowler, and a loss of spin, dip and drift if a spin bowler. This is quite common, particularly with young bowlers.

Without a strong front arm participating in the bowling action, there is a tendency for a bowler to fall away to the off side when delivering the ball. Because the body starts to lean to the off side as the bowling action progresses through to front-foot contact, the body has naturally aligned itself to head in the off side direction, as it is now out of balance. Another case of leakage or wash-off.

The front arm should be up and active, with the elbow at eye level, pointing towards the target. This acts like a rudder, directing the bowler forward. It is vital that both the front foot and the front arm head towards the target. The contribution of the front arm (non-bowling arm) into the bowling action will remove the possibility of prematurely falling to the off side.

For a seam bowler, the full participation of both arms in the bowling action, activated from a powerful stable base position will help activate the correct timing of shoulder and hip, thus acting like a slingshot catapult. For a spinner, the full participation of both arms in the bowling action, activated from a powerful stable base position will help activate the correct timing of 180-degree shoulder and hip rotation, thus providing more spin, dip and drift on the ball.

Relevant remedial drills (see Technical Remedial Work Drills section):
- Three Stump V Showing Counter-Balance Issues
- Intervention Pole Corridor
- String Line on Ground
- Stationary (Standing) and Walk-Through Sequence
- Walk-Through Using Vertical Barrier
- Spinner's 180-Degree Rotation (Two Sets of Stumps)
- Front-Arm Hand Trace
- Fluorescent Stickers

Seam Bowler's Arm, Wrist and Fingers Not Vertical

Another common technical issue is when a seam bowler does not have their bowling arm, wrist and fingers vertical when releasing the ball. Irrespective of all the other body-balance and stability weaknesses potentially encountered in a bowler's action, if the ball does not leave the bowler's fingers in a vertical position it will not swing or display seam movement off the pitch.

Even if the bowler has the perfect grip, if the wrist and fingers are at an angle the amount of swing will be greatly reduced. If a bowler has the perfect grip, it is possible for them to swing the ball, even if their arm is not vertical on ball release. This can only happen if the hand is truly vertical, while the arm is slightly off vertical. The tolerance for that orientation is very small. Therefore, it is crucial that the arm, wrist and fingers are vertical upon ball release.

The great Sri Lankan opening bowler Lasith Malinga was famous for having a very flat, round arm action, yet could swing the ball viciously, at pace. Imagine what his grip must have been like to achieve a vertical seam position upon ball release! Once again this comment is worth remembering. It is important to remember that we are all made differently, and no two body compositions are the same. If a bowler's action is proven to be biomechanically safe, (i.e. does not have a 'mixed' action), is free from persistent stress and impact-related injuries, and they are bowling consistently well, their action may not need any intervention.

Relevant remedial drills (see Technical Remedial Work Drills section):
- Intervention Pole Corridor
- String Line on Ground
- Stationary (Standing) and Walk-Through Sequence
- Walk-Through Using Vertical Barrier
- Red-and-White Ball Release
- Aggot Ball Bowling
- Bowling-Arm Hand Trace

Seam Bowlers Not Flicking Wrist

Many seam bowlers bowl medium pace and swing the ball gently. There is a place for bowlers such as this, as the lack of pace can often take wickets. In most situations, a contributory factor in their lack of pace or swing could be because they do not flick their wrist as they release the ball.

If the ball is released with a downwards flick of the wrist, it will gain extra pace. Because the ball will now be released off the fingertips, at pace, it will have considerably more backspin applied to it, which will hold the seam in a strong position, enabling more seam movement and swing to be attained.

Relevant remedial drills (see Technical Remedial Work Drills section):
- Wrist Flick (Seam Bowlers)
- Red-and-White Ball Release
- Aggot Ball Bowling
- Fluorescent Stickers

Off-Spinners Undercutting the Ball

A common occurrence is to see an off-spinner struggling to turn the ball despite having a good grip, strong finger-spin rotation and strong body action. The reason for this is that they are probably undercutting the ball upon its release, meaning that the ball is rotated by the hand, so that the side of the ball hits the ground rather than the spinning seam. This is caused by the wrist bending to put the wrist ahead of the ball on release. This is often called a 'Saturn ball', after the ringed planet.

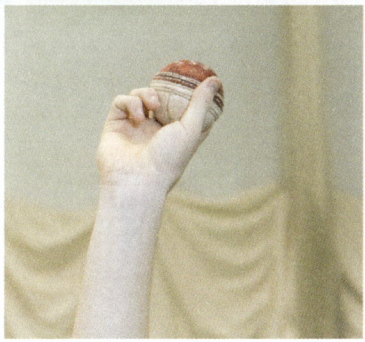

To attain more spin the ball should be released so that the wrist is stiff and behind the ball on release. This will ensure that the ball lands on the spinning seam, rather than the side of the ball.

It is worth noting that the occasional ball undercut and not turning will be a great variation ball, and remember not all wickets are suitable for spin bowlers!

Relevant remedial drills (see Technical Remedial Work Drills section):
- Red-and-White Ball Release
- Off-Spinner Undercutting the Ball
- Aggot Ball Bowling

Spin Bowler Not Rotating 180 Degrees

A common problem for spin bowlers, particularly young players, is not fully rotating 180 degrees in their bowling action. For both off-spinners and leg-spinners, spin can still be imparted on the ball by just using the fingers and wrists respectively. But if a bowler possesses a weak follow-through, failing to rotate their feet, hips and shoulders 180 degrees, they will be missing out on some more spin on the ball, and both drift and dip will be absent from the ball's flight.

The use of two stumps laid on the floor to indicate the current rotation angle, one indicating the approach target angle, the other indicating the actual rotation angle achieved, is a great visual way of displaying the remaining degree of rotation required. In most cases the bowler is normally searching for the final 45 degrees approximately, having only rotated approximately 135 degrees.

Once the bowler has achieved the more powerful completed 180-degree rotation regularly, they will experience a big increase in the amount of spin, drift and dip they apply to each delivery. Put simply, the left side of the body faces the batter as the ball is gathered at back-foot contact, then the right side faces the batter after completion of the delivery. The bowler should then jump back to face the batter in a front-on position ready to field or catch a returning ball.

Relevant remedial drills (see Technical Remedial Work Drills section):
• String Line on Ground
• Stationary (Standing) and Walk-Through Sequence
• Spinner's 180-Degree Rotation (Two Sets of Stumps)
• Off-Spinner's Knee Drive
• Leg-Spinner's Hip Drive
• Front-Arm Hand Trace
• Bowling-Arm Hand Trace
• Fluorescent Stickers

Weak Follow-Through (Shoulders, Arms and Feet)

A weak or incomplete follow-through can usually be seen by looking at the completed positions of the shoulders, arms and feet. There is an overall appearance of a lack of energy and forward momentum. This applies to both seam and spin bowlers.

In this weak follow-through condition, neither the front arm (non-bowling arm) nor the bowling arm appear to finish fully in the most desirable completed position, and the shoulders finish in a similar vein. The feet appear to have a very short follow-through stride, with the back-foot follow-through height being very low.

A weak follow-through does not allow the ball to receive its maximum potential energy in terms of speed, flight, swing, seam movement and spin. A more purposeful, energetic follow-through to the target is needed.

To create this, it is essential that the energy inherent in the delivery of the ball is continued through to the end of the follow-through. The front arm, bowling arm and shoulders should finish fully at the extent of their follow-through, the feet having a longer follow-through stride and a greater height seen from the back-foot follow-through.

The ball now receives its maximum potential energy in terms of speed, flight, swing, seam movement and spin.

Relevant remedial drills (see Technical Remedial Work Drills section):
- Stationary (Standing) and Walk-Through Sequence
- Spinner's 180-Degree Rotation (Two Sets of Stumps)
- Off-Spinner's Knee Drive
- Leg-Spinner's Hip Drive
- Front-Arm Hand Trace
- Bowling-Arm Hand Trace
- Fluorescent Stickers

Weak Back-Leg Knee Drive

A weak back-leg knee drive will not allow the bowler to attain the final element in a good, powerful bowling action. This lack of lift and momentum does not allow the ball to receive its maximum potential energy in terms of speed, flight, swing, seam movement and spin. A more purposeful, energetic drive through to the target is needed. A weak knee drive does not allow the best hip action to be activated, essential in the bowling actions of seam and off-spin bowlers. The seam bowler misses out on extra pace, and the off-spinner misses out on spin, drift and dip, as they are unable to rotate up, over and around their front leg.

By completing the knee drive correctly, extra energy is introduced into the bowling action, activating better hip movement for fast bowlers and off-spinners alike.

Relevant remedial drills (see Technical Remedial Work Drills section):
- Stationary (Standing) and Walk-Through Sequence
- Walk-Through Using Vertical Barrier
- Spinner's 180-Degree Rotation (Two Sets of Stumps)
- Off-Spinner's Knee Drive
- Leg-Spinner's Hip Drive
- Fluorescent Stickers

ABOUT THE AUTHORS

JAMES KNOTT

Having come through the junior ranks at Kent, James played professional cricket for MCC Young Cricketers, Surrey and Somerset for eight years between 1994 and 2001, making 24 appearances for Surrey's First XI. Following on from that he played nine years of Minor Counties cricket for Bedfordshire, captaining for three of those. He made several appearances for the representative Minor Counties XI and also the ECB XI (England Amateurs) that won the European Championships in 2004.

As a coach, James has been the Head of Cricket at Stowe School since 2004, finishing top of the schools' cricket league twice and finishing runners-up of the National T20 twice. Several pupils have gone on to play professional cricket in that time – Mark Nelson (Northants), Graeme White (Northants, Notts & England Lions), Ben Howgego (Northants), Liam Gough (MCC Young Cricketers & Essex), with the most high-profile being Ben Duckett (Northants, Notts & England Test, ODI & T20i). Several others have gone on to MCCU programmes at Loughborough (James Cronie, Adam King and Olly Clarke), Cambridge (Jack Keeping), Oxford (John Gurney) and Durham (Rufus Easdale). Current pupil at the school – Aadi Sharma – is on the Northants Academy and represented the Midlands at the Bunbury Festival and the Super 4s.

ANDY O'CONNOR

Andy came through the junior system at Northants, playing for both the Academy and Second XI. The remainder of his 25-year playing career consisted of playing in the Birmingham League, and predominantly the

Northamptonshire Premier League, also representing the county in the Northants Amateur League XI.

Andy is an ECB Level 3 coach, and is also a member of the Northamptonshire ECB Coach Education team. He is part of the junior coaching set-up at Northants, having coached most age groups, both boys and girls. He is currently coach of the Northants Academy, which won the ECB One-Day Cup in 2022, having also coached the U17s Boys team during their ECB National Championship three-day and one-day cup-winning seasons of 2017 and 2019. Andy was head coach of the Northants Women's squad, the Steelettos, for eight seasons, and also headed up the Northants Girls Emerging Players Programme (EPP), while also working on the boys Academy and EPP Coaching teams. He was also head coach at the Moulton College Cricket Academy for five years, one of the students being Olly Stone (Northants, Warwickshire, & England), with others moving on to MCCU cricket.

Andy has been a coach at Stowe School for the past ten years, seeing several cricketers progress to MCCU and County Second XI cricket.

In 2010 Andy was voted National Chance to Shine MCC Spirit of Cricket Coach of the Year.

ABOUT THE PLAYERS & COACHES

DARREN GOUGH

Darren Gough MBE is a former fast bowler who took 229 wickets in his 58 Test matches. In addition, he is the second-highest wicket-taker in ODI cricket for England with 229 wickets. In county cricket Darren spent most of his playing time with Yorkshire CCC, where he also captained the side, as well as three years with Essex CCC.

In total Darren played 700 times for club and country, taking 1,486 wickets. In 1999 he was one of the Wisden Cricketers of the Year. In 2000 he was the Cornhill England player of the year, and in 2001 Vodafone England cricketer of the year. Now back at Yorkshire CCC, Darren has taken on the role of Director of Cricket at the club.

DAVID WILLEY

David Willey is a left-arm seam-bowling all-rounder who has played 116 matches for England in ODI and T20i internationals, taking 151 wickets. David was a member of the England team that won the 2022 T20 World Cup as well as when they were runners-up in 2016. Domestically, David has played first-class cricket for Northants and Yorkshire as well as playing in a various franchise T20 competitions around the world, including the Big Bash, the Hundred and the Indian Premier League. Cricket runs in the family – he is the son of former England cricketer and international umpire Peter Willey.

SAQLAIN MUSHTAQ

Saqlain Mushtaq is an off-spin bowler who played over 200 internationals for Pakistan as well as having a long career in first-class cricket both in Pakistan and England, playing county cricket for Surrey and Sussex. His time at Surrey coincided with the county dominating the domestic scene in the late 1990s and early 2000s. Overall Saqlain took 208 test wickets at an average of 29.83 and 288 ODI wickets at 21.78.

Saqlain has had a long coaching career at international and domestic level, primarily as a specialist spin-bowling coach. This has included spells with the England national team as well the head coach of Pakistan.

MARTIN BICKNELL

Martin Bicknell was a right-arm swing bowler who played 288 first-class matches for Surrey, taking over a thousand wickets for the county. He also played in four Test matches for England, with the last two being against South Africa in 2003, where he helped England level the series. Martin also took 429 List A wickets and was part of the Surrey team that dominated county cricket in the late 1990s and early 2000s. After retiring he moved into coaching and is now the Director of Cricket at Charterhouse School in Surrey. Cricket also runs in his family, with brother Darren having a long first-class career with Surrey and Nottinghamshire.

PHIL ROWE

Phil Rowe was a long-serving coach at Northants County Cricket Club for 15 years. He started life as a development coach before progressing quickly to work with the county's best young players on their EPP and Academy programmes. This progressed to becoming the county's lead bowling coach, Second XI coach and then finishing his time as First XI assistant coach. During his time at Northants the county won two T20 Blast titles, the first of which was the club's first trophy for over 20 years.

IAN SALISBURY

Ian Salisbury was a leg-spinning all-rounder who played first-class cricket for Sussex, Surrey and Warwickshire in a career spanning from 1989 to 2008. During this time, he also played 14 Test matches and four ODIs for England. Across all formats he took 1,195 wickets and was an integral part of the

Surrey team that dominated county cricket in the late 1990s and early 2000s. Ian was one of the Wisden Cricketers of the Year in 1992. Upon retirement he moved into coaching with stints as Second XI and then First XI coach at Surrey CCC. Ian is now the head coach for the England Physical Disability Cricket team.

CHRIS LIDDLE

Chris Liddle had a 17-year professional playing career with Leicestershire, Sussex and Gloucestershire and had particular success in the shorter forms of the game. In 2020 Chris moved into coaching with KNCB (the governing body of cricket in the Netherlands) as their fast-bowling coach, as well as taking up the lead fast bowling coach role at Northants CCC, with a further promotion to the county's assistant coach in 2022. Recently Chris has been appointed as the England Women's Performance Fast Bowling coach.

GARETH BATTY

Gareth Batty was an off-spin bowler who made 728 first-team appearances for Yorkshire, Surrey and Worcestershire between 1997 and 2021, taking over a thousand wickets. During this time he also represented England 20 times across all formats, taking 20 wickets. After retiring in 2021 he went into coaching as the head coach of Surrey CCC, winning back-to-back County Championship campaigns in 2022 and 2023.

BRENDEN FOURIE

Brenden Fourie was a South African seam-bowling all-rounder, playing for Border, Impalas, Leicestershire and Norfolk. On his debut for Impalas he took a hat-trick, and went on to play 48 first-class matches for Border between 1988 and 1999, taking 148 wickets, with a best haul of 6 for 74. Additionally, he played in 74 List A games for Border in the same period, taking a further 84 wickets. He also played one game for Leicestershire in 1994, and represented the Northants Cricket Board from 2001–03.

ACKNOWLEDGEMENTS

We are very grateful to everyone who has helped bring this book together. Firstly, the players and coaches who gave so generously of their time and expertise – Martin Bicknell, Ian Salisbury, Chris Liddle, Gareth Batty, Brenden Fourie and David Willey, as well as Darren Gough and Saqlain Mushtaq for the forewords they wrote. A special thank you to Phil Rowe, who sat with us twice and talked in great detail – influencing much of what you have read in this book.

Several Stowe pupils also gave up part of their school holidays to feature in the photographic elements of this book. So, a big shout-out and thank you to Blake Macleod, Connor Lawford, Tristan Dickinson, William Harrison, Harvey Hughes, Zorawar Sidhu and Archie Lazarus-Ingham.

Thanks as ever to Jonathan Glynn-Smith for his hard work in taking such high-quality photos. Jonathan really does go above and beyond and we are so lucky to have had him on board for all three books.

A special thank you to Ashish Baluja, Kaylan Kumar and Riqbal Sidhu, whose company CFS sponsored this book, which helped overcome the rising printing costs and allowed for colour photos this time around.

Thank you also to the Stowe School Headmaster, Dr Anthony Wallersteiner, who allowed us to use the Stowe School Cricket facilities for the photographs. Finally, a big thank you to Peter Burns and his team at Polaris Publishing for their help in developing the book, and to our agent, David Luxton, for his invaluable support and advice.

We would also like to thank all those who have helped us both on our cricketing journey throughout the years that led us to this point – our families, our friends, our team-mates, our co-workers, other teachers and other coaches. They have all inspired, encouraged, challenged and shared their knowledge and experiences with us over many years, and without all of that accumulated knowledge neither this book nor our others would ever have been written.

Lastly, a huge thank you to you the reader for buying this book. We very much hope you enjoy it and, whether a player or coach, that it helps you out on your own cricketing journey.

Andrew O'Connor

James Knot

ALSO AVAILABLE

BATTING

'Like the best Joe Root innings, it has everything . . . easy to follow and bang up to date' – Richard Hobson, *Wisden*

'This book is fantastic. It is insightful and detailed, I thoroughly enjoyed the holistic structure, weighted heavily towards tactics and the mental approach, still with accurate and simplified technical input' – Sam Arthurs, Foundation Pathway Manager, Oxfordshire Cricket

ALSO AVAILABLE

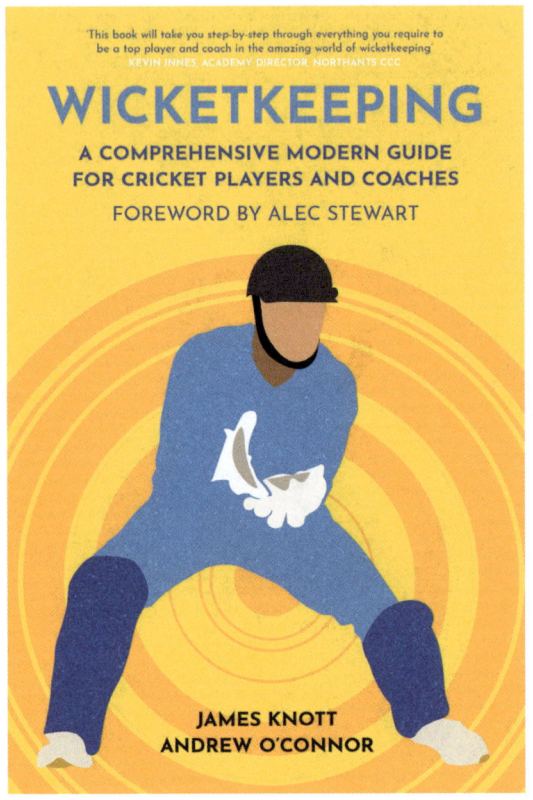

WICKETKEEPING

'In the most comprehensive book on wicketkeeping on the market, James Knott and Andrew O'Connor provide detailed and easy-to-understand insights into all aspects of wicket keeping, whether you are a player or coach, and no matter your level . . . Clear, insightful and easy to follow, this is an essential guide for improving your game or your coaching methods' – *Cricket World*

'clubs, schools and universities could all do with stocking this in their changing rooms' – Ivo Tennant, *The Cricketer*